When
Actions Speak Louder
Than WORDS

Understanding the
Challenging Behaviors of
Young Children and
Students With Disabilities

KIM DAVIS
SUSAN D. DIXON

Solution Tree | Press

a division of

Solution Tree

555 North Morton Street
Bloomington, IN 47404

800.733.6786 (toll free) / 812.336.7700
FAX: 812.336.7790

email: info@solution-tree.com
solution-tree.com

Visit **go.solution-tree.com/behavior** to download the reproducibles in this book.

Printed in the United States of America

13 12 11 10 09   1 2 3 4 5

Library of Congress Cataloging-in-Publication Data

Davis, Kim.

    When actions speak louder than words : understanding the challenging behaviors of young children and students with disabilities / Kim Davis, Susan D. Dixon.

       p. cm.

    Includes bibliographical references and index.

    ISBN 978-1-934009-60-4 (perfect bound) -- ISBN 978-1-935249-13-9 (library binding) 1. Behavior modification. 2. Classroom management. 3. Early childhood education. 4. Children with disabilities--Education. 5. Students with disabilities--Education. I. Dixon, Susan D. II. Title.

    LB1060.2.D38 2010

    371.9'04393--dc22

         2009046817

Solution Tree
Jeffrey C. Jones, CEO & President

Solution Tree Press
President: Douglas M. Rife
Publisher: Robert D. Clouse
Vice President of Production: Gretchen Knapp
Managing Production Editor: Caroline Wise
Proofreader: Elisabeth Abrams
Text Designer: Orlando Angel

Cover Designer: Rose Sheifer

Acknowledgments

From the authors:

We have been lucky enough to have been surrounded by colleagues and families who have supported our understanding about behavior as communication. The individuals who communicate with challenging behaviors who have been part of our lives deserve heartfelt thanks as well. Herb Lovett's wisdom has guided our path as we have traveled through this process. We have been forming these ideas for years, both in our personal and professional lives. It's truly been a journey of learning to listen differently.

Thanks go to all those who have helped us in the formative years, and to Dr. Cathy Pratt (director of the Indiana Resource Center for Autism) and Dr. Michael Conn-Powers (director of the Early Childhood Center), both at Indiana University's Indiana Institute on Disability and Community for allowing us the time to finally put all this down on paper.

Gretchen Knapp, editor extraordinaire . . . thank you for your time, encouragement, insights, and patience.

We are appreciative and grateful.

Solution Tree Press would like to thank the following reviewers:

Jeanne Boehmler
Special Education Teacher of Students With Autism
Thomas Jefferson Elementary
Bentonville, Arkansas

Christina R. Carnahan
Assistant Professor
University of Cincinnati
Cincinnati, Ohio

Bryan Dague
Center on Disability and Community Inclusion
University of Vermont
Burlington, Vermont

Mary Benson McMullen
Associate Dean for Graduate Studies
Professor of Early Childhood Education
Indiana University
Bloomington, Indiana

Patricia Rogan
Executive Associate Dean
Indiana University School of Education
Indianapolis, Indiana

Gen Shelton
Early Childhood Consultant
Bloomington, Indiana

Ellen Veselack
Director of the Preschool Program
Child Educational Center
La Canada, California

Stacie Ward
Special Education Teacher
Lowell Elementary School
Boise, Idaho

Lori Whitman
Director
Learning Technology Center 2 East
Loves Park, Illinois

Visit **go.solution-tree.com/behavior** to download the reproducibles in this book.

Table of Contents

About the Authors

Kim Davis began her career as a middle and high school physical education teacher before moving on to complete her master's degree in adapted physical education. In that work, she found her niche supporting young children, including children with disabilities. Currently, Kim works for the Indiana Institute on Disability and Community, at the Indiana Resource Center for Autism, located at Indiana University–Bloomington. She serves as a consultant providing assistance to teachers regarding positive behavior supports and classroom programming. In addition to presenting on behavior issues, Kim also presents at state and national conferences on topics including autism, movement difference, person-centered planning, and recreation. Her inspiration comes from the words of the late Herb Lovett, who instilled in Kim a belief in the value of all people and the importance of building relationships through active listening and clear communication. That inspiration has helped Kim become a better advocate for those children whose behaviors may be misunderstood, and who may not always be heard.

Susan D. Dixon is a speech and language pathologist who, after receiving her master's degree in that field, began her career in the late 1970s working in a large institution for individuals with significant developmental disabilities and mental illnesses. This experience led her to the seminal question of her career: how do behaviors function communicatively? She works for the Indiana Institute on Disability and Community at Indiana University–Bloomington, where she is involved in research, writing, and training. She also works for the Monroe County Community School Corporation to provide direct services for preschool and elementary-aged children. She has maintained a private practice for her entire professional career, through which she has worked with infants, toddlers, and their families; early intervention providers in several states; school-aged children; and adults both at home and in vocational settings.

Preface

We wrote *When Actions Speak Louder Than Words* following years of making technical assistance calls, providing communication intervention, giving presentations and workshops, and talking about and with individuals with challenging behaviors. Children with socially unacceptable behaviors present a great challenge to educational teams and parents. Unwanted behaviors are the most frequent topics of conversation among school staff and can literally make or break a child's experience in any group setting. It is also the single issue that families find most challenging and often impacts the child's and family's abilities to easily move through their routines at home and in the community.

The ideas we present in this book have evolved through years of interaction with workshop participants and individuals we have supported, and with the help of a vast cadre of professionals whose research and practice helped shape this book. No single philosophy or body of work is predominant.

Kim's professional career began as an adapted physical education teacher working in public schools as well as at a special school for children with developmental disabilities, specifically autism. Sue began as a speech and language pathologist working in a large institution for individuals with developmental disabilities and/or mental illnesses. She has subsequently worked in the public schools, with adults in their homes or vocational settings, and for the past several decades as an early interventionist. Our experiences with older individuals with challenging behaviors have always informed our work with young children and vice versa. It is why we do what we do as early interventionists and in our work with early childhood providers, with teachers in schools, and staff in other settings. Although we've geared most of the language in this book toward early care and education providers, the beliefs and strategies are useful for individuals of all ages and abilities. You will notice that some of our examples are of older children or adults; remember, every child will get there someday! Some little piece of what we have learned from those who have crossed our paths is contained in these pages, and we have them to thank for all we now know.

In Part I, "Foundational Knowledge and Philosophy," we explain how communication develops, define particular behaviors that can be used as communication, and explore some ways children (and adults) use behaviors to communicate. We then discuss the important factors to consider and questions to ask when attempting to discover the underlying messages in certain behaviors.

In Part II, "Practical Strategies for Supporting Behavior," we first provide proactive measures you can take to alleviate the child's need for unwanted behaviors, then discuss some reactive strategies. The final chapter focuses on child-centered approaches.

Throughout this book, you will find stories that illustrate, clarify, and sometimes amuse, as well as activities to help you and your colleagues discover where you are in your own thinking about behavior as communication.

Part I: Foundational Knowledge and Philosophy

1

Introduction

As we travel from home to home, family to family, classroom to classroom, listening to families, childcare providers, and teachers who share stories about challenging situations, we hear numerous similarities. We meet with classroom teams searching for strategies to support students' behaviors during instructional time, or ways to make transitions between activities easier for their students. We talk to parents who struggle to get their child to school without a meltdown over breakfast. In short, we observe children whose primary way to communicate is through challenging behaviors. We also find that our basic beliefs about behavior and its fundamental, functional purpose as communication, and the basic principles for proactive strategies to help teachers and families look at challenging behaviors, remain consistent across settings. The purpose of this book is to build an understanding of how different behaviors are communicative, what their messages might be, and how to begin to interpret those messages. Along with suggestions on how to reframe your perspective about the messages of behavior, we offer fundamental proactive strategies to support more acceptable behavioral alternatives.

Philosophical Foundations

Children who use challenging behaviors need to be acknowledged and to have their behaviors seen as meaningful messages. Children are still developing their skills in communicating and have fewer coping skills than we do as adults. Whether or not the behavior in which the child engaging is acceptable to us, it contains a message.

Above all else, the authors of this book value each person as an individual, regardless of her ability level or the way she communicates. Each person has a place in our community, in our schools, and in our workplaces and should be recognized for her unique abilities and talents. We also know that supporting people with challenging behaviors can be difficult sometimes and can require a team effort.

Our values greatly impact our actions when supporting others, especially those with challenging or noncompliant behaviors, who may have been written off as "unworthy" of support. The late Herb Lovett stated in *Learning to Listen* (1996) that "the label of non-compliance not only dismisses any good reasons people might have for their behavior, it also sets us up to manage people in automatic and unthinking ways" (p. 50). We believe that summarily dismissing noncompliant behaviors without looking at the deeper meaning is unacceptable behavior on our part. Individuals with challenging behavior have needs, desires, and emotions that must be understood. Applying labels to people has negative consequences. There are reasons for challenging behaviors, and it is up to us to provide the support needed to satisfy the person's intentions or desires and to improve his quality of life. In order to do that, we must learn about the person, understand him, and help him gain a sense of community, whether at school, home, work, or in public settings.

Our philosophy is that each person deserves to be heard and listened to completely, to the best of our ability. It may take a great deal of effort to understand the issues for individuals with certain disabilities or limited speech, but we believe we must seek the answers in order to understand the behaviors. Each person is important and deserves a voice.

Our Five Core Values

1. Behaviors communicate.

2. If we first ask what a person is communicating through behavior, we establish a basis for change.

3. There are basic approaches we can take to help others communicate their needs in ways that promote positive behavior.

4. We have the responsibility to provide the interactive and physical environment conducive to appropriate behaviors.

5. Each person has a place in our community—in our schools and other education settings, and in our workplaces—and should be recognized for his or her unique abilities and talents.

These core values are the foundation for this book.

What Is Behavior?

The various behaviors that are part of our daily lives can mean many things. According to Webster, *behavior* is "the manner of conducting oneself in a specified and proper way." But who decides what *proper* means? Sometimes proper behavior may mean one thing to adults and something very different to children. Imagine Tamika's mother's astonishment when she discovered that following the rule about not playing in good clothing meant that her kindergarten daughter took off her clothes before she went outside for recess!

A simplified definition of behavior is *what we do or how we act in different situations*. A child in your classroom pokes at the child sitting next to her; another slams his desk; and a third chronically forgets his homework. The reasons for the behaviors may be different for each individual in each situation. Depending upon the situation, we can choose to see a particular behavior as either good or bad, but we must remember it is the *behavior*, not the person, which is our focus. The observed behavior does not indicate that the person using the behavior is either a good or a bad person. It simply means that depending upon the situation—who is sending the message and who is receiving it—the behavior is judged to be either okay or not okay.

That is a very simple way to look at behaviors. However, from our years of experience, we believe that behavior is something more. In every situation where we have experienced a challenging behavior, we have realized there is a very definite reason for that behavior. Whether a person can speak or not, has a disability or does not, or is old or young, our definition of behavior is that *it is a way to communicate or tell others our needs or feelings.* Each of the classroom behaviors mentioned earlier—poking a classmate, slamming a desk shut, turning in work late—communicated a message for that unique situation. In another situation, the behavior could have meant something entirely different. While the behaviors may look similar, the *meanings* are always unique and must be interpreted within the context of each situation. We must learn to listen more carefully and in a different way, because behavior is a way to communicate!

What Is Communication?

Communication is more than simply the use of symbols to share ideas with others. Sharing information with others and letting others know what we think or need is vital to our lives, and we attempt to communicate in various ways. Some of us can speak eloquently, and some may not be able to speak at all. What is the common denominator? A deeper definition of communication may be *a range of behaviors used to bring about changes in the immediate physical environment, to structure social exchanges, or to exchange information.*

Communication and behavior are inextricably linked, and it is important that we begin to recognize this connection in our work and relationships with children of all ages and abilities. It is almost impossible *not* to communicate. If behavior is communication, everyone on the planet communicates all the time!

In this understanding, even so-called *misbehavior* is communication. Therefore, when someone misbehaves, a rule of thumb is to ask, What is this person saying? What is the message of that behavior? Assume that behavior has a meaning, and that serious behavior has a serious meaning, and the stage has been set for significant change. It is not easy to look within ourselves; challenging behavior can be very upsetting. But as Herb Lovett points out, "By labeling people's behavior we often feel we have the right to act on how it affects us rather than on what the person doing it might be trying to communicate" (1996, p. 56).

Assess Your Perspective

Please take a moment to consider your own perspective on specific behaviors. If you are a classroom teacher or work with a team of people to support a student, complete this exercise individually, and then compare your responses with those of your team or other teachers who work with the student.

Define the following:

- Behaviors that are always acceptable

- Behaviors that are never acceptable

- Behaviors that are sometimes okay and sometimes not okay

(See page 12 for a reproducible handout to use with groups, or visit **go.solution-tree.com/behavior** to download it.)

Take some time to create your lists. You might think of a specific student's behaviors when you fill this out. However, it is also enlightening to evaluate your own behaviors, and those of your close friends and loved ones. Think about the daily routines in which you are involved. Consider the routines in which the children in your care may excel and those in which their behavior may be problematic. Any situation you can think of is appropriate. There is no right or wrong response, and there is no limit on the number of responses you might have in each box.

Once you have completed the exercise, compare your responses with others. Usually, the people with whom you are completing this activity are a fairly homogeneous group: all work with children or students in some manner, enjoy children, and want to help them thrive in their environments. Nevertheless, there may be significant inconsistencies in responses to given behaviors. What is important to note is where the responses are similar and where they are not. Are there behaviors that are "always okay" for one person and "never okay" for another person? Are there behaviors that appear in different boxes depending upon the respondent? What factors might create this discrepancy? What messages might this discrepancy send to students you share?

We have used this activity in our workshops for years with groups of early childhood teams, school-age teams, and teams supporting adults either in their home or vocational settings. We've also used it within extended families in which different people (parents, grandparents, stepparents, aunts, and uncles) care for a single child at different times. Given the same instructions stated here, the following feature box lists some of the responses we have received. (See pages 13–15 for complete lists of acceptable, unacceptable, and sometimes acceptable behaviors from our workshops.)

Behaviors That Are Always Okay

Smiling, laughing, hugging, singing

Talking, listening, socializing

Participating, asking questions

Sharing, playing together, cooperating

Following directions, asking permission, being obedient

Behaviors That Are Never Okay

Biting, scratching, kicking, hitting, pinching

Defiance, disrespect

Whining, crying

Picking nose

Screaming, yelling

Having a bad attitude

Behaviors That Are Sometimes Okay and Sometimes Not Okay

Hugging, kissing

Refusals

Screaming, yelling

Crying

Laughing

Asking questions

Let's look at the lists, beginning with the "always okay" list—even though most people admit they start with the "never acceptable" list because it was easiest! Does that say something about how we view behavior in general? Which list did *you* create first?

One of the first items on the "always okay" list is "hugging." Let's think about this. Is it always okay to give a hug?

I Want a Hug: Mary Lou's Story

Mary Lou, a fifth grader, is almost as round as she is tall (less than five feet) and believes in hugging. Hugging has always been an integral part of the way Mary Lou interacts with others in her environment. Mary Lou has Down syndrome and does not use spoken words to communicate, so her use of hugging says a variety of things for her. She hugs when she is happy, hugs when she is excited, hugs when she comes home, and hugs when she is on her way to bed. Mary Lou hugs a lot! It is almost always a very nice social event. However, sometimes Mary Lou hugs people she does not know, and that can be extremely awkward. Mary Lou's friends need to be particularly vigilant when walking through the mall because Mary Lou has a fondness for very large men. Mary Lou can quickly become innocently attached to a strange man's leg!

And then there's laughing. Is laughing always okay? What about at a funeral, when someone gets hurt, or in the middle of a lecture?

Even talking and socializing may not always be acceptable behaviors. Think about how you feel when you are trying to listen to a presenter at the front of the room and are distracted by a conversation going on behind you. Is talking okay then? What other items on the "always okay" list might be questionable for you? Take a look at the complete list from our workshops (page 13), and examine your own beliefs about specific behaviors that typically show up on the "always okay" list. Are they always acceptable to you?

"Never okay" lists are usually fairly easy to come to consensus on as a group. (See page 14 for our workshop list.) It is generally accepted that it is not okay to hurt others, steal, lie, or use profanity. Yet in each group we work with, someone will have a very valid argument for those points. Would it be okay to hurt another person if it was in self-defense? To steal something if your children are hungry or if you were taking away something that might hurt someone? To curse if it was the only way to get someone to pay attention?

Is Swearing Ever Okay?

In the large institution where Sue started her career in the 1970s as a speech and language pathologist, violent behaviors were common. This is not surprising given that almost a thousand people with developmental disabilities and mental illnesses were housed in a facility in which the rules were made by administrators who did not know even a handful of the "patients" personally. Choice was virtually nonexistent, and having a voice was unheard of (pun intended). One of the very minor changes Sue was able to implement in her short stay there was to allow profanity. Now why would she be proud of that? Because it allowed people to express their anger and frustration in ways that were not physically violent! Not everyone swears, and we are not advocating profanity as a way to end violence. This is simply an example of one situation in which a seemingly socially unacceptable behavior might be viewed as an acceptable means to an end.

Finally, as we look at the behaviors that fall into the third category of "sometimes okay and sometimes not okay," the lines become very blurred. Some of the always-okay behaviors and never-okay actions are repeated in this "sometimes" list. (See page 15 for our workshop list.) What does this tell us as team players, whether we are teachers, therapists, school staff, or parents? *Behaviors are situational.* Teamwork is essential to help children learn what is acceptable and what is not—at home, in schools, during therapy sessions, and at all points between.

If you are on a team supporting a child with a disability, and each team member has a different response to screaming, what message does the team as a whole convey? It is probably confusing to the child to get different responses from different people at different times. Think of parents who have different approaches to a specific behavior: one is easy and one is strict. What message does their child receive? If a team of adults is not consistent in their messages about what is okay and what is not okay, how can the child learn what is appropriate? The team members must collaboratively discuss and agree on their approach. This may mean compromise, but will always result in a clearer and more consistent message.

Obviously, the list of acceptable and not acceptable behaviors is not always as clearcut as it appears at first glance. We could undoubtedly come up with many more examples of misbehaviors that might be okay in different circumstances. *If we see behaviors as "not okay," we are setting up barriers to them as communication.*

Time to Let Loose

As a physical education teacher, Kim expected her students to make lots of noise and let off steam when they came to the gym. However, at one school, the gym was in the middle of the building, and there was no hallway to the gym. The only access to the gym was to go through the classroom; if you were on one side of the door, you were in the classroom, and if you were on the other side, you were in the gym. No hallway meant no transition time or environment to indicate a change in location and expectations. Since the students were always revved up at the end of physical education (PE), they were very loud and excited when they entered their classroom. Classroom teachers did not like this and kept reminding the students to use their "inside voice." (Of course, the students *were* inside. How confusing that must have been for them!) The classroom team met and decided that the students had to be quieter when they were inside the building. Initially, this did not sit well with Kim, because she believes that PE should allow the students to "let loose." After further discussion, however, she realized that perhaps she was hanging on to this idea due to her own perceptions and even ego around what she thought was best for her situation or class. She realized she had not even considered what the students could be experiencing.

The students in this instance were, in fact, students with disabilities who had a difficult time knowing the boundaries and rules in everyday situations. All they knew was that they were in PE inside in the gym and were encouraged and allowed to yell and be loud—and then as soon as they walked through a door, they were told to quiet down. Kim realized that she needed to be there for the students and let go of some of her ideas about what was "right." The students were just beginning to learn the rules and expectations of the school, and this situation was causing great confusion for the students and displeasure for the classroom teachers as well as slowing down the learning process. She had to realize that she was there to help the students learn, not to fulfill her agenda. So she began to have PE outside whenever she could. When the class did come inside or had to be inside, they did activities that were less rowdy or calming right before they went back to class. In this way, Kim was still getting her job done in physical education, but more importantly, she was supporting the students to learn more control over their behavior—which allowed them to progress overall. It was a compromise, but in the end, it paid off for everyone. The choices were not about Kim's preferences as the teacher, but about the students and their learning abilities.

When we look at all of the lists, many threads have appeared consistently over the years. Many of the behaviors that are always okay are actually adjectives, or descriptions of the person, not the act or behavior: being *trusting, thoughtful, respectful, friendly, independent*, or *kind*; having *good manners*. What does *thoughtful* look like? What about *respectful*? In order to know what is meant by those terms, we need to be able to "see" behaviors. How team members define those traits may also be problematic. Team members will have unique personalities and belief systems, and what may seem respectful to one team member may be totally unacceptable to another. Therefore, it is imperative to clearly define or list *behaviors* along with those *traits* when creating the "always okay" list.

By contrast, behaviors that are never okay are often listed as verbs or actions and are listed very rapidly: *hitting, spitting, kicking, lying, cheating, stealing, being late, not helping, swearing, running away, burping*, and so on. These are all known factors to anyone who reads the list. Everyone knows when someone is hitting, kicking, or spitting, because those are visible behaviors. But it is still important for team members to be certain what a "hit" looks like. Is it a tap on the leg, a punch in the arm, or a pat on the back? Which is acceptable, and which is never okay?

What Does Good Behavior Look Like?

Let's take a closer look at just a few examples of what the implications of having a clear understanding of what each member of your team can mean. Choose several examples of the traits listed in the following feature box. Define the behaviors you associate with this trait, and compare with your partners. Remember to ask, What exactly does this *look* like? What behaviors can I *observe* that tell me that this person is "kind," "disrespectful," and so on?

Traits				
Kind	Thoughtful	Independent	Destructive	Rude
Cruel	Disobedient	Disrespectful	Respectful	Friendly

As you listed the specific behaviors that characterize many of these descriptors, what did you find to be true? We suspect that even if everyone agreed that being friendly was important, "friendly" looked different to different people. As we embark on teaching children which behaviors are acceptable and which are not, it is important to be clear exactly what our expectations are. For all of us, our expectations are based for a large part on our upbringing and past experiences.

One implication of this is that *what we learn is what we observe.* This means that our communication knowledge is culturally influenced. Here we are talking about culture as

> an integrated pattern of human behavior which includes but is not limited to thought, communication, languages, beliefs, customs, courtesies, rituals, manners of interacting, roles, relationships, and expected behaviors of racial, ethnic, religious, social and political groups; and the ability to transmit the above to succeeding generations. (National Center for Cultural Competence, 2004, p. vii)

As we delve into more specifics about using the elements of communication that we can see, we must recognize that there are differences in how cultures use both the spoken and the visual aspects of communication. Body language such as gestures, eye contact, and touch differs among cultures, and some cultures rely more on the unspoken aspects of communicating while others rely more on the spoken words (Jones & Lorenzo-Hubert, 2006).

Start by Changing Yourself

In all situations, whether at home or at school, children respond best to consistent expectations. Children feel safe when they can trust that each adult will provide the same responses. Our intent is to support the student with the challenging behavior in learning more acceptable ways to communicate. This may mean that teachers, team members, or parents need to change their behaviors first! You may need to learn how to communicate openly, value differing opinions, and share the responsibility in coming up with positive behavior support plans. This is especially true when teams continue to respond to challenging behaviors in the same old way only because "we have always done it this way"—even when the old way doesn't work any longer. We must strive to be open to explore new options, to release our personal biases, and to do what is best for the child. This may be challenging and frustrating for some. But if we are working to provide the best support possible, sometimes we must let go and move on. In many situations a "band-aid" approach that just "fixes" the problem for the time being will not be enough; it's time for the team or parents to see behavior in a new way and to implement a new system and a new way of working together.

Behavior may serve many different functions depending on the context in which it is used. The first step in fostering positive communication behaviors is to build trusting relationships with all our communication partners: the child, the family, and the rest of the team, if there is one. The first step in this process is to take a new look at what and how behaviors communicate.

Takeaways

- Behavior is communication, even challenging behaviors. People who use challenging behaviors have the same human need to be acknowledged and have their behaviors seen as meaningful messages as you and I do.

- Behaviors can serve many functions.

- Whether a behavior is perceived as acceptable can vary depending on the situation and the receiver of the message.

- Self-assessment and team assessment are needed to achieve clarity in defining acceptable and unacceptable behaviors.

- Establishing trusting relationships with a team and the student is the first step toward being able to listen to the message behaviors send.

Assess Your Perspective

Take some time to create lists of behaviors that are always acceptable, never acceptable, and sometimes acceptable. You might think of a specific child's behaviors when you fill this out. However, it is also enlightening to evaluate your own behaviors, and those of your close friends and loved ones. Consider the routines in which the children in your care may excel and those in which their behavior may be problematic. There is no right or wrong situation or response, and no limit on the number of responses. Complete this exercise individually, and then compare your responses with others who work and/or live with the child.

Behaviors That Are Always Acceptable

Behaviors That Are Never Acceptable

Behaviors That Are Sometimes Acceptable

Acceptable Behaviors

Following are typical responses from workshop participants who are asked to identify always-acceptable behaviors. Read and discuss with others. Which are observable behaviors, and which are traits that need more precise description? Which are the most important to you?

Hugging

Gentle touching

Sharing

Laughing

Reading together

Helping others

Crying

Playing together

Talking

Screaming

Shaking hands

Sharing ideas

Constructive arguing

Gesturing

Initiating

Making mistakes

Being nice to classmates

Using body language

Creative but safe use of materials

Interacting

Making choices

Differing perspectives

Accepting

Refusing

Personal expression of feelings or emotions

Singing

Following rules

Participation

Nonparticipation

Politeness

Communicating to be understood

Anything not hurting others

Assertiveness

Socializing

Talking out problems

Caring

Negotiating

Responsibility

Independence

Walking inside

Smiling

Using words instead of . . .

Bathroom accidents

Resting quietly

Changing activities

Yelling

Arguing

Not wanting to be part of the group

Choosing to say "no"

Staying in seat

Being quiet

Having one's own opinion

Turn taking

Being ignored

Asking questions

Needing sameness

Consideration of others' feelings

Arguing with words

Playing

Withdrawing to collect

Friendliness

Problem solving

Cooperation

Having tantrums away from others

Kindness

Honesty

Excitement

Positive physical contact

Good listening

Good manners

Respectfulness

Respecting materials

Trustworthiness

Expressing feelings

Being angry

Curiosity

Humor

Compassion

Unacceptable Behavior

Following are typical responses from workshop participants who are asked to identify never-acceptable behaviors. Read and discuss with others. Which are observable behaviors, and which are traits that need more precise description? Which are the most important to you?

Hitting	Tantrums	Making fun
Selfishness	Running in rooms	Inappropriate language
Kissing	Destructiveness	Screaming inside
Biting	Dangerous behavior	Laughing when hurt
Spitting	Being knowingly unkind	Running
Hair pulling	Vomiting	Chasing
Bad language	Physical aggression	Cussing
Pushing	Limiting others' choices	Unbuckling seatbelt
Property destruction	Hurting others or self	Taking things
Whining	Teasing others	Moodiness
Throwing at others	Being late	Name calling
Kicking	Violence	Rudeness
Pinching	Manipulation	Leaving room
Arguing	Verbal abuse	Screaming in someone's face
Being verbally unkind	Dishonesty	Biased behavior
Screaming to get attention	Sneakiness	Being judgmental
Constant moving	Defiance	Dominating behavior
Taking things from others	Disrespect	Leaning back in chairs
Lying	Attitude	Tattling
Belligerence	Yelling	Never making waves
Growling	Nose picking	Grabbing
Cursing	Taunting	Harassing others
Breaking things	Being a wet noodle (going limp)	Put downs
Overreaction of caregivers		Rough play
Self-injury	Putting self or others at risk of emotional or physical injury	Interrupting the group

Sometimes Acceptable Behavior

Following are typical responses from workshop participants who are asked to identify sometimes-acceptable behaviors. Read and discuss with others. Which are observable behaviors, and which are personality traits that need more precise description? When are these behaviors acceptable, and when not?

Whining

Playing loudly

Throwing tantrums

Fidgeting

Having noodle knees

Interrupting

Aggression

Biting in self-defense

Screaming

Teasing

Growling

Cursing

Hitting

Hugging

Asking questions

Gestures

Participating

Being rowdy

Bickering

Refusing

Crying

Angry words

Leaving group

Being angry

Hitting things

Talking

Not sharing

Yelling

Being loud

Running

Kicking

Ignoring

Touching

Burping

Throwing

Not sitting still in circle

Bathroom accidents

Throwing up

Crying fit

Directing behavior

Being excited

Needing repetition or verbal cues

Being unfair to others

Walking away

Grabbing

Physical activity

Spitting

Crying for no reason

Passive resistance

Not listening

Moodiness

Talking back

Silliness

Being very quiet

Tattling

Name calling

Making waves

Being mean

Playing

Personal Reflection

What is your perspective about behaviors being communication?

Do you and your colleagues share the same perspective? How is that helpful or detrimental?

In what situations have you experienced behavior as communication?

In those situations (whether positive or negative), what was your response?

In retrospect, do you feel your response addressed the behavior's message?

What shifts would you like to make in your response to communicative behaviors?

What support would you need in order to listen more carefully to the behaviors around you?

2

Forms of Communication

We all use behavior to communicate in everyday life. We are constantly communicating without ever saying a word. This is true for you and for us, for young children, school-aged children, college students, adults of all shapes, sizes, colors, and abilities, as well as for people who may or may not use the spoken word to communicate. Everyone communicates! To understand each other, we need to learn to listen to more than words.

Not all behaviors are *meant* to be communicative, however. Communication theorists debate as to when exactly children begin to communicate "on purpose." In fact, although as competently communicating adults we are able to monitor our facial expressions and body language, most of the time expressions and body language are not under our conscious control, and therefore are not intentional communication. Many of the behavioral cues we interpret to get information are not intentionally used to send a message. Think about your posture when you are watching a great action scene in a movie. Then think about your posture when you are impatiently waiting in the grocery line. Finally, think about your posture when you are engaged in a conversation with someone you love dearly. In each situation, your body sends a message to anyone who is "listening," even though you probably aren't conscious of sending any message at all. We can also use our posture to send a message on purpose—as when a teacher puts her hands on her hips to show she means business—but most of our communication through body language is unconscious, automatic, and unintentional.

Stages of Communication Development

From birth, infants communicate. Most movements we see in newborns are reflexive responses to stimulation, such as sucking when the nipple is presented or startling in response to a loud noise. As clearly unintentional as these behaviors are, adults look at them and use them to gain information about the state of the baby. Babies don't "mean" to communicate, but their caregivers treat their behaviors as communicative.

Soon infants begin to use vocalizations, eye contact, facial expressions, smiles, and various cries in response to their immediate environment. By using this array of signals, they communicate a variety of emotions and needs to their caregivers. As children grow, they are able to use increasingly more sophisticated and intentional ways to communicate their ideas, needs, and wishes. One of the most critical skills we learn very early is the ability to mutually attend to objects or events with a partner. When a newborn turns toward his mother's voice, when a baby plays peek-a-boo with a caregiver, or when an infant looks at a toy and then at the person holding that toy, those acts of mutual attention to the same object or action are forming the foundation for future communication, social understanding, and social interaction skills to develop (Carpenter, Nagell, & Tomasello, 1998; Schuler, Wetherby, & Prizant, 1997). The ability to call attention to one's self or to an object or activity that is mutually interesting creates the environment necessary for the interaction to take place.

So in addition to the extraordinary explosion of language skills we gain in early childhood, we also learn most of the rules of social communication and interaction. By the time we enter school, we know where to stand, how close to get to different people in different social situations, how loud to talk, what types of words to use, how to use gestures—and we learn it all through observation. We watch our parents, our caregivers, people in our communities, even the television.

Three phases are observed in the typical development of communication (Wetherby & Prizant, 1992; Warren & Yoder, 1998). During the prelinguistic phase, the child develops the ability to use gestures in increasingly more intentional ways. Infants at this stage communicate primarily to express immediate needs and wants, but are also learning how to engage a partner in a social interaction. From birth to about eight months old, typically developing infants explore their environments, learning to interact with both objects and people. The behaviors they exhibit are unintentional, nonsymbolic communication acts. During this stage, children also begin to learn the basic communicative functions and how communication works, and their caregivers work to make meaning of their communicative efforts.

Sometime between eight and twelve months old, children who are developing typically start to gain more control over their movements and vocalizations, which allows them to communicate more purposefully in a variety of ways.

In the next phase, children learn single words, which allows them to begin to communicate symbolically, a skill that explodes in complexity in the third phase when they begin to string words together to form ideas.

Nonverbal Communication

The focus of the rest of this chapter, however, and of much of this book, is communication behaviors that are *nonsymbolic* or nonverbal. The term *nonsymbolic* communication means there are no spoken words or other types of symbols (no pictures or sign language) attached to the message being communicated. When a baby cries, something is wrong. Whether that communication is intentional or not is irrelevant; if we look at the behavior and interpret it, it becomes communicative. As babies get older, the crying becomes differentiated if they are hungry, tired, sick, have dirtied a diaper, and so on. The caregivers in the baby's environment shape the baby's behavior by the way they respond to it. When we pay attention to the same object or event, and react together, we form routines that are perpetuated and become communication interactions.

For many of us, language develops out of these routines (Lifter & Bloom, 1998). Most three-year-olds are capable of engaging in interactions containing many intricate components that remain elements of our conversational interactions throughout our lives. But it is important to recognize that infants learn how to use their bodies and voices to communicate long before they have any understanding of language. For some people with significant disabilities, this use of those nonsymbolic means to "get the message across" remains the predominant way they communicate throughout their lives.

The nonverbal behaviors discussed in this chapter are representative of behaviors we all exhibit. It is not an exhaustive list, but will provide us with a basis for thinking about cues that are right there for us to see and use, if we just know what to look for! The next chapter will provide a more in-depth discussion of the communicative purposes of these behaviors.

Conventional Gestures

Waving, shrugging, or nodding our heads are understood by most people in Western culture. Gestures such as these commonly occur in conjunction with speech, are developmentally linked to speech (Capone & McGregor, 2004), and in fact, are considered to be an integral component of the overall production of the message (Kendon, 2004). As critical as they are in adding information to spoken messages, they may also be one of the primary means of communication for people who do not speak. In addition to the gestures mentioned in this section, many researchers (Capone & McGregor, 2004; Ozcaliskan & Goldin-Meadow, 2005) include some of the behaviors discussed in following sections in the broad definition of gestures.

We separate them here and in our presentation to make it easier to see them as acts of communication.

Generalized Movement or Changes in Muscle Tone

Studies have shown that even newborns are aware of their environment and changes in it. For example, infants may change their muscle tone when an interesting object is presented to them or they hear a different voice (Williams & Golenski, 1978; Bertoncini, Bijeljac-Babic, Jusczyk, Kennedy, & Mehler, 1988; Nazzi, Floccia, & Bertoncini, 1998). This is also something, as speakers, we look for in our audiences. When our workshop participants get "antsy," shifting in their seats, their behavior "announces" that it is time for a break or that the information is challenging, boring, or uncomfortable. Think of children in class; what happens when one of your lessons slows down or is too long or too complicated? The kids begin to fidget and move about, often without verbalizing much. As an adult, when you talk with a friend about an enjoyable topic, you will see a relaxed posture, a smile, consistent eye contact, and maybe the body slightly tilted toward you. Conversely, in a more confrontational or uncomfortable interaction, you are likely to notice a stiffening of posture, tightened lips, perhaps balling of the fists, changes in breathing, a decrease in eye contact, and so on. Body language speaks loudly if we pay attention and "listen."

Gazing, Gaze Shift, and Gaze Aversion

Imagine you are gazing longingly at an object. If someone else sees you, he may form some opinions about what your gaze means: interest, desire, or curiosity. If, however, you shift your gaze repeatedly from the object to the person, he might eventually understand that you want him to do something with that object. Gazing works in reverse, too. Babies frequently communicate through *gaze aversion*—for example, by looking away from the spoon of food once they feel full, or by refusing to even glance at the mashed carrots. Similarly, when we adults do not want to speak with someone, we avoid his or her gaze (Doherty-Sneddon & Kent, 1996; Doherty-Sneddon, Bruce,

Bonner, Longbotham, & Doyle, 2002). Remember in school when the teacher asked for an answer to a question, and you did not want to respond? Where did you look? Was it at the floor, your notebook, or something else? Certainly not directly into the teacher's eyes! The use of gaze, gaze shift, and gaze aversion is quite communicative.

Orientation

Orientation is simply turning the whole body (not just eyes) away from or towards something or someone. A baby who has been offered strained peas may exhibit a classic example of turning away from that undesirable food. Conversely, if we turn toward an object, person, or location, the likelihood is that we are expressing interest or acceptance.

Even a reflex present at birth, the "rooting reflex," which helps babies find their mother's breast, is an orientation of the head toward the stimulus of touch on the baby's cheek. Using this example, we can see where a clearly unintentional, neurological reflex can be interpreted as an affirmation: "Yes, I want to eat." Sometimes the orientation of the head or body may simply mean that someone has recognized a stimulus in the environment. On the other hand, orienting one's body toward a desired object, person, or activity can be very deliberately communicative, as we would see if we observed two people who are in love in deep conversation with each other.

Proximity, Assuming Positions, and Going to Places

Children move toward the people, objects, activities, and environments with which they want to be involved. This group of behaviors simply entails the placing of one's body next to or near what is desired or pleasurable, and conversely, moving away from what is being avoided. If you can picture yourself in a classroom where a group of students gathers around a computer, but no one stands by the globe, you have an idea of how this group of behaviors works.

Giving

Sometimes nonsymbolic communication behaviors do not necessarily have clearcut meanings. For example, giving can be a very nice way for children to say, "Play with me," "Do this with me," or "Get involved with me." When younger children offer objects to enter into a group-play situation, the act of giving becomes a clear offer of friendship (Honig & Thompson, 1994).

However, giving can also mean, "Get this away from me; I am tired of it." One young man we observed, Nate, used giving as a way to say "I don't want to do this," but his support staff interpreted the giving as him asking them to do it *with* him or *for* him. As they continued to misinterpret his true meaning, his behaviors escalated to unfortunate proportions, as we shall see later (page 24).

Reaching, Grabbing, and Pointing

These communication behaviors seem to go together, especially in younger children or children with disabilities. When they want something, the first thing they may do is reach for that object (or person), and if it is in reach, they may grab it. Without using any words, children make their desires quite apparent! Children reach and grab for objects they want before they learn to point. As a developmentally more sophisticated skill (Butterworth, 2003), pointing may not yet be in every student's repertoire—and can be taught as a more acceptable way to let someone know what is wanted (Dobrich & Scarborough, 1984).

Touching, Manipulating, or Moving With Another Person

There are many times when one person may physically manipulate another to get some message across. Grabbing and taking you to the door may mean, "Open the door," or, "Come and see." A child may take your hand and put it on the refrigerator when he or she wants something to eat or take you to the VCR when he or she wants to see a video.

Touching another person sends a powerful, very deliberately chosen message. Think about who you touch and when. The touch of a loved one at a time of sorrow is comforting, but the touch of a person who has power over you in your personal or professional life can be threatening. When we use touch, and when we observe others using touch to communicate, we must keep in mind that the physical connection we have with others has the ability to create positive and loving relationships or negative and destructive ones.

Hugging and Kissing

While these are wonderful to receive and are definitely positive ways to demonstrate affection, hugs and kisses are not always appropriate. Be sure that the nonverbal communication skills you encourage are accompanied by clear expectations as to when they are appropriate and with whom they are appropriate. Remember Mary Lou who loved to hug from chapter 1?

When we work with young children who like to hug and kiss, the guidelines should be discussed with the other caregivers in the child's life and carefully and clearly explained to the child. As children grow older, and the social rules change, what may have been appropriate at age three or four may no longer be acceptable in all settings and with all people.

Facial Expressions

Our facial expressions are a window to our emotions. While there is an ongoing theoretical debate surrounding how many facial expressions we use in what specific situations, when they develop, and the variation in their readability by people with disabilities (Bennett, Bendersky, & Lewis, 2002), we do know that most of us pay attention to facial expressions when we are having conversations. We can see if our listener is interested or distracted; whether there is a question or comment; whether the joke we told is funny or a flop. We see when the light bulb goes off and an "aha" moment occurs. The way someone's face reacts to the circumstances, environment, or words being said is another critical nonsymbolic cue we use to read the situation.

Laughing and Crying

Laughing and crying convey messages that seem to be clear. We generally interpret laughing or giggling as a message that things are going well and crying as a message that things are not so wonderful. In most cultures, there are clearly defined times when these behaviors are acceptable. And both laughing and crying can communicate a number of emotions. As with all communication behaviors, remember to consider the context when deciphering the message.

Have you ever found yourself laughing inappropriately? Perhaps you laughed when someone fell down, tripped, or made a mistake. In those instances, laughter may happen not because something is funny, but rather because someone feels uncomfortable, embarrassed, or threatened. People can also cry at very happy times, such as at weddings. The saying goes "I laughed until I cried," and in fact research tells us that the physical control of laughing and crying is in the same part of the brain (Parvizi, Anderson, Martin, Damasio, & Damasio, 2001). This makes it possible for us to find ourselves laughing or crying when we least expect it.

Self-Stimulation

The technical term for what many commonly call self-stimulatory behaviors is *stereotypy* or *stereotypic behaviors*. These are behaviors that stimulate one or more of our senses through repetitive movements. Most of us do things like wiggle a foot, play with jewelry or our hair, hold something in our hands, drink or eat, chew on our nails or a pen, or wiggle in our seats during a meeting or a long lecture. Some of us sit in rocking chairs while we watch television. All these behaviors stimulate our sensory systems for various reasons. We may be trying to keep our focus on a topic of conversation during a meeting or just relaxing at home. We have developed multiple ways by which we can keep our system alert and calm at the same time, and some of them use self-stimulatory behaviors.

However, some people, often those with significant disabilities or autism, have not learned how to monitor those self-stimulatory behaviors, which then become socially unacceptable to others or interfere with interactions, learning, or work. This type of self-stimulatory behavior may include spinning objects, flapping hands, or body spinning and rocking. Theories vary about why people engage in self-stimulatory behaviors; some may need increased sensory input (due to underarousal or hyposensitivity to stimulation), while others may need an avoidance or a calming strategy when there is too much stimulation in the environment (overarousal or hypersensitivity to the environment) (Murray-Slutsky & Paris, 2005; Gillingham, 1997). Because these behaviors often serve a specific sensory purpose, they will probably never disappear. However, as children become engaged in more meaningful and varied activities, and learn how to monitor their behaviors more fully, many stereotypic or self-stimulation behaviors decrease in intensity, in frequency, or in both.

While it is true that these behaviors are harder to look at as communication, they are nevertheless often very communicative! Ask yourself: When do you see these behaviors? What purpose might they be serving? Self-stimulatory behaviors often appear during periods of frustration, boredom, confusion, excitement, or fear. Recognizing that these specific behaviors appear at predictable times may help us understand them. By changing our perspective, we can begin to look at the reason the behavior exists, the message it sends, and think about ways in which both the sensory and communicative needs of the child can be met.

Self-Injury

Self-injurious behavior takes self-stimulation one step further. As improbable as this may seem, self-injurious behavior can also be viewed as communication.

Hitting a Communication Wall: Jose's Story

A young man in our past named Jose worked in a small room in a sheltered, windowless workshop made of concrete blocks. There he put together and took apart nuts and bolts. A young teenager, Jose was diagnosed with an IQ of 13. He was extremely self-injurious; he sat in the corner of this concrete block room and beat his head repeatedly against the wall. He was always scared and had large open wounds on his head. He had no way to communicate: no language, no signs, and no communication board to use. He was bored! Over several years, a picture communication system was developed for Jose. As the use of his system increased, his self-injurious behaviors began to diminish. But change does take time. Jose had spent fifteen years developing his angry behavioral repertoire, and it took years to develop other, more acceptable ways to communicate his needs, ideas, and emotions. The happy ending: years later, Jose graduated from high school and since then has successfully held down a job. When he graduated, his communication board had over eight hundred words that had been placed underneath the pictures on the board. The pictures had become faded, but were not replaced—because he had learned to read! (See page 25 for more about picture communication systems.)

Jose had been so bored and frustrated, with no way to tell anyone how he felt. The only thing he could do was beat his head and hope that someone would recognize his boredom and frustration. His behavior was saying, "I need something! Do something for me!"

Self-injurious behaviors may have the same sensory roots as self-stimulatory behaviors. Behaviors such as self-biting or head banging may indicate an increased sensory need. However, we propose that self-injurious behaviors stem from an increased need to "get the message across." When all other nonverbal cues fail, self-injury usually gets a response. Herb Lovett (1996) suggests that self-injurious behavior needs to be investigated as an indicator for undiagnosed pain. For example, if a child is hitting her face, she might have teeth or sinuses that are painful. Clearly, before we begin to explore other messages that self-injurious behaviors send as nonverbal communication, we must rule out any medical causes that might exist.

Aggression

Using aggression or hurting someone else is probably the most controversial topic in the nonverbal communication sessions that we do. Once again we need to stress that there are many possible causes for aggression, and numerous studies have attempted to describe the reasons aggression occurs (Allen, 2000). As with self-injury, the first avenue of investigation must be medical; if a student is showing aggression, first rule out any undiagnosed pain, serious depression or mood disorders, or other medical conditions the student is experiencing.

Typically, aggression does not just appear "out of the blue." Some people have difficulty with impulse control, but in our combined experience of over fifty years working with people with the most challenging behaviors, we have encountered only a handful who fall within that category. Instead, close observation of aggressive incidents often reveals many of the other nonverbal cues we've discussed—*before* the aggressive incident occurs. You might observe changes in movement and muscle tone first: a stiffening of posture, tightened lips, balling of the fists, changes in breathing, changes in eye contact, and so on. Or an increase in self-stimulatory or self-injurious behaviors might precede aggression. The aggressive incident is rarely the first thing that happens.

What Do I Need to Do to Get You to Listen? Nate's Story

The school called Kim and Sue in distress. One of their junior high students was beating up his teachers, particularly his aide and the physical therapist. We asked them to send us a video of part of his day so that we could be prepared for this critical situation.

Nate did not speak and used very little sign language to communicate. He and his aide were working puzzles in apparent good moods; lots of smiling and eager body language let us know that. After the aide pulled out the fourth puzzle, Nate began to look around the room. He waved at his friends working at another table. He turned around in his seat to look at his teacher, vocalizing and gesturing to her to come over to his work area. He slumped in his chair. He twiddled his hair and picked his nose. Finally he took the puzzle and handed it back to his aide. "Oh," she said. "Do you want to do this one with me?"

Nate hauled off and hit her right in the arm. Being a rather large teenager, and not having a great amount of control over his strength and coordination, Nate hit her hard enough to add yet another bruise to her arm.

As outsiders watching the situation unfold, it was clear to us that Nate was using all the nonverbal communication means in his repertoire to tell his aide that he was finished with puzzles. The change in his body language and facial expressions, his orientation away from the task, and his loss of attention should have given her the message—had she been listening. The final straw for Nate was her misinterpretation of his gesture of handing the puzzle back to her. By that point, aggression was the only way he had to get the message across.

It may seem as if aggression happens out of the blue because without the close observation of the preceding cues, teachers, support staff, and even parents may be unaware of the impending blow-up. If all other attempts at communication are not "heard" and acknowledged, the one behavior that always gets an immediate response is aggression. Aggression is never ignored! Although the real message may have been missed, someone at least *noticed*. When the real message is heard sooner, the child's need for aggression is diminished. Learn to listen attentively and early.

A Continuum of Communication Behaviors

Within each individual repertoire of *communication means* (the way we communicate) is a variety of behaviors that fall on a continuum, from those that provide the most information and are most socially acceptable, to those that are most difficult (see fig. 2.1).

Easier to understand and most socially acceptable ↑ Speech
                                                   Written language
                                                   Sign language
                                                   Picture symbols
                                                   Conventional gestures
                                                   Facial expressions
                                                   Giving, reaching, grabbing, and pointing
                                                   Proximity
                                                   Crying, whining, laughing, and giggling
                                                   Vocalizations
                                                   Echolalia
                                                   Self-stimulation
                                                   Self-injury
Harder to understand and least socially acceptable ↓ Aggression

Figure 2.1: Continuum of communication behaviors.

For many of us, speaking face to face is our preferred way to communicate because it provides the most information. Not only do we hear the actual words, but we also use body language, tone of voice, facial expressions, and so on to help us understand the exact message. Many of us consider written language the next-most conventional and explicit way to communicate, since it provides ample information about the text of the message. However, in reading a written message, we do not have all the nonverbal cues we would have if we were speaking in person. Sign language is a full and complete language with the capability of communicating anything that can be said in spoken language. However, because not everyone signs, it is less conventional than spoken language and may therefore not be as understandable in multiple contexts as either spoken or written language. Picture and word boards are often useful as communication systems for students with disabilities who cannot speak. If arranged in a linguistic format (not just as a dictionary of pictures), they can provide a viable language system and therefore many opportunities for interaction in a variety of environments. Because well-chosen pictures are understandable to many different people, a nonspeaking person can use them to communicate in many situations.

Picture and Word Boards

A picture communication system can be organized in several ways. For example, it may have columns that represent parts of a sentence, and each column may contain pictures of commonly used words. The purple column has question words, the green has days of the week and other time references, the orange has people words, the turquoise has action words, and so on. Vocabulary reflects individual needs and preferences for each user. When the user wants to make a message, he can generate a complete sentence by pointing to the pictures. This allows him to communicate entire ideas, even though he is not able to speak, ideas such as, "I want help please. Where pencil and paper?" or "I want to read more books."

continued on next page →

Low-tech communication systems are a good segue into electronic devices such as computers with voice output, in which the computer reads the sentence out loud, giving the user a "voice." The low-tech systems continue to serve a purpose after electronics are introduced, however, in such settings and during activities when electronics are not feasible (for example, at a beach or during horseback riding).

As we move across the scale we find echolalia, which is the use of spoken language but in a way that is not always recognized as communication. Echolalia is the repetition of what has already been heard; it can be immediate or delayed. When it happens immediately (question: "Do you want a soda?" and answer: "Want a soda?") it can often (but not always) be viewed as an affirmation. Be careful, however, since echolalia can hide the true desire of the child. Be sure to ask your question in several ways ("Do you want a soda or some juice? Juice or soda? Which one would you like?") to avoid the trap of the student always repeating the last item named. Echolalia can also be delayed, as Samuel's story shows.

Mysterious Morning Messages: Samuel's Story

In working with a four-year-old boy who was demonstrating extremely destructive behaviors, echolalia became a clue to his behavior. This behavior never occurred at night, only in the morning—but not every morning. Some mornings were fine; others were not. What was happening?

Samuel would almost always wake up happy. He would sing as he got dressed and came to the table for breakfast. At that point, things could flow easily, or they could get ugly. On some days, Samuel would sit down, eat, get on the bus, and begin his school day relaxed and smiling. On other days, Samuel would scream, stomp, upturn the entire table, and rampage through the house overturning furniture and swiping things off shelves. On those days, when the bus came, his mother would shove his arms into his coat, hand him over to the bus driver kicking and screaming, and hope his day would not be totally lost.

Sue went to observe. On the first morning of observation, nothing happened. Things were beautiful. What's the problem? she wondered. The next morning, things fell apart. Samuel and his mom were such a happy picture the morning before. What had Sue missed? Another observation on the third morning showed him going through his morning routine of singing in his room as Mom helped him get dressed. Then they went to breakfast, and the scene became chaos.

What was happening? To his mom, Samuel's singing was background noise (and possibly self-stimulation), but to Sue, an outside observer, his songs were the jingles to breakfast food commercials! His seemingly meaningless noises were a way to communicate. If he sang the jingle from the commercial and the item appeared on the table, all was well. If it did not appear, then the house was a wreck, and his day at school was ruined. Samuel was using delayed echolalia to express his desires.

With the realization that she could avoid his behavioral upsets by listening to his song in the morning, Samuel's mom modified her approach to breakfast, and everyone benefited. If the food item was available, she could provide Samuel's first choice. If the desired item was not available, she could tell him, "I don't have this. Let's go and see what else you want." He was heard; his message had gotten across, and he could move on with his choice of breakfast and then with his day.

Self-injurious and aggressive behaviors are perhaps the least socially acceptable behaviors, and usually provide the least explicit information to the listener as well. It is hard to figure out the meaning of a behavior that is threatening the well-being of the student himself or herself, or others in the environment. However, we must keep in mind that we ourselves move up and down on this continuum: think about the behaviors you exhibit when you are extremely frustrated or angry and no one is around to see. Many of us have probably wanted to scream, and some of us might express frustration through profanity or pounding our fists. If we accept the fact that all of us flow up and down this continuum, and that sometimes we use behaviors that are neither totally socially acceptable nor totally understood by our listeners, then we must accept the fact that the children we teach and support, regardless of age or ability level, flow up and down the continuum as well. If the student uses a form of communication that is at the least-acceptable and least-understandable level, then our logical next step is to teach him a more conventional means of communication to move "up" the continuum. The most crucial response, however, is to always listen to the behaviors.

When we listen to the message behind even self-abusive or aggressive behaviors, we often find that the student has something so important to tell us that he believes it is worth the consequences of the socially unacceptable and sometimes painful behavior.

Our ultimate goal is to find a way to communicate. If you can communicate with someone, you can solve problems, make friends, and get what you need. Since speech is not always available, we must explore other means of communication to help the child learn to interact without resorting to challenging behaviors.

Intentional Communication

As we expand our understanding to *what* children communicate in addition to *how* they communicate, we also need to take another look at the question of whether the message was intentionally sent, and how we know that.

There are some clues. Wetherby and Prizant (1989) have proposed several useful signs that may indicate that a behavior is an intentional message. For example:

- If a child looks back and forth between the adult and the desired goal

- If the signal persists until the goal is achieved

- If the child waits for a response from the listener

- If the signal stops when the goal is met

- If the child displays satisfaction when the goal is met or dissatisfaction when it is not

We communicate both intentionally and unintentionally throughout our entire lifetime. The fluctuations communicated by simple changes in attention and behavior give those around us information as clearly as if we say out loud, "This is really exciting!" or "Get on with it; I'm so bored I can't stand it!" Most of us will add the components of speech and language (the locutionary stage of communication development), which will greatly increase our ability to interact with information and other people. But for some people, the preverbal stages of communication behaviors may be their only means of communicating. All behavior is communicative, whether intentionally or not, and whether or not we have language to augment our unintentional, nonsymbolic behaviors. Recognizing the difference between intentional and unintentional messages can inform the way in which we react to them.

Listen When Behaviors Speak

As we have shown, sometimes we communicate consciously and purposefully. Sometimes we unintentionally communicate more than we think we do! We are all communicating at all times, whether we are aware of it or not. Children are born communicating. In the beginning, infant communication behaviors are all unintentional in nature and are interpreted by the adults who care for them. Think about the way a baby calms and cuddles into a parent's arms. This is interpreted as "I am content. I am happy. I love you." Conversely, think about the way a caregiver reacts to the loud screams of an infant: "Something's wrong! Is the baby hungry? Tired? Sick?" It is sometimes hard to interpret behaviors that do not use conventional symbols such as words, gestures, or pictures, but the consistent pairing of a behavior with a response from a caregiver shapes those behaviors into meaning.

As children pass developmental milestones and start walking and talking, adults assume that they will communicate primarily through words. However, as we have seen, communication continues to occur through a wide variety of means, and we can learn to "listen" to behavior as communication. Each and every one of us has the power to choose to open our eyes, ears, and hearts to listen and understand.

Takeaways

- We are all communicating all the time.

- Even if a behavior was not meant to be communicative, it still sends a message.

- We begin to learn in early infancy that our bodies, faces, and voices communicate.

- We can hear a vast amount of information when we learn to listen to behaviors and value them as communication.

Personal Reflection

What types of nonverbal communication do you see from the children in your class?

What types of nonverbal communication do you use in your classroom?

What messages might each convey?

Do you and your colleagues have a way to support each other when you are seeing confusing nonverbal messages from the students in your class? How do you do this?

3

Functions of Communication

Each person and each situation create a unique purpose for communication to take place. The following list outlines some of the most frequent reasons for communicating. These are called *communicative functions*. Each communicative attempt or interaction may have more than one function. Through careful observation of each situation, we may start to understand the messages of behaviors.

What Do We Accomplish Through Communicating?

Greeting or departing (saying "hi" and "goodbye")

Making requests:	Protesting or refusing
• For objects	Agreeing or disagreeing
• For actions	Describing
• For social routines	Announcing completion
• For comfort	Fulfilling sensory needs
Getting or giving information	Expressing feelings (pleasure, fear, frustration)
Getting help	Reporting internal states (illness, pain)

As we have shown, behaviors can communicate many things, depending upon each situation, the student, and his or her needs and feelings. Behaviors may convey one message in a certain situation and something completely different in another. Behaviors never happen in a vacuum. Several categories of behaviors can be consistently challenging: escape and avoidance behaviors, attention-seeking behaviors, and sensory behaviors. Let's take a more in-depth look at some situations that illustrate not only how clearly behaviors can communicate, but also how much we can learn when we take the perspective that behaviors, even difficult behaviors, *are* communication!

Escape and Avoidance Behaviors: "I Wanna Get Outta Here!"

Escape and avoidance behaviors may occur when a request is made (such as "Time to pick up," "Get out your books," or "Do the first ten problems"). We know that when a behavior is intentionally communicative, it will persist until the person's need is met. Many behaviors can be used to avoid, as we illustrated in our discussion of communicative behaviors in the last chapter. No single specific behavior can be labeled *the* avoidant behavior.

The Runner: Jerry's Story

Jerry was a ten-year-old student whose behavior announced, "I wanna get out of here!" He was a "runner." When requests were presented to him (such as "Come to the gym" or "Get ready for a snack"), he would often leave the classroom or his home by simply running away. When he ran away, his teachers or his family followed him, but this only excited Jerry more! He not only wanted to escape, but also enjoyed the attention he received during the chase.

At school, Jerry consistently ran to a particular classroom. Jerry's teachers (including Kim) talked with that classroom teacher as well as her students, instructing them to continue with their lesson and ignore Jerry. Kim promised she would be there to intervene.

The next time Jerry came to the gym, Kim instructed him, "Jerry, today I want you to shoot ten baskets in the gym." He looked at her and looked at the basket—which was less than ten feet tall—and ran away. Kim knew where he was headed and started to follow him. When Jerry showed up in the classroom, the teacher simply placed her hand on Jerry's shoulder to keep him there. He stayed there, gazing into a fish tank that he enjoyed, until Kim arrived and told him calmly, "Jerry, we have to go back to the gym to shoot two baskets. Let's go."

He did not readily agree to go back to the gym. He did need some physical assistance and a firm voice to get him started on his way. This time, Kim did not talk to Jerry on the way back about why he ran or why he should not run from class; that would have given him the attention he was seeking with his escape behavior. Once they were back in the gym, she redirected him to his task of shooting two baskets.

Jerry grimaced, crossed his arms tightly across his chest, and said, "It's too low! I wanna shoot outside!" and pointed to the baskets on the playground. Kim said, "You know what, you're right. This basket is too low. Do you want to go outside to shoot baskets?" He nodded. "Okay," she told him, "we will go outside, and I want you to shoot two baskets, and then we will be finished." They went outside, where he immediately shot two baskets.

A Communication Puzzle: Tina's Story

Tina was a seven-year-old girl who had limited verbal communication through echolalia. Kim was asked to supervise Tina as she put together a four-piece noninterlocking puzzle. As they sat down, Kim disassembled the puzzle and instructed Tina to put the puzzle together. Tina looked at Kim, looked at the puzzle, and immediately swung her arm, clearing the table of everything. The school staff had decided that the response to this type of behavior was to say, "You knocked it off, so now you need to pick it up," which was what Kim said next. Tina followed this instruction perfectly. Kim thought they were on the right track and again said, "Tina, put the puzzle together." She got the same response not just one more time, but numerous times! Kim was at a loss. Finally, their time together was finished, and Tina gladly went with the speech and language clinician to her next lesson. As Kim stood at the table, slamming the four-piece noninterlocking puzzle together, the classroom teacher came over to see how things went. It was obvious that Kim was not happy and the lesson had not gone well. Kim pointed to the puzzle and told the teacher, "I told Tina to put the puzzle together." The teacher covered her mouth with her hand, stifled a laugh, and said, "Is that the puzzle you were using? No wonder you had problems. Tina does twenty-five-piece interlocking puzzles very well. That one is totally boring and beneath her!"

Tina's avoidance behavior is not as blatant as Jerry's running away, but it is still a clear message that something is not right with the activity in which she is being asked to participate. In both scenarios, the children sent the message "I don't want to do this" loud and clear through their behavior. Yet the two situations ended differently. Why?

In the first scenario, Jerry's behavior indicated that he was not pleased with the activity he had been instructed to complete. Kim had to "listen" to his behavior and try to figure out what he was trying to say and why. Was the problem the activity, the environment, the instructions, a combination of them, or something entirely different? Fortunately, Jerry was able to verbally say that he thought the basket was too low and that going outside would be better. By listening to his behavior and his verbal responses, and adapting the activity, the conflict was resolved. Jerry's challenging behaviors were changed when the teacher listened to the message, acknowledged it, and then *the teacher changed.* The teacher needed to rethink the way the activity was presented, where it was being done, the level of difficulty, and Jerry's need not only for physical challenge but for an activity that allowed his self-respect to remain intact. Jerry's behavior was "heard."

In the scenario with Tina, a number of challenges arose—some of which could have been prevented if her regular teacher had informed Kim about what types of puzzles Tina could do! Since that did not happen, Tina communicated the best way she could that Kim had chosen the wrong puzzle. But that time, Kim did not listen. Instead, she repeatedly used the strategy she had chosen and created for that type of behavior, natural consequences ("You knock it down, you pick it up"). When Tina's message was not heard, and Kim simply followed the protocol for unwanted behaviors, neither of them got their needs met, and it ultimately caused more frustration for both of them.

If Kim had listened to Tina's behavior more intentionally, she could have changed the outcome of the activity. Tina was telling Kim that the activity was incorrect and that a change was needed. In one strategy, for example, Kim could have had many different puzzles available. When Tina knocked one off the table, Kim could have ignored that behavior and presented her with another puzzle. A better strategy would have been to say to Tina, "I guess this isn't the right puzzle. You go over and get the right one so you can do it here at the table." Tina would have retrieved the right puzzle—and would have been given some power in the whole scenario. The challenges could have been avoided—as well as hard feelings for everyone!

In both of these scenarios, it was not simply the student who needed to change; instead, the *teacher's instructions and the activity* needed to be respectfully changed to meet the learner's needs.

Attention-Seeking Behaviors: "Hey, Look at Me!"

Often, teachers or parents will say in an exasperated voice, "Oh, he's just doing that for attention!" Generally, that seems to be the case. The child wants attention. What child doesn't? Quite frankly, who among us does not like to be noticed or receive the attention of others? Many adults want to be recognized for everything from a new haircut to a major accomplishment. How we get attention has an impact on how others see us, just as how a child gains attention defines him as either a proud, self-assured child or a braggart, bully, or all-around troublemaker.

There are times when some children may need more attention than others, but every child desires and deserves to be noticed. Sometimes that attention can be eye contact, a wink intended for one specific student, a pat on the back, or a simple smile.

When we think of our fast-paced days and everything we think we should get done, it can be quite eye opening to also examine when children receive any attention. Often, when children are "good" or "quiet," the adults in their lives—whether parents or teachers—breathe a sigh of relief and continue with their daily routines. The children are left to themselves. Suddenly there is a cry or yell that demands attention. The adults must stop what they are doing to attend to the child and situation. The child may need comforting, may need some time to talk with an adult, or may simply need someone to notice she is there. Some children resort to acting out simply to receive the attention they crave and deserve. In this way, they receive attention for "negative" behaviors. Adults reinforce these unwanted behaviors by attending to them, essentially making them a "good idea" from the child's perspective, as a way to gain the attention needed.

One positive strategy in reducing unwanted behaviors is to catch the children being good. The next time the children in your care are quietly engaged in an activity or actively participating in a positive and productive manner, make a point to notice them. Give them the praise and positive interactions they crave. In that way, they can begin to learn that positive behaviors can get them wonderful and fun reactions or interactions from the adults.

Attention is important to everyone, but especially to children. Sometimes children may feel the desired interaction is worth the consequences of being "bad." Just as this teacher learned, it is more pleasant for everyone to notice the good and to reinforce positive behaviors. There is a wonderful list, easily found on the Internet, titled "101 Ways to Praise a Child" (author unknown) that has great ideas for ways to catch children being good and let them know it. In the end, when the goal is to foster positive, socially acceptable behaviors, the best time and place to give attention is when the kids are being good.

The Pincher: Billy's Story

Billy was a cute kindergartener who, according to his teacher, pinched "all the time." She felt she spent all day dealing with him pinching the other children. Kim went to observe her classroom. At the start of the day, an adult greeted the children and told them to go to their respective areas to play until everyone was present. The teacher and her assistant stood at the teacher's desk, chatting and preparing some activities for the day. As they were chatting, the cry came, "Billy's pinching me!" The teacher sighed, tossed her materials on the desk, and groaned, "See, this is what happens all the time!"

The teacher crossed to where Billy stood by his "victim," who was rubbing her arm and had tears in her eyes. The teacher said, "Billy, why do you do this? Ming, honey, you'll be all right soon. Go get a drink and you'll feel better." She then turned her attention back to Billy and proceeded to ask him why he did this every day. She told him that it made her stop what she was doing because she had to go over to see what had happened and then had to talk with him. On top of that, the other kids watched this happen, and she wondered why he continued to pinch when all it did was cause a scene. As she talked at him, Billy sat with his arms crossed over his chest, listening to her. Then he looked up and smiled, as if to say, "See, I got ya where I want ya!!" This behavior did occur several more times, but at specific times and during specific activities, and definitely not all day long.

At the end of the day, Kim asked the teacher why she thought Billy pinched. She stated that she thought he did it for attention. "That seems reasonable," Kim said, "but if you go to him every time he pinches, what are you giving him?"

"Attention," the teacher said, "but I have to do something about the pinching!" Kim agreed. Pinching is not acceptable. But if Billy pinches to receive attention, and he in fact does receive attention—even negative attention—what is likely to happen? The pinching will increase because he is being positively reinforced for his actions.

The teacher pondered this challenge. After some discussion about reinforcement and catching Billy being good, she decided to make some changes in her classroom environment. She decided to move her materials to different areas of the room, so that instead of always preparing at her desk, she could sometimes be near Billy's area. As Billy and the others gathered in their morning area, she greeted them all and began having conversations with them. For example, she would tell one child she had seen her parent at the grocery store, or she would tell Billy that she had enjoyed the story he told her the day before at sharing time, and so on. As she initiated the positive interactions with Billy and his classmates, she realized that something shifted *in herself*. She began to notice more positive aspects of each child, including Billy. All of the children loved to chat with her when she was not being "Teacher" but instead was simply talking with them. The teacher, in turn, enjoyed learning things about each child, such as who liked Disney© movies, who was into Pokémon©, and whose Grandma or dog had died, and began to find the unexpected teachable moments during the day as valuable as her planned lessons.

The teacher used this strategy for two weeks and then called to report that the "miracle" had happened. The pinching had not gone away but had decreased dramatically. She was feeling better about giving more positive attention to all the students, but especially to Billy. "And," she said, "Billy seems happier as well."

Sensory Behaviors: "That Feels Good"

Many children engage in specific behaviors because they feel good, are calming, or fill a void of some sort. Very young children suck their thumbs, for example, and preschoolers rock back and forth as they sit on the floor at group time. At times those behaviors may also serve a physical or emotional need; this may be particularly true for children with autism spectrum disorder. We all engage in sensory behaviors when we need to keep our systems awake and alert. However, most of us can monitor those behaviors and use actions that are not distracting or disturbing to those around us. Sensory behaviors that occur in the classroom that may seem challenging can include clicking a pen, twiddling hair, fiddling with a toy or object, humming, talking to oneself, bouncing feet or legs, doodling . . . you get the idea. As noted earlier, these behaviors are referred to as self-stimulation behaviors, and if unmonitored (as in students on the autism spectrum), they may appear odd to others or interfere in the completion of a required task.

Teachers who have been asked to describe when they see children engaging in self-stimulatory behaviors often list the following:

- When they are bored and don't know what else to do

- When they are annoyed, frustrated, anxious, confused, or excited

- When they need comfort

Clearly, the self-stimulation behaviors are already communicating feeling, emotion, or need—and yet most of us think they are simply a socially unacceptable behavior to be eliminated!

Since children exhibit these behaviors for a reason, it will be nearly impossible to make them disappear through strategies or behavior interventions. Behavior is communication, so perhaps it would be wise to listen to the behavior and make the necessary changes to the environment. If one tries to extinguish a self-stimulation behavior without listening to the message or giving a replacement behavior, it is guaranteed that some other behavior, equally if not more interfering, will take its place.

Communication on a Shoe String: Martin's Story

After spending a good deal of his young life in an institution, ten-year-old Martin came to live at a residential center (when that was still considered to be an acceptable option for some people with challenging behaviors). He had minimal language and few academic skills. When Martin arrived at the center, where Kim and her colleagues would be working with his parents and his home school, all he had that was his very own was a shoestring. He held the shoestring in one hand and snapped it with a whip-like motion.

Most of the time, Martin seemed very anxious and constantly flipped his string. It was almost impossible to get him involved in any sort of academic activity. His string was interfering with his ability to work because it was constantly in his hand. One day, an unsuspecting teacher took away his string to "help" him do his work—three colleagues had to take the young boy off the teacher as he fought to get his string back. Martin was furious and scared; he reacted in the only way he knew to get his string back, which was to attack. The string was his sole comfort. Martin's message was, "I am scared. That activity is meaningless to me. Don't you dare take my string." His behavior sent his intended message loud and clear to the classroom staff.

The staff put their heads together and asked his family and people at the institution if they could list anything that he enjoyed doing or playing while he was with them. The results were slim, but they did share that he liked farm animals. That was at least a starting point the staff could use to create activities for Martin, so they shopped for everything they could find that had farm animals. There were posters to throw beanbags at, puzzles, books, coloring books, markers, plates, silverware, cups, sheets, towels, balls, popup toys, and all sorts of fun things with farm animals on them to attract Martin's attention to something familiar that he enjoyed.

The next step was to devise a plan to get Martin to put his string down, complete the activity, and not feel threatened. The staff decided to use a puzzle with two easily recognizable animals; they purchased two copies of the puzzle, one for Martin to use and one for the staff to use as a model of the entire activity sequence. The sequence also included a small index card with a circle on it where Martin could place his string. When Martin approached the table, the puzzles were ready with the index card nearby. The adult model went as follows: "Put down the string, put the cow in the puzzle, and then you can take your string back."

Kim modeled this sequence of behaviors a number of times while Martin watched and flipped his string. He was intrigued because of his interest in the subject of the puzzle. As he stood watching, one teacher said, "After two more times, it will be Martin's turn to do the puzzle." Martin continued to watch, and as the staff counted out, "One, two, now it is Martin's turn to do the puzzle," he didn't retreat. One of his teachers said, "Let me help you with this," and very gently but swiftly helped him place his string hand down on the index card and use his other hand to place the puzzle piece—and then released his string hand. It happened almost immediately. There was no incident to report other than positive smiles and praise—success! The staff put this system into place in every environment for Martin: index card for the string, very limited expectation, and then return of the string. Every staff member consistently presented the same expectation in the same fashion. Over time, Martin came to the work areas, tossed his string in the circle, did his work (which was increasingly more difficult and lengthy), and then got his string again.

Martin was beginning to trust the staff and become engaged in activities, but he still had the string. When he was out in the community, the string continued to make him stand out, so it was still an issue for some staff members.

Christmas came and Martin went home for a two-week break. Two days into the break, his mother called and said that Martin had lost his string, but that things seemed okay thus far. Staff told her to call if she needed any assistance over the break, but she never called. Everyone believed that since Martin had lost his string, now they could really make some progress, because

continued on next page →

he must be feeling safe and trusting the people in his various environments. Everyone waited anxiously for his return following the break.

Dad entered the classroom building first, looking very ashamed; Mom followed, saying, "I'm so sorry. I'm so sorry." The staff was puzzled. When Martin walked in, he no longer had his shoestring. Instead, he had replaced it with something equally if not more obnoxious: an eighteen-inch holiday snowman candle! Clearly, he still needed something calming to "do" and to hold.

Over the next few months, things happened that dramatically changed his situation. Martin went home every weekend, where his father burned the candle. It melted, of course, and over time, all that remained was a wad of wax that Martin held in his hand. Martin would go to his activity, toss the wax onto the index card, do his work, and then grab his wax and walk away. He was working longer and doing more involved activities, so things were getting better.

Then one day, Martin walked into the classroom without his wax. The classroom teachers were stunned and immediately called his residential staff to find out what happened. The residential staff said they didn't know; they thought the classroom teachers had kept it, because Martin went all night without the wax or any behavioral incidents. For the rest of that day, the teachers were on pins and needles trying to act normally as they engaged Martin in his activities. He got through the day with only a few minor incidents. As time went on, the incidents became fewer and fewer, his involvement in activities grew, and Martin seemed to be more at peace.

What happened? Why did Martin no longer "need" his string or wax? As everyone involved in Martin's life discussed this, we realized two significant breakthroughs had happened for Martin. First, he felt "listened to" by the staff at the center. Whenever he had used his string or wax during the day or his activities, we let him know we understood that he was frustrated, confused, bored, anxious, or was not sure what to do. We talked to Martin as if he understood what was being said, and apparently he did! Second, our staff started his program of activities by utilizing *his* interest areas and creating activities that held meaning to *him*. Even though Martin was ten years old and could not tie his shoes, we didn't start with that activity. Instead, we started with farm animals, so that he would have some desire to get involved and have immediate success on which to build. If we had started with an age-appropriate skill, we might never have engaged him. By listening to Martin, we established a safe, caring, and respectful environment for him to live, work, and play without fear or frustration.

It's important to recognize that Martin presented no easy victories. This young man was so violent when he first came to the center that the staff recommended that he return to the institution because he was beyond help. The supervisor at the center, however, said, "No, Martin is ours to support, so do it"—and we found a way. Today that young man holds a job through supported employment, lives in an alternative family situation where he shares a home with another adult without a disability, and has made friends at the local YMCA and other community venues. His friends include not only other individuals with disabilities, but also community members who like him and want to be around him. Martin is part of the fabric of his community.

Self-stimulation is part of our human nature. If there's an unplanned increase in a student's physical activity during a lesson, it may be time for a break. If you notice that Jaquee is spending more time fiddling with her hair than doing the classwork, maybe she needs a little more assistance. If we can value the behavior as communication, listen to it particularly carefully when it is interfering with classroom and/or social interaction, and provide acceptable alternatives that meet the same needs, we will take an important step for the student and ourselves as teachers.

Context Matters

We have spent some time thinking about nonsymbolic behaviors, whether or not they are intentional in nature, and what functions they could serve. The communication behaviors that happen all around us function in such a wide variety of ways and can provide us with vast amounts of information if we are paying attention. Now let's ask some questions about what we personally need to have in place to be at our communicative best, and how we can collect simple data to help us understand what behaviors a student exhibits and what she might be communicating. In the next chapter, we will take a look at the big picture—the entire situation that surrounds communication behaviors.

Communication Best and Worst

There are moments in our lives when we know we are communicating clearly and effectively, as well as moments when we struggle to express ourselves or find ourselves completely at a loss for words. This activity explores what enables us to do well and what causes us stress or failure. (See page 42 for a reproducible form for group work, or visit **go.solution-tree.com/behavior** to download it.)

First, think of the times when you were right on target, saying exactly what you wanted to say and felt good about it; list what made that experience happen. Perhaps you were rested, felt healthy, or were only speaking to one other person. What works for you? Then take some time to think of the times when you felt just the opposite. What made it harder for you to communicate effectively? Were you hungry, defensive, speaking to a large group, or put on the spot? There are no right or wrong answers. This is a personal check on your own needs as a communicator.

Communication Best and Worst

I am at my communication *best* when . . .

I am at my communication *worst* when . . .

When we look at our lists, it is interesting to note what helps or hinders our ability to communicate. Do we have a hard time when confronted, when unfamiliar with the topic, when tired, depressed, or mentally occupied for some reason? Do we do well when we feel comfortable with our conversational partners and know they are listening and agreeing with us, when we feel informed about the topic, when we have had time to prepare? There are many reasons that could be listed under each heading, and they will vary depending upon the student and the situation. (See pages 43–44 for lists of communication bests and worsts generated by our workshop participants.)

When looking at your lists, think about what children might have on their lists. Are they always prepared to talk about topics? Do they feel rested, healthy, or heard? Are they ever put on the spot with no time to prepare, and yet expected to be at their communication best in those moments? Perhaps, if we are to expect them to be at their communication best, we should consider what they would need and ensure they have it. If competently communicating adults, teachers, and parents have certain needs to be at our best, we should allow those needs to be met for our children and students as well.

A Simple Communication Assessment

For some teachers or parents who have been told that a child does not communicate, a simple communication assessment can offer great hope and joy. It is almost impossible *not* to communicate, and the Simple Communication Assessment (page 45) can help illustrate what a child is communicating with various behaviors. This chart, adapted from one originally developed by Anne Donnellan (1984), can be used for a very basic, functional communication assessment of non-speech communication behaviors. Across the top are many behaviors that are used to communicate, and down the side are the possible functions of the behaviors, or what we accomplish through our communication acts. During observation, check the appropriate squares. How does the student request an object: gazing, gaze shift, pointing, gesturing, vocalizing, proximity, asking with words? How does the student express fear or protest: gaze aversion, vocalizing, pointing, giving, gesturing, aggression? There are many possible variations. (Completed examples of this chart for several of the stories contained in chapters 2 and 3 can be found on pages 46–48 and used for team discussion.)

This tool is, in a way, a summary of the preceding topics. In the behaviors presented across the top, you will see many of the behaviors discussed in the previous chapter, and down the left side are the messages that those behaviors can send. If you are noticing that frustration is expressed frequently with behaviors that you find unacceptable, you can look across the top of the chart to identify a behavior that can replace the unacceptable one. It is advisable to choose a behavior that the child already has in his repertoire and is using to send a less stressful message. So if you see that a student uses gestures to greet (waving), or to indicate confusion (shrugging shoulders), but uses touching or yelling to get your attention (which disrupts the flow of your teaching), you can work to replace the unwanted behaviors with a more acceptable gesture.

Note: The Simple Communication Assessment is indeed a *simple* tool to help discover what the meaning behind a behavior might be. It is *not* a substitute for the involvement of a speech and language pathologist who can provide a more in-depth and thorough picture of the student's full communication capabilities.

Takeaways

- There are many reasons why people communicate. Each person and each situation create a unique purpose for communication to take place, which we need to consider before attempting to understand the message.

- Some of the things we as adults need to be at our communication best are the same things we need to put into place for our students.

- Once we have understood the message of the behavior, we can provide support for the student to learn alternative ways to express him- or herself.

Communication Best and Worst

I am at my communication BEST when . . .

I am at my communication WORST when . . .

Communication Best Factors

Following are typical responses from workshop participants who are asked to identify circumstances when they are at their communication best. Read and discuss with others. What trends do you see?

I am at my communication best

When I am . . .

In a good mood

Rested

Not preoccupied

Organized

Not hurried

Supported

Treated equally

Confident

Not frustrated

Talking one to one

Comfortable with the setting, person, and subject

Happy

Knowledgeable

In a small group

Relaxed

In familiar surroundings

Prepared

Understood

Not tired

Not hungry

Not hot or cold

Interested

Healthy

Not stressed

Focused

In a role

Undistracted

In a crisis

Alone

Talking

Being observed

Face to face

In control

Enjoying myself

Among friends and family

With kids

Being listened to

Calm

Aware of others' perspectives

Angry

Challenged or confronted

Stimulated

When I have . . .

A good listener

A comfortable environment

Routine

Someone's full attention

Eye contact

Responsiveness

Cooperation

Rehearsed

Something to say

Coffee

Acceptance

Respect

Trust

Time to think

When . . .

I feel strongly

I can write down my thoughts

I get feedback

I understand the language

There are consistent expectations

I know the audience

It's Friday 4:40–5:30

It's a positive situation

There's humor

I've had past positive interactions

There's no noise

I feel like it

It's early morning

I can express myself immediately

I can use my hands

Communication Worst Factors

Following are typical responses from workshop participants who are asked to identify circumstances when they are at their communication worst. Read and discuss with others. What trends do you see?

I am at my communication worst

When I am . . .

Tired

Sick

Bored

Eating

Depressed

Disorganized

Intimidated

Mad

Hungry

Unknowledgeable

Too hot or cold

Confused

Impatient

Being evaluated

Hurried

With new people or situations

Caught off guard

With a lot of people

Personally involved

Not objective

Overwhelmed

Forced

Emotionally attached to the outcome

Questioned

Pressured

Interrupted

Ignored

Uninvested

Underinformed

Put on the spot

Being verbally attacked

Stressed

With strangers

Uninterested

Trying to communicate bad news

Not prepared

Frustrated

Preoccupied

Nervous

Threatened

Worried

Anxious

In pain

Uncomfortable with the topic

Surprised

In an unfamiliar setting

In a loud, chaotic environment

Not getting my point across

Not stimulated

In large groups

Irritated

"Hormonally challenged"

Oblivious to the situation

Being interviewed

In trouble

When . . .

No one is listening

I have a hostile listener

I have an uninterested listener

I don't have enough time to think of an answer

There are different agendas

There are cultural differences

The topic is provocative

There's a language barrier

I don't know what's going on

I don't feel understood

I have to write

I don't care

It's a bad time of day

It's a confrontation

It's too noisy

I have to "go"

I just woke up

It's a rainy day

I receive no responses

There is a misunderstanding

Everyone is talking

I have no voice

Simple Communication Assessment

Name: _____

D.O.B./age: _____

Date of sample: _____

Context: _____

Behaviors/Communicative Means

Preverbal Behaviors:
- Gazing
- Gaze aversion
- Gaze shift
- Giving
- Reaching/grabbing
- Pointing
- Gesturing
- Proximity
- Hugging/kissing
- Facial expression
- Self-stimulation
- Self-injury
- Aggression
- Vocalizations
- Crying/whining
- Laughing/giggling

Verbal Behaviors:
- Echolalia
- One-word utterances
- Multi-word utterances

Communicative Functions
- Request object
- Request action
- Request social routine
- Request comfort
- Greeting
- Agree/disagree
- Protest/refusal
- Share information
- Get help
- Announce completion
- Express feelings
- Report internal events (illness)

Simple Communication Assessment: José

Name: *José*

D.O.B./age: *13 years*

Date of sample: *10/15/09*

Context: *Pre-vocational class—nuts & bolts activity*

	Behaviors/Communicative Means																				
Communicative Functions	*Preverbal Behaviors*	Gazing	Gaze aversion	Gaze shift	Giving	Reaching/grabbing	Pointing	Gesturing	Proximity	Hugging/kissing	Facial expression		Self-stimulation	Self-injury	Aggression	Vocalizations	Crying/whining	Laughing/giggling	*Verbal Behaviors*	Echolalia	One-word utterances	Multi-word utterances
Request object		X		X		X	X	X	X		X					X						
Request action		X		X		X		X	X		X					X						
Request social routine		X		X	X		X	X	X	X	X					X						
Request comfort									X	X	X					X						
Greeting								X	X	X						X						
Agree/disagree			X						X		X		X	X		X						
Protest/refusal			X	X				X	X		X		X	X		X						
Share information																						
Get help	*X*						X	X			X					X						
Announce completion									X				X	X								
Express feelings													X	X								
Report internal events (illness)																						

Simple Communication Assessment: Samuel

Name: Samuel
D.O.B./age: 4 years
Date of sample: 11/5/09
Context: 3rd observation—Samuel from wakeup to bus

Behaviors/Communicative Means

Communicative Functions	Gazing	Gaze aversion	Gaze shift	Giving	Reaching/grabbing	Pointing	Gesturing	Proximity	Hugging/kissing	Facial expression	Property destruction	Self-stimulation	Self-injury	Aggression	Vocalizations	Crying/whining	Laughing/giggling	Echolalia	One-word utterances	Multi-word utterances
	Preverbal Behaviors																	*Verbal Behaviors*		
Request object	X				X			X				X						X		
Request action	X				X			X				X						X		
Request social routine								X				X						X		
Request comfort					X							X								
Greeting												X							X	
Agree/disagree					X			X				X						X	X	X
Protest/refusal		X			X			X				X						X	X	X
Share information												X								
Get help					X							X						X	X	X
Announce completion												X								
Express feelings											X	X								
Report internal events (illness)												X								

Simple Communication Assessment: Billy

Name: *Billy*

D.O.B./age: *01/26/04, 5 years*

Date of sample: *3/20/09*

Context: *Observed after arrival in K class—other children arriving over time*

Behaviors/Communicative Means

Communicative Functions	*Preverbal Behaviors* — Gazing	Gaze aversion	Gaze shift	Giving	Reaching/grabbing	Pointing	Gesturing	Proximity	Hugging/kissing	Facial expression	Self-stimulation	Self-injury	Aggression (pinching)	Vocalizations	Crying/whining	Laughing/giggling	*Verbal Behaviors* — Echolalia	One-word utterances	Multi-word utterances
Request object	X					X												X	X
Request action	X			X														X	X
Request social routine	X			X			X	X		X			X					X	X
Request comfort								X										X	X
Greeting	X			X				X		X								X	X
Agree/disagree	X	X								X								X	X
Protest/refusal		X						X		X								X	X
Share information	X																	X	X
Get help								X										X	X
Announce completion																		X	X
Express feelings										X								X	X
Report internal events (illness)										X								X	X

Personal Reflection

What behaviors do you personally use to get someone's attention or to avoid/escape something?

What behaviors do you see the children in your class use to gain attention, or to avoid something?

What did you learn from the Communication Best and Worst activity? What do you need to be at your communication best?

Did this activity cause you to rethink your perspective on what the children in your class might need?

How will that impact your teaching and interaction with the children?

4

The Big Picture of Challenging Behaviors: Six Critical Questions

In our busy lives as teachers, how can we listen to behavior? What must we do to understand its potential messages? Among the many behaviors we observe daily—whether exciting or challenging—how do we even start to seek answers as to the message the student is sending? First, we must realize that the "problem" does not lie only within the child with challenging behavior. There are other people involved, to say the least! Behaviors occur within a context and a situation. There is no "behavior dictionary" that will give you the exact message that a child consciously or unconsciously tells through behavior. Messages must be understood one by one, situation by situation. Therefore, to hear and decipher any behavior, we must examine its big picture.

Usually, behaviors are described in isolation and without all the necessary details. When Billy pinched or Tina swept materials off the table, all the staff mentioned was the behavior itself: that was the instant or "memorable moment" that represented the "problem." But nothing can be solved by looking at a snapshot. What happened the instant before or after that moment in time is never apparent in a photo. To understand the message of any behavior, we must look instead at the "video" of the entire event and ask six basic questions:

1. What was the child doing before the behavior?

2. How did the adult respond?

3. What was the activity?

4. Who was involved?

5. Where did it happen?

6. When did it happen?

Question 1: What Was the Child Doing Before the Behavior?

Consider this scenario: it is early morning, and you have been resting peacefully all night. You are completely relaxed. Then, suddenly, the alarm snaps on, indicating it is time to get up and change activities. *Do it NOW!!* the alarm screams.

How many of us hit the snooze alarm and buy more time for ourselves so we can wake up gradually instead of having to move on to the next activity immediately? Perhaps we are not unlike children who hesitate, protest, and don't immediately follow the prompt.

Children are engaged in many activities throughout the day, whether at school or at home. They may move from one activity or location to another rapidly or become so engrossed in one activity that they stay with it for a long time even when we want them to do something else. Do we interrupt them without giving them a chance to finish what they are doing, or do we prepare them mentally, physically, and emotionally for the next activity? If adults have trouble with sudden, unexpected, or unexplained changes, perhaps we can understand why children respond as they do when we surprise them with requests or demands.

In looking at challenging behaviors in the classroom, the first question to ask is, did the behavior occur when *you* interrupted the child in an activity? Was the child involved in a fun, exciting, and engaging activity that he was not ready to leave? Could *you* have created a challenging situation by not allowing the child time to finish and demanding that the child start the next activity immediately? Is it understandable if the child hesitates, protests, and doesn't comply at that moment? When we don't consider children's processing patterns, interest areas, and ability to shift gears rapidly, adults can become part of the "problem."

Everyone experiences interruptions and transition times throughout the natural course of a day; however, to some children, these may seem to be an unending barrage of directives that provoke challenging behaviors. Warnings for transitions are a simple and effective way to help decrease challenges. Following are some strategies for easing transitions.

Give Visual Warnings

Many early childhood classrooms post a visual schedule of the day's activities. These schedules may simply be words (such as "free time," "circle time," "snack time," or "recess") or may also include a picture of that activity. Teachers can then point to the visual schedule to help children move through their day.

Give Verbal Warnings

The simple act of stating, "In two more minutes, it will be time to clean up [*or* come in, have a snack, *and so on*]" can give children the information they need that a change is coming, and they need to take action to prepare for that transition.

Give Individual Warnings

Some children need individualized warnings about transitions. You may have to speak to the child directly, use both verbal and visual reminders of the next activity, and tell the child what she should do to get ready.

Question 2: How Did the Adult Respond?

Everywhere they go, children hear adults talking, making comments about life, questions, reprimands, and information that make no sense to them at all. The adults may not be paying attention to what they are saying and how they are saying it, but children still hear them. For some children, especially those with a disability, listening is a challenge. It can be especially challenging if the speaker seems unaware of the listener. Imagine what all of that adult racket sounds like to children—is it any wonder they sometimes just sit and look at adults as if they were speaking a foreign language?

There are some significant, yet simple factors to consider when talking with children. As adults, we must monitor ourselves to give children a better chance at processing and then understanding our messages. The following strategies will help.

Don't Talk Too Fast

In this age when time is of the essence, we tend to speak rapidly and believe that any listener can keep up with any pace. This is not always the case, especially when the listener is a child, has a disability, or is momentarily distracted. For many people, adults and children, trying to listen to someone who is talking too rapidly may not allow enough time to actually process all of the information. Some people may need as much as fifteen seconds to process all the information and then respond. However, most of us are used to listeners understanding what we've said within one or two seconds. If we have to wait longer, we often assume something is wrong with the listener and accuse her of misbehavior or being rude.

Don't Talk Too Slowly

On the other hand, a speaker may talk too slowly for the listener. This is especially true for those of us who are not used to being around students with disabilities and who may believe that talking more slowly enhances the listener's ability to understand. In some cases this is true, but if the speaker continues to speak *too* slowly, any listener will have difficulty staying on track and paying attention. Speaking too slowly can cause the child to become disengaged with the interaction and focus on things that are more interesting and stimulating.

Prevent Interruptions

It becomes even more challenging for a child to pay attention and be engaged when a speaker is interrupted or actually interrupts him- or herself. A classroom can be interrupted naturally for many reasons: for example, by announcements that occur throughout the day or by a classroom discussion that does not necessarily include the entire group. These interruptions are usually unavoidable. However, other interruptions can be avoided. If someone knocks at the door, or if the classroom phone rings, for example, the teacher may stop instruction to answer the door.

When interruptions happen, children find ways to entertain themselves. What they decide to do may not be exactly what the adults want. However, the lack of adult communication, instruction, or interaction during these interruptions has created the situation. It is not the fault of the child. Teachers may request that no one knock on the door or call the room unless there is an emergency, or state that they will take calls or messages only during a certain timeframe. These strategies minimize the chance of unnecessary and unwanted interruptions and allow the classroom activities to continue without the chance for unwanted behaviors.

However, given the fact that unplanned interruptions will happen, the class should know the expectations for behavior when the teacher is attending to an interruption.

Don't Give Too Much Information at Once

Often we bombard children with too much information or too many options. While it is wonderful to present choices, when we present too many, children have little time to process and understand them all. Making things absolutely clear by stating all the facts is great only if the child can absorb all the facts, make sense of them, and then make distinctions in order to follow through. Instead of giving all instructions at one time, break the information down into groupings that are easier to hear. Small bits of information are easier for anyone to remember.

The first year Kim taught preschool PE was only a year after she taught high school. She was used to a certain way of giving instructions to her students. When she went to gather her preschool class, she would sometimes forget the abilities of her young students to take in information as compared to her high school students. Her typical greeting to her preschool students went something like this:

> "Hi there, kids, it's time for PE! Today we are going to go into the gym and sit in a big circle. There is a carpet square for each of you to sit on for our circle game, which is Duck, Duck, Goose. You all know how to play Duck, Duck, Goose, right? Once we finish that game, we will go outside to play on the swings and slides, and it will be a blast. After that, we will come back into the gym and sit in the circle once again on the carpet squares to do some relaxation and sing our goodbye song, and then you will come back to class and have your snack. Now come on!"

Students simply sat and stared at her. Some got up ready to go outside; others were waiting for their snack. Clearly, Kim had presented too much information at one time, and each child reacted to the piece that meant something to him or her.

Give Enough Information

For many students, not having enough information can cause stress and anxiety. For example, for one child, not being told enough about a class trip created anxiety. She was told, "We are going to the zoo. All of us are going together." Her response was, "Mommy?" Staff told her that Mommy was not going, but that her class was going. She continued to ask, "Mommy?" and staff continued to tell her what she would see, who would be there, that she had been to the zoo before and enjoyed it, and so on. By the end of the discussion, the student was sobbing and still crying, "Mommy, Mommy?" Finally, a staff member leaned down and said, "We are going to the zoo—*and then coming back so you will see Mommy.*" The student was satisfied and quieted almost immediately; she had just needed more information. The staff all knew they were coming back that day because as adults, we know these things and assume everyone else does, too. However, for the student, who had autism and was a very literal thinker, the staff had not made explicit all that *she* needed to know. Just as we need to be careful that we do not overwhelm some listeners with too much information, it's important that we check with others to be sure they have all the information they need.

Get the Listener's Attention

Having the attention of all the children is important when you are speaking, especially having the attention of the one who is of most concern. This can be done by moving over to stand near that child, putting a hand on his or her shoulder, or even saying, "Tom and Sally and everyone else, listen to what I have to say." Proximity and touch engage them from the start. Be sure the kids are "with" you and not otherwise occupied before speaking.

Use Visual Supports

Photos, calendars, lists, or objects can help some children process information. Those who have difficulty with verbal instructions—whether due to a disability or limited English proficiency—will do better when there are visual supports as well. Presenting a photo of the activity—even something cut from a magazine or catalog—can increase understanding and, ultimately, compliance.

Question 3: What Was the Activity?

From the time a child gets out of bed until bedtime, he goes from one activity to the next; some activities may be acceptable to the child, and others not. Everyone has reasons for liking or disliking certain activities, and yet even those reasons can from vary day to day. So when challenging behaviors occur during a specific activity or during a change in activity, ask yourself, is there something about this activity *or the next one* that might be contributing to the challenges? If an activity is fun and a favorite, the "challenging" behaviors may show excitement or happiness; for some reason, these behaviors are easier to tolerate. But if the child displays behaviors that seem to show something other than enjoyment, ask yourself the following questions:

- Is the activity boring or too simple?

- Is the activity meaningless?

- Is the activity frustrating, too difficult, or confusing?

- Has the child tried and failed at this task before?

Is the Activity Boring or Too Simple?

In schools, especially in special education classes, activities are often repeated for long periods of time to ensure that students have mastered the activities. Many times, the students *have* mastered it and are ready to move on, but the staff has not modified the activity in a timely manner. This can also be true at home. If a toy has been around for some time and is no longer developmentally appropriate, the child can become bored. Changing activities, even a little bit, can keep the interest going.

Some activities are too simple and may not include anything of interest for the student. If there is nothing of interest in any activity, it is harder to remain engaged and attentive to it. Everyone works better if their activities include aspects that are interesting to them.

If students appear bored, increase the complexity of activities. For young children, that may simply mean using a puzzle with more pieces or books with different words to sound out. As will be discussed in chapter 11, an excellent way to incorporate the interests, strengths, and preferences of a child into activities is to spend time getting to know that child and what makes him or her tick. All young children seem to have favorite cartoon characters, types of toys, or games to play, and those activities can be noted and then incorporated into portions of the child's day.

Is the Activity Meaningless?

Does the child see a reason for doing the activity? Does it contribute to her life in some way, or is it simply "busywork"? Some children may not see the merit in cleaning their rooms, doing the dishes, or helping around the house. Those same children may not see the merit in sitting still, coming in from recess, or learning certain subjects at school. Many adults who were poor math students wonder why they had to take algebra or geometry because they still seem meaningless in their adult lives—and can recall trying to think of ways to avoid going to those classes.

Ask yourself, why are the children doing this activity, and how will it contribute to their life? Is the activity relevant? Once you have answered those questions for yourself, it may be easier to explain to or show children the value of the activity. For example, learning to identify letters can lead to reading, which means children may choose books they like to read; learning how to count and use numbers can help them purchase a cookie or lunch at school. Here again, emphasizing the child's interest areas can be useful.

Is the Activity Frustrating, Too Difficult, or Confusing?

How many times do children have to do something that is hard for one reason or another? More than likely, their first reaction is to whine and say it is too hard. As adults, we often reply, "Oh, it is not. Just keep trying!"—and then take our attention elsewhere. But sometimes, the child can try and try, but simply not be able to make it "work." The longer children try, without an adult really listening to their words and behavior, the more frustrated, confused, or angry they can become. To prevent challenging behavior, it may be better to listen the first time and accommodate their feelings in a simple way. Try demonstrating the activity, changing an aspect of the task, or working with the child to build his confidence.

Has the Child Tried and Failed at This Task Before?

No one wants to go back and do something they *know* they cannot do. It simply is not fun or ego enhancing! If the child has failed to complete the activity in the past, a drastic change may be in order. If she *continues* to fail, something must change, or negative behaviors will continue to occur. For example, if a child is not coordinated and has difficulty in doing a certain activity in physical education, on the playground, and in her neighborhood, she won't want to repeat it over and over again without improvement, only to incur the added insult of ridicule from peers. This principle also applies to academic tasks such as reading in front of a group, doing math at the board, or sharing toys. If a child has experienced failure, he may feel no reason to try again.

Teachers must be ever vigilant in assessing each situation and making accommodations that are needed to help each child find success. Certain tasks will be more difficult for some children, perhaps due to a disability; however, accommodations can and should be used to augment activities. Tasks can be broken down into smaller segments; some children may even need some individual instruction time to help understand concepts. Changing the way you present material or structure participation may be all that is needed for a child to be successful.

Question 4: Who Was Involved?

Many different people come into contact with children throughout the day, both in school and at home. Each adult creates a personal relationship with each child, and how each adult interacts with the child can influence that child's success or failure, depending on two issues:

1. How the adult addresses the child

2. What the adult communicates to the child

How the Adult Addresses the Child

In any interaction, how we are addressed and regarded has an immediate impact on us and influences how we respond. Ask the following questions when considering a challenging interaction:

- Did the adult treat the child with respect? That is, did the child feel valued and welcomed in the particular situation?

- Could the child feel a sense of worth and importance from the way the adult interacted with him?

- Did the adult stand over the child when talking, or did the adult make sure that they saw eye to eye?

- Did the adult speak in a threatening or condescending tone?

- Did the adult intimidate the child?

- Was the adult seeking positive outcomes in her approach or merely describing the negative?

- Did the adult simply react to behavior or try to "get the message" of that behavior?

By asking themselves these questions, the adults involved in each interaction can further ascertain what impact their interaction style has on their relationship with the child.

The more information adults can gather from the child about the situation, the better the outcome. When asking the child questions, phrasing should be as neutral as possible (asking for facts, not placing blame or shame) to create an atmosphere in which the child can help create a solution. Like most of us, when children feel valued and safe, they are more likely to share freely and explain their feelings, reactions, and behaviors.

What the Adult Communicates to the Child

How an adult communicates to the child creates an initial impression, but other conflicts can arise from *what* the adult communicates. Many times, it is not the person but rather what is said that can create positive or challenging situations. The child's behavior may be more related to how *clear, consistent, and concrete* the adult's instructions are than to how the child perceived the adult's attitude.

While clear, consistent, concrete instructions are important for all learners, they are especially crucial for children with disabilities or learning challenges. Here are questions to consider:

- Did the adult inform the child about changes and requirements and explain expectations?

- Was the adult explicit and exact in giving instructions and asking questions?

- Did the adult rephrase or repeat as needed?

- Were instructions exact and clearly presented with any additional means to help clarify them?

- Has a schedule been reviewed? Depending on the situation, either a daily or activity schedule might be helpful to clarify expectations.

- Have the rules been reviewed, to clarify expectations for behaviors?

- Are the rules always the same and reinforced in the same manner?

- How did the adult ensure that the child did, indeed, understand questions or requirements?

- Was the adult consistent in his approach to teaching or dealing with behavior?

There are many other issues to take into account when working with children who exhibit challenging behaviors. The first step is to realize that, and then begin to create a "big picture" of each behavior.

Clear Expectations: Tyrone's Story

Tyrone was just entering fourth grade at a new school. In fourth grade at that school, the children began rotating teachers for different classes to help prepare them for middle and high school, so Tyrone had three teachers instead of one that year. Each teacher was a good teacher and got to know the student prior to him entering their classes. Each teacher took a different approach, but each was respectful and kind. Two of the teachers were polar opposites in their approaches to class organization and style; the language arts teacher was very structured and seemed almost inflexible, while the math teacher was less structured but more flexible. Math was Tyrone's best and favorite subject, which made sense for an autistic child, because math is very concrete, and in math, a right answer is a right answer.

As the year progressed, Kim received a call for help. She thought it would be from the seemingly inflexible language arts teacher, but to her surprise, it was from the math teacher. He said he could not understand what the problem was in class. He gave Tyrone lots of choices—letting him pick his seat and do his work during the class sometimes, and free time as well—but Tyrone was still struggling. The teacher also said that Tyrone was doing fine in the other classes, especially in language arts. That was surprising to Kim, because language arts is a very fluid subject with less-obvious answers and fewer rules.

The difference was that Tyrone's language arts teacher was so completely clear about her expectations that Tyrone never had any question about what to do, where to do it, when to do it, or what to do when he finished his work. Tyrone never had to wonder about anything; he understood the concrete and consistent expectations in that class, and he was thriving in it.

Remember, how well children respond is based on a combination of the manner of delivery and the clarity of instructions. What counts is not only how we talk to children, but also what we say to them. They need a clear message delivered in a respectful manner.

Question 5: Where Did It Happen?

Throughout a day, we move: from room to room; building to building; inside to outside; home to school, a restaurant, a store, or a bank; regular life to vacation. With all of these changes, is it any wonder that some children become anxious, frightened, confused, or challenging? Think about these frequent movements in a typical school day:

- From one's own desk to a group or partner setting at a bigger table or on the floor
- From the classroom to the gym, cafeteria, library, art room, or music room
- From inside to outside for recess
- From home to the bus, then from school to the bus again
- From the school to a museum or other field trip site

In all of these instances, when children exhibit challenging behaviors, we should ask:

- Did the children know all of the rules and expectations in each situation?
- Have they been there before?
- Was it a positive or negative experience? Why?
- Did they know what would happen once they got there?
- Did they know the structure would return to the usual at another point during the day?
- Did they know what they would do when they arrived?
- Were they prepared for each location?
- Did others involved behave "appropriately," or did they cause challenges as well?

These questions are not atypical of the questions that many adults ask when taking a vacation trip or traveling to a conference in a new location. If adults seek this information, it makes sense that children need to have the same. Everyone wants to know what to expect. Once the unknowns become known, children's anxiety and fears decrease, and they have less need for challenging behaviors.

Question 6: When Did It Happen?

When we're faced with challenging behaviors, it can feel as if they are happening "all the time," when in fact they are occurring at specific times during the day. It may feel more frequent at school because teachers are busy with other students. At home it may be overwhelming because parents are busy with other children and household chores. Charting when the behavior happens can focus our attention. A simple scatter plot may reveal a pattern and thus assist in looking at the big picture around that specific time, activity, or interaction.

Scatter Plots

A scatter plot can be designed for use during an academic week at school or a calendar week for use at home (see fig. 4.1). List activities and times down the side and days across the top, and create a key showing what mark you will use for each behavior. When a target behavior occurs, mark it on the appropriate box. This allows support staff to see first when specific behaviors happen during the day and then to pay closer attention to other aspects of that time, such as environment set up, instructions, activity, and so on. Once you have determined the time frame, make a concentrated effort to decipher the messages of the behavior.

	Monday	Tuesday	Wednesday	Thursday	Friday
Arrival Opening Activity					
Reading					
Math					
Spelling					
Departure Closing Activity					

[Unwanted behavior 1] = /   [Unwanted behavior 3] = 0

[Unwanted behavior 2] = x   [Unwanted behavior 4] = +

Figure 4.1: Sample scatter plot.

Let's consider this scenario: A teacher asked Kim to observe her class because she felt as if one of her students, Max, was always disruptive. He would talk to classmates, not have his homework completed, refuse to participate, or simply go to sleep in class. She felt as if she was spending her entire day taking care of Max. During the observation, Kim did see the behaviors, but they were not happening the entire day—just at certain times or with certain activities. Kim suggested that the teacher use a scatter plot to pinpoint the times and/or activities where Max lost his focus or became disruptive (see fig. 4.2).

	Monday	**Tuesday**	**Wednesday**	**Thursday**	**Friday**
Arrival Opening Activities	///0	////00	000x	+0	xxx
Reading					x
Math	x		0		x
Spelling					0
Departure Closing Activities	xx	++	00	////	xxx

Not participating = /   Uncompleted homework = 0

Talking during class = x   Sleeping = +

Figure 4.2: Max's scatter plot.

For behaviors that occur first thing in the morning as Max arrives at school, we should consider:

- How was the ride to school; did anything unusual happen?

- Did he come in a bus, van, or car?

- What happened at home before Max came to school?

- How does Max feel? Is he healthy or does he not feel well or safe?

If the behaviors start before Max is going home, we can ask similar questions:

- How is the ride home? Is it a long ride? Does anything unusual happen?

- Who is there at home to greet Max? Is anyone there?

- What does Max have to do at home? What play or engaging activities await him?

- How does Max feel? Does he seem anxious, sad, or ill?

Even when the teacher or support staff cannot control some situations, such as what happens on the bus ride or at home, it is still important to ask questions. Information provides insight into behaviors. For example, perhaps Max has an exceptionally long ride to school and gets bored along the way. Perhaps on a particular day he woke up not feeling well and was sent to school because his parents were unaware of the illness. Perhaps Max witnessed a parental argument, his dog died, he didn't get breakfast or medication, didn't sleep, or was cold or hot all night. Many "invisible" reasons for behaviors are exposed through questioning.

Behaviors happen for many reasons, and often, adults can be part of the problem. But we can become part of the solution if we pay attention to our part in creating environments and interactions that support children's positive behaviors. By looking at the activity, what we say and pinpointing the times that appear challenging, we can begin to decipher the messages the behaviors convey.

As we will see in the next chapter, sometimes there are deeper, more hidden reasons for behaviors that require more vigilant observation and assessment.

Takeaways

- Behaviors are not frozen moments in time like a snapshot, but part of an ongoing story, like a video.

- Answering the six critical questions of the big picture is a good place to start when attempting to discover the message of any behavior.

- A scatter plot can assist in identifying specific times, activities, locations, and people involved when a challenging behavior occurred.

Six Critical Questions of the Big Picture

Use your responses to these questions to understand the big picture of a child's challenging behavior. Answer these questions for each adult involved in the incident.

1. What was the child doing before the behavior?

2. How did the adult respond?

   - Did the adult talk too fast or too slowly?

   - Were there interruptions?

   - Did the adult give too much information at once?

   - Did the adult give too little information?

   - Did the adult have the child's attention?

   - Were any visual supports used?

3. What was the activity?

   - Is the activity boring or too simple?

   - Is the activity meaningless?

   - Is the activity frustrating, too difficult, or confusing?

   - Has the child tried and failed at this task before?

4. Who was involved?

   - How was the child addressed by the adult involved?

     - Was the child treated with respect? Did the child feel valued and welcomed?

     - Could the child feel a sense of worth and importance from the interaction?

     - Were the adult and child at eye level, or did the adult stand over the child?

     - Did the adult speak in a condescending or threatening tone?

     - Did the adult intimidate the child?

     - Was the adult seeking positive outcomes or merely describing the negative?

     - Did the adult simply react or try to get the message of the behavior?

   - What did the adult communicate to the child?

     - Was the child informed about changes, requirements, and expectations?

- Was the adult explicit and exact in giving instructions and asking questions?

- Did the adult rephrase or repeat as needed to clarify instructions?

- Has a schedule been reviewed with the child?

- Have the rules been reviewed with the child?

- Are the rules always the same and reinforced in the same manner?

- How did the adult ensure that the child understood the rules?

- Was the adult consistent in his or her approach to teaching or dealing with behavior?

5. Where did it happen?

- Did the child know all of the rules and expectations in each situation?

- Was the child prepared for each location involved?

- Has the child been to those locations before?

  - If so, was it a positive or negative experience? Why?

- Did the child know the day would return to the usual routine later?

- Did the child know what would happen upon arrival?

- Did others involved behave "appropriately," or did they cause challenges as well?

6. When did it happen?

- Upon arrival

- During the day

- At departure time

Personal Reflection

When you experience anxiety or discontent (that in a child with fewer coping skills could lead to unwanted behaviors), can you see the "big picture"? How would a video of the event (as opposed to the snapshot) help you decide what has happened to create your feelings?

What is your reaction to the questions of the big picture? Would you add others? What are they, and why do you feel they would add to the information you need?

Why does answering these questions help you to support a child who has challenging behavior?

5

Hidden Issues

Answering the six critical questions surrounding a behavior can paint a big picture that allows parents or teachers to put together a positive support plan. But sometimes there are hidden reasons for behaviors that indicate an imbalance in a child's life. When behaviors indicating stress, anxiety, and fears are persistent, it is time to question the unquestionable and find out what might be happening in the life of that child—especially a child at risk. Seeking answers to tough questions can open the door to solving challenges and allowing a child to live in a more stable and peaceful manner.

What are the observable behavioral clues that might lead you to begin to look beneath the surface? Remember all behaviors have a message, but to assign a specific message to any of the following behaviors listed would be a mistake. However, if you know a child whose typical behaviors start to change, who is exhibiting different and perhaps unacceptable classroom behaviors, you may need to ask questions such as the following about hidden issues:

- Is the child having more frequent unexplained absences?

- Is the child having more difficulty attending in class? Getting assignments done?

- Have the child's peer relationships changed?

- Has the child become withdrawn, passive, or overly compliant?

Paradoxically, hidden issues are sometimes so obvious that they are overlooked. How can something obvious be overlooked? Simply because they are very sensitive issues to explore and can often lead to other more serious issues. But when the well-being of children is concerned, we must make every attempt to understand. Hidden issues we'll discuss in this chapter are:

- Language competency

- Health

- Family dynamics

- Home environment

- Rules, expectations, and routines

- Cultural values

- Emotional needs

- Sensory needs

- Teaching and learning issues

Language Competency

Sometimes a child can appear to completely understand the language used at home or in the classroom, but still has difficulty complying with simple instructions. This can cause the caregivers to assume deliberate defiance. While defiance is always a possibility, there are other possibilities that we must consider. These options are especially important for children with disabilities and for English language learners. Previous compliance does not necessarily indicate language competence. The following examples illustrate cues that a child may use to successfully follow directions or complete routines, despite language difficulties.

Familiar Routine

Routines make up a substantial part of our day, and children become adept at following them. Upon arrival at school, for example, children may be greeted, told to hang their coats up, put their backpacks in their cubby, use the restroom, wash their hands, and begin the first activity. When this occurs every day, it may appear as if the child can understand and follow a five-step direction such as, "Hi, Maria. It's good to see you today. Please hang up your coat, put your backpack in your cubby, use the restroom, wash your hands, and then find a book to look at until we start circle time." But later in the day, when Maria is given an even simpler two-step direction that is novel or out of context, she may have a difficult time following through. Though she may have appeared to understand the instructions in the morning, Maria has probably learned the morning *routine*—and had no need for the verbal instructions.

Environmental Cues

When we enter a room, we scan the room to get clues about what to do or where to go. If there is a line, we know to enter the line to get where we want to go; no one has to tell us. That is an example of an environmental cue. Classmates going to the cafeteria, changing shoes for PE, or putting on their coats are also providing environmental cues. Sometimes following the cues (rather than the verbal instructions) can make it appear as if the child has greater language competence than he does, simply because that child is doing what everyone else is doing.

Parts of an Utterance

As we discussed in the last chapter, sometimes when adults provide instruction or directions, they pack a great deal of information into them and then expect that children will have heard and understand every word. In many instances, not only have they said a great deal, but they may also have said it very rapidly and assumed that the children were paying close attention from the very beginning. We all know this is not always true. Some children may only hear part of the information and respond to that specific part—the word that is most meaningful to them within the string of sentences. For example, when giving instructions to a preschool class, we observed a teacher who very rapidly listed three to five activities they would do before snack time: "Today is a big day. We are going to finish our circle time, and then we are going to look at what is in the centers for us today. We will go outside, and when we come back in, we will all use the bathroom and wash our hands. Then it will be time for a snack." The teacher may expect comprehension and compliance with this list, but instead, what many of the children will hear as "next" is the snack!

Other children key into the first thing they hear. Consider the teacher who told her class, "Don't forget that we have a demonstration by the high school football team this afternoon, so we will be going outside right after lunch. But first, we will need to get together in our groups and work on the social studies presentations that are due at the end of the week, and we also have all-school reading time before lunch, so let's get busy!" Later, when several students in the class had a hard time attending to the academics at hand, the teacher was annoyed. After all, she had given them clear instructions. But to some of her students, the demonstration was all that they could think of. She had sabotaged the rest of her directions by mentioning it first.

What could she have done instead? By giving only the morning schedule at the beginning of the day, and waiting to remind students of the afternoon fun until just before lunch, she may have been able to keep the excitement level under control.

Intonation

There is a melody to our communication that can indicate our moods, emotions, or the intent of what we are saying. We use intonation patterns to add information to words: our voices go up at the end of a question ("What are you doing?"), fall at the end of a statement ("I'm going home"), and get firm in a demand ("Please give that to me *now*"). Sometimes the intonation pattern can convey meaning irrespective of the words. The intonation may not always convey the correct message, however. Sometimes children hear the intonations in the voice of an adult and respond accordingly; though they may not understand the words, they have learned how to respond according to the tone of the message. For example, "Are you ready to throw that away?" may be heard as a question when it was meant as a direct request for an action. Failure to read the message as a direct request can cause the child either to not throw the item away or to answer no, both of which could easily be misconstrued by the adult as deliberate noncompliance, when it was really a lack of understanding.

In all of these situations, we may see a child as being disobedient and not realize she doesn't understand the language involved. We must take care to listen to the behavior and assess all of the possibilities before reacting to suspected misbehaviors. The ability to read the cues in the environment is a crucial skill in getting along in our world, and is a great way for people whose understanding of language is limited (English language learners, people with disabilities, and others) to use nonverbal cues to understand the situation. However, if frequent unwanted behaviors occur when information is provided through spoken language, we must consider whether the child actually understands what has been said.

Health

Anyone can become sick or feel internal pain. Some children are fortunate enough to have parents or other caregivers who can see the signs, some subtle, that indicate the child doesn't feel well. Children who cannot speak or have limited language might not be able to let anyone know they don't feel well. Unless there is a visible wound, others may not know any pain exists, and behaviors may seem to occur out of the blue. Parents, caregivers, and teachers should all be aware of the potential ailments that can impact a child's behavior.

An important question to ask is whether the child has a regular doctor (also called a "medical home") that he sees for well-child check-ups and for immunizations. This will also let you know if the family has access to regular medical care when the child is ill or hurt.

A child who does not feel well—whether for one day or chronically—has a hard time behaving. It is hard for anyone to be on best behaviors when feeling sick, and for children, it can be difficult to sit still, listen to instructions, do activities, and maintain an acceptable classroom demeanor. There are many health issues that teachers should keep in mind that can impact the learning and behavior of children in their classroom. Remember, sometimes children do not have the words to tell teachers exactly what they are feeling, so it is up to teachers to be very observant. The following health issues can have a detrimental impact on behavior; look for them in the children in your classroom:

- Poor hygiene
- Earaches
- Headaches
- Sore throat
- Poor nutrition
- Vision impairment
- Hearing loss
- Constipation
- Stomachache

- Dehydration
- Medication
- Allergies
- Ringing in the ears
- Secondhand smoke at home
- Toothache
- Internal pains
- Seizures
- Insufficient sleep

How many of us have experienced one of these issues and have felt too awful to get up or to move forward with our day? How often might a child feel bad and still be made to get up and go to school or daycare? When children are very young or have limited vocabulary, they will use their behaviors to let adults know what hurts. It is up to caring adults to check out all the possibilities and remedy the situation. Illness and not getting enough sleep cause everyone to behave differently, and accommodations are generally made for those who are ill. Children especially need to receive those accommodations.

Family Dynamics

Family dynamics are as varied as the individuals in the family. Each family system creates its own culture, values, and expectations that can influence the behaviors of people in that family. When a family dynamic is different from what is considered the norm, others may misinterpret the behavior of the children in those families outside of that family system.

Family factors are often hidden and unknown to school staff or even others in a neighborhood. When young children are involved, these factors can be especially hard to discern. Some family situations encourage behaviors that we tend to consider acceptable and positive, while others can cause anguish or stress, and hence behaviors that appear negative or out of the blue.

Here are some questions about family dynamics that can influence behaviors:

- Are the parents together, separated, or divorced?

- Does the family appear loving and kind, or more argumentative and harsh?

- Do the family members get along, or are there abusive behaviors?

- Are parents agile and ambulatory, or elderly?

- Is this a single parent family with a job or without a job?

- Is this family accepted or stigmatized by others (for having gay or biracial parents, for example)?

- Are the grandparents involved in support and assisting, or are they the main support?

- Are there siblings? Are they younger, older, disabled?

- Is the extended family involved? How much?

- Are there safe family pets?

- Do the children have friends in the neighborhood?

- Are caregivers consistent, capable, and respectful, and do they pay attention to the children?

- Are the parents working? Have they experienced an increase or decrease in work time?

- Are the parents under unexplained stress?

Family issues are private; however, if the issues begin to impact the behavior of a child in ways that are detrimental to education, relationships, or well-being, it is imperative that a caring adult attempts to bring about understanding. It is not a matter of judgment; it is a matter of what is in the best interest of the child's abilities and safety.

There are several avenues that teachers can take to help bridge the gap between home and school to better understand family dynamics. Home visits at the beginning of a school year can help the teacher get a feel for the home situation as well as get to know the family members. The social worker would be able to see firsthand who lives in the home and how compatible residents are, and gain a beginning understanding of any stresses that the family might be experiencing. Schedule parent/teacher meetings throughout the school year to keep communication open. If parents are too busy and the only time the teacher sees them is pick up or drop off time, the teacher could walk the child out of the building to the parent and personally chat with the parent.

Electronics have offered teachers and families multiple ways to stay in touch, even if personal visits aren't possible. A class Facebook page can provide general comments, while emails should be used for comments that are more personal in nature. New ways to keep in touch seem to emerge almost daily, and while they all take a commitment of time, they also let families know that teachers recognize their vital role in the lives of the children in their class.

If issues become larger or more serious, the school social worker would be the next logical person to become involved. Social workers are trained to deal with family dynamics and can serve as that bridge in a neutral manner while keeping communication open. Teachers are among a handful of professionals who are federally mandated to report suspected abuse or neglect, and in many districts, the social worker makes the first family contact, and then follows through with the process if necessary. Check with your school, district, or state guidelines for details on how to approach these issues.

And remember, there are many possible messages for any one behavior. For example, in one school, a special Mommy's day was going to be held in which each child could invite his or her mommy to come to school for a special party. All of the children were very excited except one little girl, Amanda, who was very quiet and did not want to talk with anyone. She withdrew each time this day was discussed and cried quietly. The teacher could neither get any information from her, nor could she reach anyone at home during the school day, so she called the social worker. The social worker was able to make contact with the family and asked to talk to the parents about the little girl's behavior. A meeting was established, and that one meeting helped to answer questions. Amanda's father was the main contact because Amanda's mother was away from home helping her own mother recover from surgery. Amanda did not fully understand what was happening and thus was upset that a Mommy's day was going to happen and she did not know if her mommy was coming back. A face-to-face meeting or personal contact can quickly facilitate resolution in many situations like these.

Home Environment

We are all greatly impacted by our immediate environment, whether it is home or where we work, go to school, shop, eat, or play. Though we may take environment for granted, it should not be overlooked, especially in the lives of children.

A child's home environment is often an unknown; most school staff do not make a habit of home visits. While it is true that school staff cannot do a great deal to change a student's home life, they can learn more about the child's home environment in an effort to understand potential reasons for his behaviors at school. Most schools have a social worker on staff at least part time. School social workers are there to assist teachers when there are concerns about how a specific child's home environment may be impacting his school success. Here are some questions to consider:

- Is the home stable, or does the family move frequently?
- Is the home shared with another family or relatives? How many people live there?
- Is the home an apartment, condo, duplex, or single-family home?
- Is there a long bus ride to school? Does the family have a car? If not, is it hard for family members to get rides?
- What is the neighborhood?

- Are there weapons in the home? Are they locked and inaccessible to children?

- Are all utilities (electric, gas, water) working?

- Is there enough money to meet personal and/or family needs?

- How many rooms are in the home? Is there privacy?

- Does the child have his or her own room or share a room?

- Does the child have to share a bed? With whom? Does the child sleep well?

- Are there choices at home regarding comforts, play, clothes, and so on?

- Is the child toilet-trained?

- Is there a television, DVD player, computer? What type of programming is typically available (for example, age-appropriate or adult, educational, talk shows, soap operas, and so on)?

- Are there appliances for preparing food, cleaning laundry, and so on?

- Are there interesting, appropriate materials and activities for a child?

- Is there a safe outdoor play space?

For many of us, our home is our haven where we can do no wrong; there, we retreat from our daily stresses through quiet time alone in our comfortable dwelling. While reviewing the previous questions, consider how your own behavior would be impacted if your situation was different: if you were surrounded by people, there was no heat or air-conditioning, it was loud, the only television shows were action-packed and violent, you were trying to sleep on a pallet on the floor in the middle of all the activity (and your little sister urinated on the blanket and you didn't have a washing machine at your house), and you couldn't even go outdoors because it was not safe. While these are not issues all children experience, they are real issues for some. While they do not make problem behaviors acceptable, they do make them more understandable.

Rules, Expectations, and Routines

As we will learn, we all enjoy daily routines that give us consistency and predictability in our lives; not everyone enjoys surprises. Children rely on predictable daily routines at home, at school, and elsewhere to help them learn the rules and feel safe and secure in their various environments. Changing their daily routine can cause confusion and discomfort, but once they return to the routine or realize the day's events will be back on track and they are safe, most children will relax.

However, not all children come from families where there is a safe, consistent routine. Their families may be constantly moving, dinner may be served at different times or not at all, various people may move in and out of the home—all of which can make a child feel uncomfortable. The following questions might be used to explore the routines in the life of a child:

- Is there a consistent schedule or routine?

- When is bed time, meal time, bath time, and so on?

- What happens after school?

- Who is there after school?

- What can the child do at home?

- What are family values around

  - Back talk

  - Homework

  - Violence

  - Cussing

  - Doing chores

  - Faith

- Does the child care for younger siblings?

- How independent is the child expected to be?

- Does the child lose privileges if he does not "perform" or obey? For example, does the child have to stay inside if he doesn't wash the dishes or clean the bedroom?

Once again, the school social worker is invaluable in bridging the gap between home and school. Schools cannot control what happens in the home, but with an understanding of how the home runs, the language used there, and the expectations placed upon the children, teachers can begin to structure a safe and consistent learning environment for the children. If any of the issues regarding family dynamics, home environment, or home rules and regulations become a greater concern, perhaps due to signs of potential physical abuse or neglect, the social worker should be notified to call for further investigation. In these cases, the school has a legal obligation to report to the child protection service. The social worker will let the teacher know when papers have been filed so the teacher knows her legal responsibility has been completed. Each school system may have its own protocol, however, all schools have the legal responsibility to report serious cases. While these do not happen frequently, they must be taken seriously.

Cultural Values

The conversation around *culture* is complicated. That term usually brings to mind broad ethnic cultural delineations. However, as complex as that picture may be, there is much more to consider. Cultural differences can be seen between the United States and Canada, East Coast and West Coast, British Columbia and Quebec, New England and Florida, the Bronx to Manhattan—from block to block, and from family to family. Religious differences fall within this conversation, some racial differences, socioeconomic differences, and even political differences. The point we need to remember is that the rules and social mores may not be stated or discussed, but are nonetheless strictly adhered to. A seemingly blatant show of disrespect may in fact be a sign of honor. Don't make assumptions; think about the true message of the behavior in each situation and within each context.

While we may recognize that a student comes from a unique culture, that culture's rules and mores may not be well known or discussed with outside people. Many cultures have values that are not shared in North American culture, and that can cause misunderstandings. For example, in many cultures, eye contact is not respectful: children are taught to look down and remain silent when an adult is speaking to them. In a typical North American classroom, however, that child might be seen as belligerent and given detention or time out. It is vital that school staff educate themselves on the traditions, expectations, and rules that children from other cultures follow.

Home life can also have a cultural influence on the way children respond in other environments. For example, some children live with extended families. The rules about how physically close is too close may be different for a child living with many family members under the same roof. For that child, bumping into other children in line, sitting very closely during groupwork, or touching others may be acceptable under the guidelines of the family culture.

While variations in family culture may cause difficulties when translated to school expectations, it is important to remember to value the many opportunities afforded to the child who is growing up in a rich environment with a wide range of ages. Identifying that the unwanted classroom behaviors are due to cultural differences provides information as to how to approach teaching alternatives. Children can learn to switch behaviors between home and school, given the information, support, and practice to do so.

Emotional Needs

We all want and need to feel safe and secure. Our sense of security comes initially from home and family, where we either learn to feel safe or begin a life of fear and distrust. Understanding a child's emotional state and what might contribute to his feelings of trust or distrust can help us understand his behaviors. Some children may act out simply to be noticed or receive some attention. Some may be reclusive or shy due to name calling at school or being disabled or dressed differently. To many adults, these issues may seem trivial, but to children they can be monumental. Consider these questions:

- When and how is the child noticed?

- Does the child fight for attention, food, clothes, or space?

- Does the child fear:

    - Abandonment, separation, or being alone

    - The dark

    - Strangers

    - Starving

    - Failure

    - The unknown (places, people, activities, food, and so on)

    - Arguing, violence

    - Being criticized

- Does the child worry about her appearance, body changes, or sexuality?

- Is there abuse at home? Do the adults grab kids or each other?

- Is the child being bullied while at school? Is the child being called names, taunted, or teased?

- Does the child have an unusual name that might be culturally based or simply atypical (such as Rain, Apple, Zowie, or Bong)?

- What is the peer pressure in school? Is there pressure to be one of a crowd or to make friends? Does the child feel excluded?

- Is the child starting at a new school and having to make new friends?

- Does the child feel jealous (even if unable to name it)?

- Does the child feel ugly, slow, too smart, or different in other ways?

When people don't appear to be in step with what is considered the norm, they are often described as "not getting it." Those who don't get it may exhibit strange behaviors in attempts to fit in and can often be targets for abuse. What "it" is that the child doesn't "get" is often elusive to define. It may refer to innuendos or other hidden context of conversations, or to the manner in which a child interacts with others, when talking at home, answering questions at school, or simply chatting in groups.

If we think back to our own youth, all of the emotions we experienced along the way would be a varied list that would depend on many of the factors listed earlier. Even children who come from an apparently stable and loving home can experience fears of abandonment, failure, or of anger and arguments. Those fears may cause the child to become timid, afraid to stand up for him-or herself, or a perfectionist in the classroom because failure is not an option.

Most children experience varied emotions. Those in frightening or uncomfortable situations may react even more strongly. Goleman (1995) says that "the power of emotions can disrupt thinking itself" (p. 27). He further states that "when we are emotionally upset we say we 'just cannot think straight' and continual emotional distress can create deficits in a child's intellectual abilities, crippling the capacity to learn" (p. 27). Therefore, for children who are reacting emotionally, understanding may be more beneficial than accusations. By realizing that emotions are powerful influences on behavioral responses, we can take a step back and rethink our responses to behaviors and the potential causes and messages. Ultimately, we empower ourselves and the child to find alternative, more acceptable ways to get the message across.

Sensory Needs

How many of us have gone into a room and been overwhelmed by the sounds, sights, or even smells there? This happens to children regularly. At school, the cafeteria can be full of smells and sounds, the gym may sound like an echo chamber or have too much undefined space, a classroom may be too bright with too many windows, or too many people may talk at once. Sensory overload can happen to anyone and can really alter behaviors: an otherwise calm student may become agitated and excited. If there is too little stimulation, however, that same student may look disinterested and daydream in order to create positive stimulation. He may create noises to fulfill the need to hear something or flip a pencil to create a visual stimulation.

Sensory issues are very difficult because they are not usually visible. For young children, people with disabilities, or even the elderly, explaining their feelings to others may be very challenging. Consider:

- Is it hard for this child to listen and do something at the same time?

- Is the child seated or standing to do work?

- Is the child wearing clothes that scratch, irritate, or tickle?

- Is the room too bright, chaotic, noisy, or loud?

- Has the child's space been invaded? Does he feel trapped?

- Was there decreased sensory stimulation when the child was young? That is, was the child held and cuddled at a young age or left alone in a playpen for long periods of time? Did the child have someone who would read books or simply talk with him about the events of the day?

- Was there decreased movement and creative play when the child was young? For some children, being able to move freely and discover ways to use their bodies in play can be greatly inhibited by playpens or small areas that restrict movement. Play and movement are both great ways that everyone learns, and when they are inhibited, learning is as well.

Become aware of your own behavior while you teach, and make any necessary and simple accommodations. If you stand in the front of the room to speak to the class, perhaps stroll around the room instead, or seat any children who are having difficulties toward the front where you can keep a closer eye on them. Take note of the varied scents in the room, and eliminate those that are unnecessary, such as scented candles, tissues, or even markers for the board. If you have natural lighting, keep the blinds open; if not, use halogen lamps instead of overhead fluorescent lighting. Be aware of where children sit, and be sure the children who wiggle or have trouble sitting next to peers are on the outside of a circle time or on the end of the bleachers during an assembly. These accommodations can be done to diminish the chance for challenges and are not costly or difficult to achieve. Chapter 7 will include more information on creating effective environments.

Teaching and Learning Issues

Some school issues have already been mentioned regarding the environment, sense of security, or sensory challenges. All children may experience difficulties in school at one time or another. Some of them can rise above the challenges and do fine, while others may feel so challenged that they use their behaviors to avoid some tasks or distract the teacher's attention. School staff should constantly be evaluating and monitoring classroom participation as well as their teaching strategies. Consider the following questions:

- Is the child bored?

- Does she have test-taking anxiety?

- Is there too much competition in games or for grades?

- Is the child fearful about speaking aloud in class?

- Is the child given choices?

- Is the work interesting?

- How are directions given, and how can responses be made—only verbally?

- Are directions given too fast, too slowly, with too many words, or without pauses?

- Does the child have enough time to process information?

There are many issues within a classroom that require constant monitoring to maximize the success of all children. These questions can lead a teacher to explore his own teaching style, types of activities, and interactions with the children.

Looking Past the Surface

Clearly, understanding the big picture involves more than simply describing a challenging behavior. So much happens in the daily life of a child that can go unnoticed, unless the adults in the child's life are vigilant and alert to troubling signs and signals in the child's behavior. Some signs may be subtle and others more obvious, but each one deserves further exploration. Some are truly personal issues and may not be comfortable to directly discuss with those involved, but can be addressed via conversations about a child's ability or inability to maintain appropriate learning behaviors. We may be able to connect a family to additional information or resources that are just what is needed to help mend an uncomfortable or unhealthy situation.

Sleeping in Class: Elijah's Story

In Illinois at a very small rural school where the hardworking families did not make much money, a young boy in one of Kim's fifth-grade classes always seemed a bit dirty, tired, and hungry. By the end of every day, Elijah would put his head on his desk and fall fast asleep. She asked him why he was always so tired, and he explained that his mom and dad both worked the third shift and left him at home in the care of his older brother. This brother was out of school and had parties at the house with alcohol and drugs on a regular basis. Not only could Elijah not sleep, he was introduced to secondhand smoke and intoxicated behaviors. This young student was in danger, and his parents either did not know or ignored the situation. Kim spoke to the social worker, who then spoke to the family. The situation improved somewhat, but the situation had gone on for so long that Elijah had fallen behind in his development. If someone had "listened" to his behavior and investigated his situation earlier, his learning abilities might not have been so affected. As it turned out, he needed the services of special education to help him attempt to catch up in his academic areas.

Teachers must be ever observant and not be afraid to ask the tough questions or seek additional assistance from other professionals when the well-being of a student is involved. That effort can change a life for the better. Behavior is always sending messages; listening can change a life.

Takeaways

- Not everything that impacts a child's behavior is obvious.

- When language competency is an issue, routine, environmental cues, key words, and intonation patterns can assist a child's understanding of verbal instructions.

- Health, family dynamics, the home environment, emotional needs, changes in routine, and sensory needs can create confusion, anxiety, depression, or fear that expresses itself as challenging behaviors.

- Behaviors that may be related to cultural values can be misinterpreted as disrespectful or disobedient.

- Teaching and learning issues can affect a child's behavior.

Personal Reflection

Create a list of times in your life when hidden issues impacted your own behavior. How did you respond in each situation?

Do you believe that any of the hidden issues discussed in this chapter are issues for a child in your classroom?

What steps will you take in order to understand and address, if possible, those hidden issues?

6

Disability Issues

Disabilities can occur at any age and may or may not be obvious from birth. According to the Department of Health and Human Services Centers for Disease Control and Prevention (2004):

> developmental disabilities are a diverse group of severe chronic conditions that are due to mental and/or physical impairments. People with developmental disabilities have problems with major life activities such as language, mobility, learning, self-help, and independent living. Developmental disabilities begin anytime during development up to 22 years of age and usually last throughout a person's lifetime.

In particular, when the central nervous system (CNS)—the spine and the brain—is compromised, it can impact every aspect of a child's life. Disabilities that involve a central nervous system dysfunction include learning disabilities, cognitive delay, cerebral palsy, autism spectrum disorder, hearing impairments, visual impairment, and Down syndrome. We know the brain is the control center for everything we do, so when a child has a disability and the CNS is compromised, we can expect learning challenges. We might also expect that the child could behave in ways that, at face value, do not make sense. Teachers need to begin to look a bit deeper into what might be happening within the child and how disability, including the CNS component, impacts that child.

Children with disabilities such as cerebral palsy have many struggles that are immediately obvious. Other struggles, due to the nature of the disability—such as a learning disability, autism, or cognitive delay—may not be as readily obvious. But unless we are aware of and sensitive to the realities of the big picture for a child with a disability, other issues can cause behaviors or reactions out of shame, embarrassment, anger, frustration, or withdrawal. Consider the following:

- Are there mobility issues that prevent the student from engaging in all the activities of his or her classmates?

- If so, does the child have access to a wheelchair or walker?

- Does the environment accommodate the use of a wheelchair or walker?

- Does the child have independence in skills such as eating and toileting?

- Can the child work and play with other children?

- Can he or she sit at a table, in a circle, or at a desk?

- Can he or she speak or use an alternative means of communication to ask for help, say hello, play with others, answer questions, and so on?

Supporting children is a full-time job, and when a child with a disability is in the classroom, the daily demands can be overwhelming. A teacher may enter the classroom already exhausted, only to have a child follow her closely, constantly tapping her on the leg until she acknowledges that child. Another child can't sit still to do his work or eat a meal at lunchtime. The teacher can keep telling him to sit still, and he may for a short time, but soon he starts moving again. Other children may have bowel accidents, scream when they are overly excited or frustrated, or simply melt into a heap when asked rapidly and repeatedly to do something. These behaviors can add to the annoyance and frustration of the adults involved. But are these behaviors really under the child's control? Can the child simply "stop it" on demand? Why do children continue to exhibit behaviors that the adult has said are annoying or negative?

As we have discussed, there are messages in every behavior. It is up to the adults to consider all of the issues and to listen to the behaviors in order to provide the appropriate support. Instead of seeing children with challenging behaviors as "pests" or "trouble," we must begin to separate our perceptions of the child's behavior and the real person. Too often, our perceptions can color our interactions based on false or incomplete information. It is critical to dig deeper and seek reasons for challenging behaviors instead of jumping to conclusions and blaming the child.

As Herb Lovett notes (1996, p. 110), "We as a society need to listen to people other than knowledgeable experts. We need to hear not only from academic theoreticians and the whole range of intelligentsia that we have attended to in the past, but also from the people who are living the lives we sometimes so casually discuss." Children with disabilities have messages to share, and behaviors such as the tap on the leg may mean, *Notice me and love me*. The child who can't sit still may be working as hard as he is able to; the child who has bowel accidents may be just as ashamed of having them as the adults are of them happening. By putting ourselves in the shoes of others and understanding their perspective or situation, we can become more understanding and accommodating.

When teachers view challenging behavior as actions children use to get their needs met, they can reframe problem behavior as a skill-learning or skill-fluency issue. *Skill fluency* refers to a child's ability to use a skill consistently and independently. Children with problem behavior may not have appropriate social or communication skills or may not use those skills well in all situations. Reframing problem behavior as a skill-instruction issue opens the door to the development of effective strategies teachers can implement in the classroom: if young children with problem behavior are missing key social and communication skills, the next step is to teach them those skills!

Central Nervous System Dysfunctions

Children with disabilities that impact their central nervous system may struggle to control communication, bodily functions, behavior, and bodily movements. For some people, participation at home, at school, at work, or in the simplest activities of life requires accommodations, understanding, and support. Central nervous system dysfunctions include autism spectrum disorder (ASD) and attention deficit hyperactivity disorder (ADHD). Sometimes children who have been diagnosed with mental retardation, cerebral palsy, learning disabilities, multiple sclerosis, and other disabilities display symptoms of neurological disorders. These impact each individual differently—sometimes dramatically.

When Martha Leary and David Hill (1996, p. 40) began to research these types of challenges (more specifically with individuals with autism spectrum disorder), they used the term *movement difference*: "Movement difference is a difference, interference, in efficient and effective use of movement that cannot solely be accounted for by paralysis or weakness. Movement disturbance is synonymous with a disruption in the regulation of movement." They report that research has found that people with autism spectrum disorder and other central nervous system interferences or dysfunctions have characteristics and behaviors that are similar to Parkinson's disease, Tourette's syndrome, and catatonia (see table 6.1).

Table 6.1: Movement Difference Characteristics

Parkinson's Disease	Tourette's Syndrome	Catatonia
Difficulty initiating or switching movements Freezing movements Stopping movements Slowness in movement	Vocal tics Verbal tics Physical tics Obsessive-compulsive traits	Muteness Echolalia Repetitive movements Odd hand postures Automatic obedience Interruption or freezing of movements Stupor, frenzy, or excitement

In fact, many of these movement differences are quite difficult to control. When we hear or read about these characteristics, we may nod in apparent understanding. We understand that someone with Tourette's syndrome who yells obscenities cannot simply stop when asked, and that someone with Parkinson's cannot simply stand up and move without a great deal of physical and mental effort. We are quick to offer people with these diagnoses accommodations, understanding, support, and encouragement. However, when confronted with a child who experiences a central nervous system dysfunction, we may forget that these characteristics are the result of an internal central nervous system challenge and respond by telling the child to control herself. Consider this example: the lack of movement or freezing in people with Parkinson's disease is called *akinesia,* while the same phenomenon for people with central nervous system dysfunctions such as autism, attention deficit disorder, learning disabilities, or cognitive disabilities is often called *noncompliance!*

Before we can more closely examine the challenges of movement difference, we must understand that the body is a dynamic system that responds to a variety of environments. This means that our bodies are composed of many systems (such as vestibular, proprioceptive, tactile, visual, and auditory) that work simultaneously and constantly to adjust and adapt based on the input from our immediate environment to our central nervous system. We automatically interpret incoming information, organize it, and then respond. Think of the readjustments and accommodations we have to make to cross a street, to stop one activity to do another, to look, to listen, to eat a meal, or to drive a car: starting, stopping, continuing, switching, executing, combining, and so on. We can do all of these activities without too much of a challenge because our central nervous system works well and in an integrated manner. Sometimes the organization of an environment can give us information to help support our responses. For example, we may remember who someone is more readily when we can recollect meeting him or her in a specific context or environment: "Oh, that's right—we had that swimming class together at the YMCA."

For children with central nervous system dysfunctions, the dynamic system works, but *differently*. They may shift, change, and accommodate to their environmental needs, but may do it slower, faster, in unique ways, or only with outside support or accommodations. They may have to consciously think about every move or every sound they make, while keeping their minds focused. What seems simple and automatic to us may be quite arduous for them. The key is they *are* responding, but *differently*. They may need additional support or accommodation to truly fit into specific environments due to their movement difference. When we stop seeing these children as merely willful, we start to gain a better understanding of how hard it might be for someone with a central nervous system dysfunction to control his or her body without a great deal of thought, effort, and support.

In *Movement Difference and Diversity*, Anne Donnellan and Martha Leary (1995) provide further insight into how movement difference can impact individuals with autism spectrum disorder; their information applies to other disorders of the central nervous system as well, and perhaps to young children without disabilities who are still developing and refining their skills. Their insights raise questions regarding communication, body control, and challenging behaviors, and provide new ways of looking at and understanding these issues. To examine movement difference more closely, Donnellan and Leary created a simple chart, that when discussed further, explains some of the impact of movement difference (see table 6.2).

Table 6.2: How Symptoms of Movement Difference Impact Responses

Difficulties in . . .	May impede . . .
Starting or initiating	Postures
Stopping	Actions
Executing (speed, intensity, timing, direction, control, rate, rhythm, coordination)	Speech
	Thoughts
Continuing	Perceptions
Combining	Emotions
Switching	Memories

Source: Donnellan & Leary, 1995, p. 50.

These "difficulties" are symptoms that can create situations that are both challenging and puzzling to the person with central nervous system interferences as well as those who provide support. Each symptom manifests itself in unique ways and may impact more than one area. It is important to look more closely at each of the issues and consider all the possibilities. Those of us without disabilities may even experience some of these challenges even with an intact central nervous system. If we are challenged, imagine what it might be like for someone who has a central nervous system disorder.

The Symptoms

The following are ways that movement difference may manifest in children with central nervous system interferences.

Starting or Initiating

In any situation, we can be asked to start or initiate actions, thoughts, memories, or speech. Sometimes this may prove challenging. Have you ever needed extra time to recall information you "should" know easily, such as a name or phone number? This may be considered an *initiation* difficulty. Consider the initiation challenges that occur during the day in a classroom, at home, or even on a job. Initiation is one of the many challenges for people with central nervous system disorders. They may have trouble moving place to place or getting out of a seat, car, or pool, for example. They may have trouble answering a question when called upon because they may freeze or not be able to think and speak immediately. Initiating a greeting, starting a conversation, and then being able to begin to leave the conversation once it is completed can be difficult. Retrieving information on a topic during a conversation or a classroom discussion may take more time than deemed reasonable. Remembering where a specific room is located, what someone's name is, where something has been placed, how to do an activity, when to go someplace in particular, or what to do at a given time are challenges for many of these students. They may not be able to begin the thought process needed for a specific activity on command and may freeze, seeming as if he or she is not responsive or does not know what to do. In fact, he or she is "stuck"! Responding with an "appropriate" emotion (such as sadness at a funeral instead of "inappropriate" laughter) may also be difficult.

Stopping

Sometimes, it is hard to stop once we start something. Have you ever arrived at work only to have the last song you heard stuck in your head all day, or to be focused on thoughts of your upcoming vacation or the illness of a loved one? These difficulties in stopping also affect children who are experiencing movement difference. They may not be able to stop impulses to stand up repeatedly, ask repetitive questions, sing or talk out loud, have sudden outbursts, constantly touch or rearrange objects, wonder what will happen next, daydream about a pleasant or unpleasant memory or activity, shut out sensory input such as a scratchy tag in clothing, or even engage in self-injurious behaviors. All may be a result of a central nervous system inability to regulate body responses.

Executing

Executing consists of skills such as rhythm, timing, speed, and accuracy. Think of dancing with a partner, and then suddenly stepping on your partner's toes—what happened to all the wonderful execution of the dance steps? The ability to execute may vanish only to return after moments of puzzlement or may never quite come back. Much of our day involves accuracy, timing, or rhythm.

Writing on lined paper, eating with a fork, moving down a hallway, taking turns in conversation, tying a shoelace, brushing teeth, combing hair, coloring, building blocks, inserting letters into envelopes, using a computer, riding a bike, playing ball, giving a class presentation, and sharing supplies all involve accuracy, timing, and rhythm. If execution skills are skewed, the resulting actions can be altered just enough to create noticeable differences.

Continuing

Many adults experience the strange phenomenon of talking about a particular subject only to have their thoughts mysteriously disappear suddenly for no reason. Being able to continue a thought or concept may be challenging at times. Continuing a specific movement, even one as simple as walking down the hall, may be complicated if we are distracted by something in a window or a conversation. Continuing or maintaining a seated posture during a long story or sermon, being quiet, staying on task, remaining on a conversation topic, doing all the math problems, reading the entire chapter in a book, staying with a group, finishing a meal, cleaning a room, or playing a game may all prove challenging for students with movement difference.

Combining

On some level, everyone experiences regular difficulties in combining actions (what we sometimes call *multitasking*), whether we are watching and listening; listening and doing; listening, looking, and talking; or any other combination of activities. We are constantly receiving input via our sensory system, and at times, we are bombarded. Most of us are able to filter out those sensations that are not needed or might bother us. For example, when driving in heavy traffic on unfamiliar roads in a snow storm while looking for a particular address and listening to the radio, many drivers turn the radio off. Why? The driver is receiving too much input and needs to shut out some.

Now consider children in a classroom with the teacher talking, other students whispering, announcements blaring, room temperature fluctuating to extremes, books and papers cluttering the desks, posters covering the walls, mobiles hanging from the ceiling—all while sitting next to someone who is eating candy that smells wonderful! A child must consider all this input and also look at the board, listen, and then focus on the task and write—while remembering all the directions. Filtering through all of the input and focusing on what is most important at a given moment can become a monumental task, especially for a child with disabilities.

Switching

Transitions happen constantly throughout the day, externally as well as internally. We move from place to place, from activity to activity, or from person to person. We change the way we walk outside in the winter when the ground is dry as compared to how we walk if a storm suddenly erupts. We also shift in thinking, action, perception, or even from one emotional state to another. We may watch an extremely sad movie, and then later make the mental and emotional switch to engage in a lively, happy conversation with friends.

Many people can make a switch instantaneously and, sometimes, without apparent conscious thought. For students with central nervous system dysfunctions, however, those shifts may only be accomplished with a great deal of effort and conscious thought. Kim's friend Ian, a person with autism spectrum disorder, once told her, "I couldn't often make my body do things that I'd like it to do" (I. Wetherbee, personal communication, February 19, 1999). His mind and body did not agree, thus making life quite challenging.

The Responses

As shown earlier in table 6.2 (page 84), these movement differences can affect many aspects of our responses to input. Because our body is a dynamic system that continually works in unison to adapt to each new environment, it is impossible to discuss challenges in isolation. Nothing in our bodies works totally in isolation. For the majority of people, most responses are automatic and do not require direct thinking. For students with central nervous system dysfunctions, however, these responses are not always automatic due to the dynamic system and movement difference. Instead of simply responding automatically, they may have to extend a great deal of energy to think directly about their posture, action, speech, thoughts, perceptions, emotions, and memories in order to respond or interact in an "acceptable" fashion. Following is a discussion of the different responses exhibited as a result.

Postures

Our knowledge of our body in space (*proprioception*), whether sitting or standing, can be impacted. When we walk, most of us maintain our typical upright posture. However, we can also change our stance when we walk with a toddler or an elderly person to accommodate their size and pace. When seated, we can maintain our posture and not jump up out of our seat at an inappropriate time, such as during a church service, a class lecture, or a presentation. Our posture may also change when we are driving and the weather changes from dry to rain to sleet to snow and to ice. We can regulate how we position ourselves. Children who have trouble in this area may appear to have a lack of coordination, use odd hand and body postures, or freeze in abnormal-looking postures (Leary & Hill, 1996).

Actions

Students who experience movement difference may not be able to control the many changes in action experienced in a day. Again, think of how differently you walk up steps to your home when they are completely dry, wet with rain, or slippery with ice. Without conscious thought, we are able to regulate the speed, touch, and placement of our footsteps. We can automatically decide how much force to use when lifting a heavy object versus lifting a baby. We can adjust when, for example, we lift a glass mug to find out the mug is actually plastic and much lighter than expected. Many times, our actions are better when we are alone and practicing them. You may be able to line dance in your kitchen, for example, but when you dance in public or have to perform the steps on command, your feet may suddenly "not remember" what to do.

Children with central nervous system disorders may have difficulty controlling their actions, including how fast they move, or difficulty maintaining a constant rate of movement. In *festination*, the person moves faster and faster. A child who starts out walking down the school hall, for example, may gradually increase her speed until she is running. She is not "choosing" to run, however; she is just having difficulty regulating her movement. In other kinds of festination, a person's writing speed increases, his speech quickens, or he has "racing thoughts." Difficulty moving in a line with the class down the hall to the library or banging and breaking toys instead of playing with them in a more acceptable way are other examples of behaviors that can indicate a movement difference resulting from the central nervous system dysfunction.

Speech

Speech is a highly complex motor function involving highly skilled movements. Not only are we able to coordinate an amazing array of muscles and structures to produce speech sounds, we are also able to regulate the volume of our voices to accommodate speaking in a large room, a library, or face to face as well as when talking to someone across a classroom. This is not always true for some younger students or those with some types of disability; they may speak out loud, yell, or make noises even when asked to be quiet. As we have discussed, festination can also impact speech through an increasing rate of speech or thoughts. This speeding up of processes can be disturbing and quite frustrating not only for the speaker, but for those attempting to listen and understand. *Confrontational naming*—when someone is asked to label, describe, or simply speak on command— can also create difficulties. Most people have experienced some freezing, slow memory recall, or inability to speak in those instances. Remember, in chapter 3, our workshop participants said that being called on in a large group or when unprepared was on the list of situations in which they felt they were at their communication worst. Some can laugh it off, while others become withdrawn, frustrated, or even angry when confronted.

Thoughts

Thinking is impeded if we have trouble staying focused on one issue or topic. Many of us can think of all that needs to be done during a day, *and* be concerned about a sick family member. We can work on the computer writing an article, *and* also be thinking about what we will eat for dinner. But if we experienced any of the symptoms of a central nervous system disorder, we could have great difficulty maintaining our mental focus and getting our tasks done.

Perceptions

Noise, visual stimulation, smells, touch, balance issues, proprioception, and taste constantly bombard our senses. How many times have we had to listen to a speaker or in a noisy environment and be expected to filter out the unnecessary noise? Some say mothers of newborn babies can sleep through anything except their baby's cries. When we buy new clothes, they often have annoying tags that we must "tune out" while we are out in public so we do not make a scene yanking them out of our clothes. We are able to focus our attention on one detail within a large area; we can pick out and watch a bird sitting in a tree surrounded by other trees.

Perception is critical in the classroom to be able to find the correct spot on the page, worksheet, or board. Students must look at many words on a page or worksheet and discern the exact place that needs attention; they must be able to look to the front of the classroom where the teacher is pointing to a specific word or symbol on the board for identification. There are also sounds that children are expected to listen to (teacher instructions) while shutting out others (peers playing). Challenges in filtering these perceptions are taxing for some children.

Emotions

Emotions may be hard to regulate or change. Imagine walking out of a very sad movie and immediately meeting someone who is in a fantastic, silly mood. As much as we might want to, it's difficult to stop feeling one emotion and start feeling another. We may be extremely excited about an upcoming vacation or visit from a friend, or we may be afraid of going to the dentist or a meeting and unable to "shake it off" even if we rationally know things will be fine.

Strong emotions can also cause a movement difference to be more prominent. When a child with a movement difference experiences fright, frustration, or surprise, she may not be able to respond as readily as usual. If she is angry, sad, or jubilant, those emotions can also create barriers to rapidly accessing required actions, thoughts, perceptions, or memories. If a child with central nervous system dysfunction has movement difference, any extreme emotion can magnify that challenge and make it even more difficult.

Memories

When the central nervous system is intact, we are able to balance thoughts of past experiences with the present situation and to realize the difference. We can recall our way home, where the bathroom is, how to tie our shoes, how to eat our lunch, how to use the phone, where to write our name, who is sitting next to us, and on and on. However, we may experience some challenges in this area as we grow older. How many of us have gone into a room and forgotten why we were there and had to retrace our steps to help us remember why we entered the room in the first place?

Now imagine if your entire life was like that on a regular basis; think of how frustrating that would be and how you might react and feel. Students with central nervous system interferences who experience movement difference may struggle with memory issues on a regular basis. These children may be labeled as showing challenging behaviors, lack of motivation or interest, or even lack of intelligence.

To put yourself in the child's shoes, try brushing your teeth, writing, or eating with the opposite hand; driving an automatic after driving a clutch for a long time; or speaking with someone and not saying the letters *n* or *s*. It can be quite challenging! We may have to think "harder" or move differently to be successful, but we *can* be successful—given support, encouragement, time, and understanding.

Commit to Continuous Learning

When we give children with movement difference the support, encouragement, time, and understanding they need, they too can be successful. As Donnellan and Leary (1995, p. 100) point out, we need to seriously consider "what we *believe* versus what we *know* about people." Many unknowns surround autism and other central nervous system disorders, but we continue to learn. Our job is to be open to new knowledge, incorporate that new knowledge into our frame of reference when possible, and be ever vigilant in creating the most supportive environment possible through our continual learning. That may mean letting go of what is "comfortable" and allowing ourselves to be "uncomfortable" with new insights that ultimately may allow us to do our job better.

Takeaways

- Our central nervous system must be dynamic and intact in order to be perceived as capable, responsive, and on task.

- Central nervous system interferences can often be mistaken for challenging behaviors.

- Children with central nervous system interferences may need to work harder to get any task done; they may accomplish it more slowly or make some mistakes along the way.

- Children with disabilities are often doing the best they can, and teachers could support them through acknowledging their issues and making accommodations.

- Any of us can experience a movement difference such as loss of memory or inability to find the right word at any time, but for most of us it will pass. For some children with disabilities, the inabilities remain forever.

- Learning more about central nervous system disturbances can help teachers create better and more supportive learning environments for each student's unique needs.

Personal Reflection

Have you ever experienced any difficulties with stopping, starting, executing, continuing, switching, or combining that might give you insight into central nervous system interferences? What were the circumstances? What was the impact?

Are there children with identified disabilities in your class (children with IEPs)? What are their disabilities? What types of central nervous system interferences do your children experience?

Are there children with unidentified disabilities in your class? What types of difficulties are they experiencing that lead you to believe this?

Can you name instances in which you thought a child was misbehaving and perhaps he or she was experiencing a central nervous system interference? Describe those situations.

Part II: Practical Strategies for Supporting Behavior

7

Supportive Learning Environments

In schools, behaviors evolve in an environment that reinforces them—a physical, social, and instructional environment. In other words, existing behaviors (positive or not) worked to get the child what he or she wanted or needed, and they are unlikely to change spontaneously. Thus, a child's behavior changes because people around that child become more aware of their role in shaping the child's behavior. They make *outside* changes to the environment that motivate the behavior change *inside* the individual. Though it can be difficult to remember when we become enmeshed in real-life situations, teachers, parents, paraeducators, therapists, and others who deal with challenging behaviors do usually have some control over those behaviors.

There are many ways to support positive behaviors. This chapter will discuss proactive strategies to create a learning environment in which positive behaviors are more likely to occur. Chapter 8 will discuss proactive behavioral strategies, chapter 9 will address proactive instructional strategies, and chapter 10 will explore some reactive strategies to use when all else fails. Finally, chapter 11 will show how to put these pieces together in a child-centered approach.

The Goal of Proactive Strategies

As children grow and develop, one of the most critical changes is the ability to self-regulate their behavior. Elena Bodrova and Deborah J. Leong (2008), researchers and writers in the field of early childhood development and school success, describe self-regulation as follows:

> Self-regulation is a deep, internal mechanism that enables children as well as adults to engage in mindful, intentional, and thoughtful behaviors. Self-regulation has two sides: first, it involves the ability to control one's impulses to stop doing something. Second, self-regulation involves the capacity to do something (even if one doesn't want to do it) because it is needed, such as waiting one's turn or raising one's hand. Self-regulated children can delay gratification and suppress their immediate impulses enough to think ahead to the possible consequences of their action or to consider alternative actions that would be appropriate. (p. 56)

The ultimate goal for the positive approaches discussed in the following chapters is to help children develop the capacity to manage their own behaviors.

Self-regulation is a developmental process. While kindergarteners are still in the beginning stages of learning to use language to discuss their emotions, to regulate their own behaviors, and to influence others, they still rely on adults to provide clear expectations and guidelines, and to give them structured opportunities to practice their emerging skills.

By primary school, development of self-regulation skills is well under way. Children grow increasingly capable of living by both the explicit and implicit rules of school life. This includes the ability to:

- Use language to interact positively with others in academic and social settings

- Independently engage in negotiation and problem solving

- Consciously control their behaviors around movement, attention, and learning strategies

- Maintain the internal motivation to be competent behaviorally and socially (Bronson, 2000)

As teachers, we must know where our students fall developmentally in order to know which of the strategies presented in the following chapters apply, and to what extent external supports are needed.

Behaviors can be changed and supported in various ways, but a team approach is best:

> The late Herb Lovett is credited with coining the term *positive approaches*. In the spirit in which Lovett intended the term, it is important to recognize that every approach that does not rely on aversive procedures is not by default a positive approach. Positive approaches are only those which enhance the lives of the people with whom we work; they are characterized by collaboration versus control. (Weiss, 1999, pp.1)

Our first response to challenging behaviors should use collaborative efforts to determine the message of the behavior and identify sensible changes that can enhance the lives of those involved, rather than methods or strategies to make the behavior go away. Lovett stated:

> Positive approaches are about behavior changes through personal growth and mutual responsiveness. This work starts with each person and each group, and as experiences widen and deepen some principles emerge, but they emerge from the lives of the people involved, and are not imported mechanically. (1996, p. 233)

Positive approaches can be quite simple and can be adjustments made to the environment, which includes the physical setting, materials, and social interactions. Many of these supports can be put into action *before* the behaviors occur, to eliminate or diminish the child's need for any challenging behaviors; hence they are *proactive* behavior supports. These strategies are commonsense techniques anyone can use. We need only *choose* to implement them—to establish an inclusive environment or to wait and see what happens. The proactive approach may be more involved and time consuming initially, but dealing with challenging behaviors that could have been avoided with preplanning also takes an enormous amount of time and energy. Proactive approaches to support behavior can enhance relationships, build self-esteem, and ultimately create major changes in behaviors that enable learning to happen.

The Impact of Environment

Our discussion of supporting positive behavior starts with looking at the environment. *Environment* can be defined as the physical and social setting and conditions in which people live, learn, work, and play. We are engaged daily in a variety of environments, and how they are organized and "feel" shapes our behaviors. Each of us reacts differently depending on the places we have been, the impact those places have upon us at that time, and our upbringing.

Consider how you feel in the following places, simply by entering them:

- A huge, beautiful cathedral

- An airport terminal

- A five-star restaurant

- A sporting event

- A hospital

- A rock concert arena

- A classical concert hall

- A favorite store with a great sale

Entering each of those venues creates a specific feeling in each of us, and that feeling calls for a certain type of behavior. No one tells us to be quiet and walk softly in a cathedral, but most people do anyway. In an airport terminal, some people are anxious and fearful and may pace or get testy, while others smile and laugh because they love the excitement and anticipation. We behave differently in different settings simply due to the powerful influence of the environment and its inherent expectations. The environment is always affecting us, either positively or negatively.

Space speaks. Why do many children need to be reminded to walk in the halls at school? To children, those long empty hallways say *"Run!"* In fact, the arrangement of any environment has an impact on everyone in it, and at school, at work, or at home, the environment can be adapted and modified to support positive behavior. Establishing a positive environment is the first step in proactive behavior support; by altering context, we can alter behavior.

In this chapter, we will consider four aspects of environment:

1. The physical setting and use of space

2. Material type, selection, and storage

3. Sensory and natural elements

4. The social environment (the amount and type of interaction)

Two handouts are included to help you apply the information in this chapter to your classroom as you read. "Your Current Learning Space" (page 112) will help you generate information about your current learning space, including a drawing of your current space and lists of critical intangible qualities, such as the number and kinds of social interactions that take place there. After you've finished reading the chapter, you can use "Your Improved Learning Space" (page 114) to re-envision your space. Together with the information in this chapter, these handouts will help you visualize each feature of your learning environment and adapt each to positively support children's behaviors and create a proactive learning environment.

The Physical Setting and Use of Space

As we begin to think about your current learning environment, let's take a few moments to get it down on paper. (You may follow along using "Your Current Learning Space," Section I, Question 1, located on page 112, or visit **go.solution-tree.com/behavior** to download it.) Think about your space; what are the bare bones of the room or setting? How big is the space, and where are the doors, windows, closets and storage space, and so on? What is the shape of the room? Are there any permanent objects in the room such as pillars, sinks, water fountains, or bathrooms?

Mapping the Basics

For now, draw just these aspects of the space—nothing else. For this exercise, you can draw any space in which your children spend time, such as a classroom, the gymnasium, or the art room. Look carefully at your drawing. Does it represent the specific space you are thinking about right now? Remember, this drawing is just the "footprint": the shape, doors, windows, bathrooms, and so on. It does not have to be to scale, but should represent your current space fairly well.

Adding Special Features

Next, we will discuss qualities such as color, lighting, flooring, storage, and entryways (these items are addressed in the handout in Section I, Questions 2–6).

Color

As with any new space or room that will be used for a specific purpose, before the larger items are moved in, some of the aesthetic qualities of the room should be considered. Aesthetic qualities play a significant role in shaping behaviors (Mahnke, 1996; Meerwein, Mahnke, & Rodeck, 2007). Colors send messages to our brain even if we do not pay specific attention to them. They can influence the way we feel physically, mentally, and emotionally. They stimulate and nurture our varied moods, and can contribute to our ability to attend to the business of school: learning. Color often gets overlooked since most teachers have limited influence over the color of their walls. Since teachers do have many choices about the colors included within the rest of their space, however, they need to be conscious about the impact color has on mood, concentration, and level of activity in general. Imagine the effect of spending all day in a classroom painted either a highly stimulating neon orange or an unpleasant gray-green.

Colors have different meanings across cultures. (As with the rest of this book, this discussion of color takes into account the predominant beliefs of Western culture.) Softer colors are generally considered to be more calming than bright colors. Greens and blues are said to promote more calm moods, and some prisons have experimented with pink paint in the belief that even violent criminals could not be aggressive in pink cells! Red, on the other hand, increases energy, can evoke a fight-or-flight response, and can actually increase blood pressure and make the heart beat faster.

Pale yellows or an almond color are thought to be least likely to annoy anyone and are often recommended for hallways or study halls (Mahnke, 1996; Meerwein, Mahnke, & Rodeck, 2007).

Lighting

Overhead fluorescent lights can cause eyestrain for some students, create headaches for others, and for some students (especially those with a central nervous system dysfunction such as autism spectrum disorder), may actually bother their hearing. Fluorescent lighting emits sounds that some people can hear and find very irritating. If the lighting is too dim or too bright, some students may have challenges attending to the learning task, challenges that can come out as behaviors. To solve these problems, many teachers have placed colored tissue paper in the overhead fluorescent lights to change the brightness of the lights. Others use floor lamps instead of overhead lighting. The intensity of halogen lamps can be controlled or pointed upward to provide indirect light.

The best lighting is natural light from windows. It is wonderful to have windows to see outdoors and to allow sunlight to flood a space; curtains or blinds can control the amount of sunlight. Additional lamps can augment sunlight, of course. If you see children leaning forward to see the board, squinting to read, or placing materials close to their faces, there may be a lighting problem. If your district has a vision specialist, and you suspect that the lighting in your room could be enhanced, consult the expert. If there is not a vision specialist in your local area, each state has a school for the visually impaired, and there are vision specialists there. Many times they can be contacted for assistance. Alternatively, you could contact a local optometrist to visit your classroom to give you feedback on the lighting arrangement in your learning space.

Flooring

Flooring can be an issue, especially in a single space that is used for varied activities that would benefit from varied flooring. Carpeting is suitable for quiet activity spaces, such as a reading area, and for group gathering spaces where children can sit on the floor. Tile is best in areas where there is water, paint, science experiments, or anything that will need to be cleaned frequently. Having the proper flooring can eliminate worry for the teachers about potential clean up and can also provide the children with visual information about activity space boundaries and the expectations for certain activities.

Storage

Storage cabinets and closets are a necessary part of each learning setting. They are usually built into the existing structure, so you may not have control over their location. You may also have purchased additional cabinets to create more storage space in your room. Where are your storage units now? Do you have adequate storage space? Are you using your space wisely?

Entryways

Other aspects of the physical setting impact behaviors as well. How simple is it for students to get into the room? Well-designed entries allow for transitions that are physically and emotionally smooth. Have you ever entered a room and felt immediately uncomfortable—feelings that then impacted your behavior in that room? Does your behavior change if you feel welcome and comfortable when entering a room? Just as entering a room can impact our behaviors, the same goes for children. So, what does the entry to your current learning space "say" to the children as they walk into the room? Is it welcoming, producing happy anticipation and comfort, or overwhelming, producing anxiety and fear? Consider whether the door opens up into a space that appears crowded with people and furniture. Maybe the room is devoid of anything that is interesting to the child. Maybe the door opens up into a wide-open space that says "Run!" Remember, space speaks. Does the entry give the children cues about what might be expected of them when they walk into the room?

Take the time now to really look at your current learning space. What does the entry to your classroom say? Is it a welcoming entrance, or does it send confusing messages to the children? Would children enjoy coming through your doors?

Stop, Look, and Listen

When Kim was teaching preschool and elementary physical education for classes with children who had a wide range of physical and cognitive abilities, the children came through the doors into the gym and saw a large space. They immediately started to run around in the space because that is what it "said" to them—"Run and play!" In order to help them learn a different behavior, she had to devise an entry that would tell them a different message. She got some of the yellow tape that road construction crews use and some orange cones. After putting tall sticks into the cones, Kim wrapped the yellow tape around the sticks, and created a small traffic pattern that led students to an area called the "parking lot" where they had to wait for directions. Each student had a "parking space" (a carpet square) that became their safe zone throughout the class period.

In some elementary classroom settings, the cubbies that are used for coats and book bags are moveable and can be set up to create a small hallway as children enter the classroom. The students can be greeted at the beginning of the year and given the entering guidelines: "Come in, hang up your coat on your hook, put your book bag in your cubby, and then go into the room." This helps them learn the routine and will also help them develop independent skills as the year progresses.

Filling in the Space

After mapping the basics, the next step is to fill the space with large furnishings and show how they are arranged, how various spaces are defined, and how densely they are filled (Section I, Questions 7–12).

Large Furnishings and Arrangement

On the drawing of your room, add the furniture and larger objects such as desks, tables, chairs, bookcases, wastebaskets, computers, computer tables, and any other large furnishings. (Do not include smaller items such as books, puzzles, art materials, and so on.)

Following are some questions you should be asking yourself regularly about the arrangement of these large objects in your space:

- How are the tables, chairs, desks, and other larger furniture arranged in the space?

- How many objects can the space handle? Are there too many objects for the size of the room or too few? If you are fortunate to have a large space, you'll have leeway in the number of large pieces of furniture that you can use. However, if your space is small, you will have to identify which pieces are essential.

- Are all of the tables, chairs, and desks in the space really necessary? How can you reduce the use of furniture so the room is free of distracting clutter?

- Does the size of the furniture match the size and need of those children who will utilize the area? For example, are there low tables, chairs, bookcases, and so on for younger children?

If your environment is not filled with the right furniture or objects, you may see children fidgeting at their desks, asking to sit on the floor instead of a chair, bumping into objects or each other as they walk through the space, or exerting a lot of effort to see you, the board, or the work station. They may wander the room looking for a space to hold their work groups or overuse one spot instead of taking advantage of the entire room. Younger children may spill drinks at snack time or water colors during art due to improperly sized tables, chairs, or easels. All of these little things can add up to a general feeling that the children are "just misbehaving" when in fact their behavior is sending a message about the design of the physical environment.

There are many ways to arrange learning environments. In his book *Caring Spaces, Learning Places*, Jim Greenman (2005) describes various room arrangements and their impact. In what he calls the racetrack layout, all the furniture is pushed toward the center of the room (creating the "racetrack" around the outside of the room). In the maze layout, activities are offered in various spots throughout the space, breaking up the open area. In the perimeter strategy, the center of the room is left open for group activities and the work areas are positioned around the perimeter of the room.

The racetrack layout allows children, who learn well from their interactions with others, to always be in close proximity. However, for those less inclined to engage, it can put distractions close at hand or invite students to race around the open pathway. In the maze layout, the space is divided up among the activities; "children can see and move into other areas but they are always within a closed space" (Greenman, 1988, p. 141). For some children there may be less distraction if activities are further apart, and this layout may also provide a clearer indication of what to do in each learning space. The perimeter layout creates one central meeting place surrounded by all the classroom activity centers. Children are more readily accessible at all times to the teacher, who can use the central area as her observation point while keeping the flow of the class going.

Clearly, there are many ways of arranging a learning space depending upon the needs of the children, your teaching style, and your educational goals. The needs of students in any given classroom may change not only from year to year, but from month to month. The one thing to remember is that the arrangement of the space is another proactive strategy in supporting positive behavior.

What layout does your room use? Does it seem to work for you and your children; that is, do the children engage in the activities and with their peers easily? Do they roam aimlessly? How does the layout impact their learning, playing, and peer interactions? Every room has the potential for numerous layouts such as those mentioned. Careful consideration should be made when creating the classroom layout.

The Changing Classrooms

Sue was surprised when she came to school on a Monday morning and found the first-grade classroom totally rearranged. What had happened? Ms. Jackson explained that this year her students were having more trouble working in teams, and they needed some practice with group work in more structured settings. She had separated the desks into a more conventional configuration for the time being, based on the needs of her students.

Apparently this was not an unusual occurrence in that school. Mid-year, Sue found Mr. Mays' classroom in a new arrangement to facilitate the type of teaching he was planning for a new set of academic units. His room arrangement was part of his instructional strategy. Clearly, room arrangement was not an afterthought to these teachers.

Spatial Variety

Spatial variety—meaning the use of both open spaces and smaller, more individualized spaces—can also be manipulated to enhance positive behaviors. We can plan open space for larger group work and closed spaces that provide a quieter, closer space for small group or individual work. Some children work best when they have space to themselves instead of always being around other people. Others don't seem to mind being in a crowd. What kind of spatial variety does your current learning space offer? Take a look at the layout you have created with the placement of the larger furniture, desks, and computers; is there any variety? How is that variety indicated or created? The makeup of each class and your instructional and interactional goals will determine the types and variety of spaces needed.

Defined Work Spaces

Once the children have entered the room and can see what awaits them, does the layout in your current learning space provide for the various needs that children have while learning? Have your spaces been designed to help students do the following?

- Focus attention on activities and learning

- Organize their actions within the space

- Associate activities with equipment

- Categorize materials

- Use the work space independently

- Care for and clean up materials

Defined spaces help children learn the behaviors that are acceptable in each area and, therefore, can be an easy way to proactively support behavior. You can use many creative methods to divide space. Different flooring can signal an activity change; tile flooring may be used in snack or other messy areas where spills are likely, for example. Folding cardboard screens can create individual space anywhere in a room, as can latticework made from plastic six-pack rings. Some classrooms have used real or artificial plants for walls. Shower curtains hung from the ceiling can be opened or closed depending on the space needs; clear curtains allow students to see into the area or can be decorated. For younger children, low bolsters may be all that is needed to define a learning center. Other more symbolic dividers and boundaries include usher's ropes, taped lines on the floor, or chalk on the carpet. Mark your classroom's defined work spaces on your drawing.

Pathways

As more classrooms are set up to encourage group learning, from the learning centers in preschools to the group learning environments in elementary schools, it will be essential that the room has clear pathways. Without clear pathways, the space becomes like a huge unmarked parking lot where teachers must become traffic police to avoid collisions. Meandering pathways allow children to learn what activities are available and to observe others engaged in them, while straight routes allow quick movement from one side of the room to another without disrupting others. Pathways must be accessible to all children, including those in wheelchairs. There will always be some accidental bumping in a classroom, but careful consideration in the way pathways are laid out can help reduce the number of "traffic jams." In most cases, the basic room arrangement can create natural pathways.

You can use innovative methods to create paths that stimulate children's independence and positive behaviors. Some pathways may be marked on the floor with colored tape. For example, a green line may lead to the door to go outside, a red line to the bathroom, a blue line to the snack area, and a brown line to the block area. The visual supports created by the furniture, tape, colors, and other dividers can help students learn what each space has to offer and where different kinds of activities take place.

How have you created the pathways among the defined learning areas in your current learning space? How are the pathways indicated? What have you used to define or divide the learning areas? Do these work well for the children? Sketch in the pathways on your drawing.

Social Density

Finally, one other crucial aspect to consider when arranging a classroom is social density—that is, how many children and adults will potentially occupy the entire space and each specific center or area used throughout the day. Are there areas that are more crowded than others in your current learning space? Remember, each class is different, so the arrangement of space and the consequent social density that worked for you last year may not work this year. Consider which activity areas are the most popular or heavily utilized, then consider how many children are optimal in each area. What impact would limiting (or not limiting) the numbers of participants in any given area or participating in a specific activity have? Ask yourself:

- Is there enough room in each area for a few students to be engaged in the learning opportunities without crowding each other?

- Does the group or large area have plenty of space for movement?

- Have you taken into account any special mobility needs? Sensory integration needs? Visual or hearing needs?

Behaviors can be greatly impacted if there is not enough room for everyone. Even adults packed into tight spaces find it natural to react negatively. If there are too many children in one space, they can start fidgeting and poking each other. This can create stress and cause ill feelings, potentially leading to aggression or withdrawal. Therefore, always think about the number of people who will use the space as you are arranging the room, creating learning centers, and establishing pathways.

Material Type, Selection, and Storage

Once the space and all of the furniture are in place on your drawings, the next step is to fill the space with the necessary materials. The activities, books, manipulatives, and art materials are the tools for learning in any classroom environment. These materials can make any learning situation either fun and interesting or dull and frustrating. It takes thoughtful planning in order to incorporate the appropriate materials to engage the children and their desire to learn.

Whatever the space may be, the manner in which the materials are presented and organized can have an impact on the behavior of the children in that environment. Most of us try to create areas for ourselves that make sense, lack clutter, and allow us to function without major distractions. Materials that are organized so that everyone knows where to find and store them add to the sense of order and clear expectations in a physical environment. (See Section II, Questions 1 and 2, of "Your Current Learning Space" to adjust your drawing in the following sections.)

Identifying Material Types

Think about the materials in your classroom and create a list of materials you have and use in your teaching. Don't get overwhelmed with this task. Every crayon does not need to be listed; just indicate, in general, where your supplies are kept.

The materials and activities that happen within a specific area all need to be carefully considered to ensure they are appropriate and interesting to the students using them. Simply having many materials in a learning space does not mean it will encourage the children to engage in activities and actually learn. In fact, too many or too few materials can have negative impacts on the children. To establish a proactive learning environment, consider the selection of materials first, then their presentation.

Selecting Materials

Materials can only be selected after the program goals and curricular expectations have been created and are understood.

Developmental Levels

In every classroom, there will always be a range of ability in children's ability to use toys, books, materials, and activities. For that reason, when choosing materials, ask, how widespread are the developmental levels of the students? In a preschool class, some may be reading simple words, while others still only look at the pictures in books; some may be able to build with interconnecting blocks, and others may only be able to use larger blocks; some may have the fine motor skills to use pencils or markers, and others may need to have writing utensils with larger grips in order to write or draw.

Student Interests

Student interest in toys, books, materials, and activities will also vary. Most of us remember how much more enjoyable it was to go to school when there were activities we liked or materials that matched our interests. If there was nothing that captured your attention, what did you do? Did you try to create an activity that you enjoyed? Did you try to attract attention to yourself in order to attempt to change an activity? Children today will do the same. The more interesting and meaningful the activities are to them, the more they will engage.

When trying to match the interest areas of the children, be aware of what children are asking for or talking about. Pay attention to the fads and crazes that attract media attention, or simply ask some children what they enjoy. In some cases what they enjoy may not be appropriate for the classroom (for example, violent videos or computer games), but when possible, be sure to incorporate the materials they like and enjoy into the curriculum and environment.

Physical Characteristics and Implied Use

The physical characteristics of materials also impact the way in which children interact while using them. By their nature, some materials encourage individual or solitary use. Art supplies with 8½ x 11 pieces of paper indicate individual work, while butcher paper that covers an entire table or wall cries out for a collaborative mural. Books can be used to encourage either solitary reading or reading with a friend. Building with blocks encourages the imagination of children as well as cooperation during group building. Creating a medieval town requires a collaborative group effort, not just in the creative phase, but also in the construction phases. Materials that encourage paired or group work facilitate the social networking and peer interactions around a topic that will benefit not only academic learning in a subject, but also social growth.

Quantity and Variety

Two other aspects of material selection that can have an impact on behaviors are amount of materials and variety. We all find ways to fill idle time. Having enough material for all of the children to actively participate in tasks such as gross motor time or group music time will eliminate the probability of them finding other things to occupy their hands while they "wait their turn." Doing a demonstration or experiment? Have enough equipment and materials so your students can be actively involved. Sue remembers watching a student teacher struggle to keep the attention of a class when using one student to experiment and report on how the senses of taste and smell worked together. How much more fun and what a greater impact she could have had by having enough materials for each student to participate in at least some of the activity. Not only that, she would not have needed her supervising teacher's help in maintaining positive behavior.

Children can also get bored if they use the same materials repeatedly, hear the same stories, do the same puzzles, or color the same pictures (younger grades), or do the same type of workbook activities (older grades). Infuse variety to maintain the interest levels of the students. In particular, in our world of ever-growing electronic resources, the range of available curriculum enhancers continues to expand, and the Internet is a boundless source of information and learning materials. Some children may connect with material electronically that causes them difficulty in other formats.

Storing Materials

Next, consider where materials are located or stored. Indicate the location of materials in your learning space on your drawing.

In most classrooms, materials have a place they belong when not in use. The materials that are acceptable for the children to have during the day should be made accessible to them—on low shelves or in places that they can reach themselves. This promotes independence and less reliance on the adults. Conversely, the materials that are not acceptable for them to have should be put away—out of sight, out of mind! To keep things out of sight, simply turn shelves around or cover them with cloth or screens. Is this how materials are stored in your current space?

Young children who are still in the process of learning how to categorize and classify items will benefit from logical organization for storage. In other words, in play environments, the shapes of the blocks could be outlined on the shelves to help with the reshelving. Bins and shelves can have photos of their contents or the toy that belongs on that specific shelf. Not all materials need the detail of a photo or outline of the object on the shelf, but for some children, a visual gives an additional cue as to what belongs where. When clean-up time comes, the children will know where things go and need less adult direction.

Sensory and Natural Elements

You've drawn your space, placed the large objects, and designated the materials and their placement. Yet there are still other aspects of the environment that can impact the behaviors of those students. They are more subtle, but nevertheless can impact behavior. Remember, space speaks and can make or break a situation. Five more subtle aspects in every environment that can speak to anyone are the sensory elements of temperature, sounds, smells, visual displays, and the use of nature. Each of these contributes to the energy, attention levels, and types of interaction in the environment. (See Section III, Questions 1 and 2, of "Your Current Learning Space" to follow along.)

Stop a moment and consider your current learning space, thinking especially of the five areas mentioned: temperature, sounds, smells, visual displays, and the use of nature. What impact do they have on your current space? Do they seem to enhance the space and therefore the learning of the children, or do they sometimes impede their progress? Take a couple moments to think about your current learning space, and make a list of the sensory aspects that have been mentioned as they appear in that space.

Temperature

Temperature may speak the loudest. No one likes to remain in rooms that have temperature extremes. Being aware of the temperature and regulating the thermostat can be a behavior support for not only the children, but also the adults in the room! What is the temperature in your current learning space?

Sounds

Sounds are abundant in many early childhood classrooms. Generally when younger children are engaged, there is a playful din. Sometimes it may become too overpowering, and the children are reminded to quiet down. Sometimes it may become too quiet, causing the adults to wonder what is going on that they might need to investigate! As children grow into more academic learning situations, there is still a productive sound that comes from groups of students learning together. As a speech and language pathologist, Sue loves to walk into classrooms where children of any age are talking about their learning.

We have other ways to help create the type of sound environment that is conducive to the type of learning we want to promote. When young children are too wild and noisy and need to calm down or to take a rest, the use of quiet music can help change their mood, their energy, or their behavior. Soothing music can create a quieter environment. The opposite is true as well; music that has a faster tempo can be used to get the students up and moving perhaps for a gross motor time or simply to help them get all their energy funneled in a more positive way. Remember that some children with special needs may overreact to loud sounds in the form of challenging behaviors; these behaviors then need to be deciphered using the big-picture questions.

Music can be used in classrooms for older students as well. Be sure it has no words, has a fairly regular beat, and isn't widely variable in volume, and you have good study music. Some teachers like to use white noise during testing times to block out the incidental sounds that can distract attention from the task. What sounds are apparent in your current learning space? Remember to listen for sounds that might be coming from outside of that space.

Smells

Smells can also impact behaviors. Some physical and occupational therapists use smells in their sessions to either perk up or slow down the student. While odors are sometimes hard to regulate, it is wise to remember that some smells may cause challenges. In the course of a day there may be very different odors in a room: your own perfume or cologne, cleaning solution, food from the cafeteria, markers, and the unmistakable odor after physical education class. For some students, specific smells can cause headaches or sting their eyes. Young children may not know what is happening or be able to express themselves clearly; in those instances, they may simply resort to using behavior in an attempt to communicate. Because odors are invisible and a sensory issue, they can be much harder to figure out as a reason for a behavior and, then, are often overlooked. Be aware of that some children deal on a regular basis with sensory issues that they may not understand or be able to express yet. Are there abundant fragrances in your current learning space?

Visual Displays

Consider the way you have used display in your current space. This is one way you can impact the color without painting the walls, and also a way that you can place student-created art on public view. While art and display are wonderful, sometimes it can be overdone and create more distraction for some students. Not only can the basic wall color impact us, but the use of too many complex patterns can be overwhelming. If every spot on your walls is covered with some form of artwork, it is too much. Too much on the walls can cause confusion and blend everything together. Instead, use a bulletin board or two to indicate a special place for their work and draw attention to their creations. How is art displayed in your space?

The Use of Nature

Bringing nature into the classroom through plants and flowers can help create a warm and inviting environment (be sure they're not poisonous, don't produce pollen, don't have thorns, and so on). Living creatures such as goldfish, rabbits, hamsters, and gerbils can also be another way to teach various skills to children, including how to take care of someone or something else in a positive and nurturing way. Nature keeps a room from being sterile and creates a feeling of welcome. In what ways is nature present in your current learning space? Be sure to list them on your drawing.

Refining the physical set up of the environment is the first step in supporting positive behaviors.

Sensory Overload: Chae's Story

Kim's observation in a third-grade classroom started out typically. A student with autism, Chae, was having trouble concentrating and working in the classroom. He also was using some behaviors that were not acceptable.

Kim walked into the classroom and immediately wanted to walk out. It was like a visual and auditory assault! The walls were covered with posters that third-grade students would enjoy. The alphabet was posted high on one wall, the solar system on another, and tiny planets hung down from the light fixtures, as did papier-mache birds and butterflies—every inch of wall space was covered. The room had an alternative arrangement with desks in the middle of the room for working and various workstations on the perimeter. In two corners of the room, computers were running different programs with various sounds; in another corner, a student was listening to a book on tape loudly enough to be audible to others; in the fourth corner, an aquarium bubbled away. There were plants used as dividers, large fig trees, and even a small cage with hamsters running in their exercise wheels.

No wonder Chae was rocking and holding his ears! He was in sensory overload. There was too much going on in the room for him to tune out. His behaviors were indicating, "Get me out of here! Help me concentrate."

Chae could speak but was unable to interpret his own internal feelings sufficiently to tell the teacher what exactly was bothering him. He reverted to his behavior, which was misunderstood without looking at the big picture.

In response, the teacher created a small work space for Chae to keep the sensory stimulation to a minimum. A divider cut out much of the visual distractions, and he had headphones he could choose to use if the auditory stimulation became too much—and he chose to use them often. His behaviors changed dramatically in the next week as he grew more accustomed to his new seat and routine.

The Social Environment

Our discussion of the learning environment has covered many topics. We have talked about the varied pieces of the physical aspects of the learning environment and about how the materials used in that space can have an impact on the behavior of the children. The last, but certainly not the least, feature to consider is the social aspect of the environment. (See Section IV, Questions 1–4, of "Your Current Learning Space" to follow along.)

Every place that we go has a social aspect, whether it is a classroom, a store, a home, or playground. A social environment is created through the amount and type of interactions and communications that happen there, which impacts the behavior of people. How are the people in your current learning environment interacting with one another? Is it pleasant, positive, and genuine, or is it nagging, negative, and robotic? Are the children engaged in friendly and fun interactions with their peers, whether silently playing or working alongside them or talking to one another? Are they interacting with each other in ways that reflect the models they have seen and heard from the adults in their lives? How many times do they hear positive statements from you, and how many times do they hear negative remarks? These interactions and communications set a tone for every learning space and produce a social environment.

Although this part of any environment is not tangible, it can produce very tangible results. Sometimes those results are wonderful when children engage in activities and communicate with their peers. At other times, the results are misunderstandings or behaviors that are not expected or wanted. Those unwanted behaviors are the tangible results of an environment that does not support positive behavior.

Children can learn more appropriate social communication and interaction skills if the social environment provides them with models of better ways to express their feelings, desires, and needs. We are constant role models, especially when children are young and impressionable. As teachers, we have a huge responsibility to help our children act and react in ways that support their engagement with others and their ability to be successful. Students learn more from us than reading, writing, and arithmetic; they are constantly observing us—how we interact with others, how we respond to different or difficult situations, how we initiate entrance to a game or conversation, and so on. According to Albert Bandura (1977, p. 22), "most human behavior is learned observationally through modeling: from observing others one forms an idea of how new behaviors are performed, and on later occasions this coded information serves as a guide for action." We must take care to always model those behaviors we wish to see copied. How do you create a safe space for your children? What might you be saying with body language that the children notice? Being a role model and maintaining a safe environment is a never-ending job, one teachers take on as soon as they enter any classroom.

Unfortunately, sometimes interactions and communications we model are not positive. Some children earn reputations that are passed on from teacher to teacher, and our social relationships with them can become biased. Instead of speaking to those students conversationally, as we would to anyone else, our tone can become harsh and directive. We use more instruction and programmed talking rather than making conversation. Conversely, when we speak to children who are successful in school and not seen as challenging, we use more praise and encouragement.

Take a moment and think about your interactions with your children. What types of interactions happen in your space? Be sure to write down the phrases that you use on a regular basis—the positive and the negative. Think about all the children in your class. Do the positive comments outnumber the negative—for all the children? Do the children in your current learning space model the behaviors they see and hear coming from you? Are those the behaviors you wish to see and hear?

An Improved Learning Space

As we have noted, space does speak to children very loudly. The environment is a key component of a positive approach to supporting the behaviors of students. Teachers should be very intentional in the creation of their learning environment, leaving nothing to happenstance. The physical set up, materials used, sensory elements, and the ease of interaction for each and every person in the room all contribute to the vitality of the learning that takes place. Every aspect of a classroom plays a part, and you, as the teacher, can control the impact each feature plays. Creating a wonderful space is the first step in ensuring the behaviors of your students will support learning instead of the need for challenging behaviors. Use "Your Improved Learning Space" (page 114, or download at **go.solution-tree.com/behavior**) to put your new knowledge into action.

Takeaways

- Ensure that physical environments are safe and accessible for all children so that each child can engage in every activity.

- Provide a sufficient number of materials so that several children are able to play and work together at once; reduce the waiting time.

- Consider the type(s) of collaboration you want to have happen as you arrange your space and choose materials.

- Provide materials that meet curricular needs.

- Ensure that lighting is adequate and not too harsh.

- Consider:

  - Temperature

  - Noise level

  - Smells

  - Visual displays

  - Natural elements

- Provide opportunities for interactions among students and adults that focus on encouraging and advancing not only academic skills, but social development.

Personal Reflection

How do you define the term *positive approaches*? What do you do that you believe are positive approaches that support your children?

Reflect on the physical environments in which you are most comfortable and most uncomfortable. What are the characteristics of the two sets of physical environments?

Now do the same for social environments. What are the characteristics of the social environments in which you feel comfortable and those in which you prefer not to spend time?

In what environments have you seen your children succeed or fail? What about those environments contributed to those results?

Have you discovered any aspects of your current environment that you are going to change?

Your Current Learning Space

Use this handout and the discussion in chapter 7 to create a drawing of your current learning space and to identify its critical components.

Section I. The Physical Setting and Use of Space

1. Draw your current learning space on a blank piece of paper.

2. What color are the walls?

3. What type of lighting is in the space?

4. What is the flooring throughout the space?

5. Where are the closets and cabinets?

6. How does your entryway appear? Is it welcoming?

7. Add the following to your drawing:

Bookcases	Chairs	Water table	Other
Tables	Easels	Sand table	
Desks	Lamps	Kitchen set	
File cabinets	Toy shelves	Gross motor equipment	

8. What does the room layout look like?

9. Do you have spatial variety in your learning space? How is it created?

10. Do you have defined work areas? Label them on your drawing.

11. Are there clear pathways in your classroom? Indicate them on the drawing.

12. Which areas are the most heavily used? Which the least? Indicate high- and low-density areas on your map.

Section II. Material Type, Selection, and Storage

1. What materials do you have in your current learning space (books, blocks, toys, maps, globes, art supplies, and other standard teaching materials)? Create a list.

2. Where are these materials located? Indicate them on your drawing.

Section III. Sensory and Natural Elements

1. What do you have in your current learning space that impacts the senses: temperature, sounds, smells, visual display?

2. Do you have elements of nature (plants, class pets, and so on) in your classroom? List them.

Section IV. The Social Environment

1. How interactive are the children in your class with one another?

2. What types of interactions does the space support?

3. How many children are in your current learning space?

4. How many students can occupy defined work areas at one given time?

Your Improved Learning Space

Once you have read chapter 7, drawn your current learning space, and defined its critical components, use this handout and your new knowledge to go back to the drawing board and create a blueprint to improve your learning space. Write your responses here and label or indicate your answers on your drawing as well.

Section I. The Physical Setting and Use of Space

1. Since you most likely cannot actually rebuild your space, redraw your learning space on a blank piece of paper.

2. What color will you make the walls, if you can change them?

   If not, what can you do to change or add to the colors in your classroom?

   What colors will help students concentrate?

3. How can you improve the lighting in your space?

   Will you use lamps?

   Do you need to improve the current overhead lighting? How?

   How can you increase and/or control any natural lighting?

4. Can you augment the flooring in your space? How?

   Do some areas need activity-appropriate flooring?

   Do some areas need less conditional flooring (where spills are okay, for example)?

5. Where will the closets and cabinets be?

   Do you need more storage space?

   How will you obtain it?

6. What are the larger objects and furniture in your improved learning space? List them, then locate them on your drawing.

7. How will you change your entryway?

   What will you do to make it more welcoming?

8. Will you have defined work areas or specific topic areas in your improved learning space? How many?

   How will you create them?

   How will you make their use clear to the children?

9. How will you change your overall layout?

What will it look like? Create the layout on your drawing, and remember to consider the specified learning centers or topic areas.

10. How will you create clear pathways?

Indicate the pathways on your drawing.

11. How will you ensure there is spatial variety?

Indicate the large- and small-group areas on your drawing.

12. What is the appropriate social density for each area?

Section II. Material Type, Selection, and Storage

1. What materials will you have in your improved learning space? List them.

How will you ensure that the materials reflect the developmental levels of the children?

How will you ensure that the materials reflect the interests of the children?

How will you ensure that the materials entice children to work together?

Will you have activities children can do alone? What will they be?

How will you be sure you have adequate quantity and variety of materials?

2. How will you store the materials in your improved learning space?

Will you need additional storage?

What kind? How will you obtain it?

Where will it be located?

How will you ensure the materials are stored in a convenient location?

Section III. Sensory and Natural Elements

1. What temperature will you maintain in your improved learning space?

Can the temperature be regulated?

If not, what can you do to help maintain an optimal temperature for learning?

What is the optimal temperature?

How will you know when it is optimal?

2. What will the noise level be in your space?

   Are there interfering noises within the space?

   How will you control those noises?

   Will you use music? What type? When?

   Will you allow a certain amount of child chatter in your space?

   How will you let the children know when it is too loud?

3. How will you control the various scents in your improved learning space?

   Do you want to use candles, scented tissues, cleaners, and so on?

   What other scents will you need to be aware of? List them.

   What will you do to improve the odors in your improved learning space?

4. How will you create new or different visual displays?

   Whose art will you display, and how?

   How much will you put up in your improved learning space?

   Will the art be seasonal?

5. How will you bring nature into your improved learning space?

   What will be safe for your children?

   Will the natural objects be used as a learning tool?

   Will they take up valuable space?

Section IV. The Social Environment

1. How will you promote positive interactions?

   What types of phrases will you use when you interact with your children?

   How will you create your space to encourage children to interact with each other?

2. How can you manage the number of children so there is enough space and time for positive engagement?

   Will you limit how many can occupy centers or topic areas at a given time?

3. How will you ensure that your improved learning space feels like a safe space for the children?

4. How will you change your interaction style?

   How will you monitor your own behaviors, body language, and interactions to be a good role model?

8

Proactive Behavioral Strategies

Most schools have guidelines that are specifically geared to "behavior management." Faculty and school administration receive annual handbooks that explain the rules of behavior, as well as what to do in the case of disruption and unwanted conduct. Not only that, but many classrooms have their own additional rules. But encouraging positive behaviors involves more than rules. It involves a shift of attention and energy. Lovett's statement that "our energies are better put to eliminate the need for difficult behavior than in trying simplistically to eliminate the behavior itself" (1996, p. 94) summarizes this philosophy.

How adults communicate with children sets the expectation for the behaviors we see and experience in different environments. What we do, what we say, and how we interact make a difference. The measures that we can take to support positive behavior are seldom written into faculty handbooks.

Proactive behavioral approaches are simple, straightforward ways that a teacher and school staff can work together to help students learn not only the academics, but also the behaviors necessary to engage in the learning and social environment that defines school. To implement these approaches successfully, the education team must work together and be consistent in all techniques. This can be challenging in some instances, but it is vital that the team stick together and stay on course with the supports they create.

Look for the Positive

All too often we only comment on children's negative behaviors or call attention to naughty activities. This gets tedious for everyone and drains energy. Instead, retrain yourself to see the positive, and comment on those aspects of the child or the day. Imagine how wonderful the days could be if you reframed your thinking; remember the saying "you get what you ask for." Start asking for a more positive outlook from yourself and others.

Praise Honestly, Descriptively, and Judiciously

We often hear staff say phrases such as: "You're working well, Johnny." What is "good" working? More importantly, if teachers all use the same sort of generic praises regularly, they won't sound genuine to children. Instead, tell children exactly what you are praising so they can learn what they are doing that gains them favor. Be explicit. Call attention to the behaviors you want to perpetuate. Try, "Thank you for reading quietly at your table. It looks like you are getting a lot accomplished," or "That poem you wrote shows a lot of hard work." These statements give students much more information about what, exactly, their behaviors allow them to do.

Praise needs to be used judiciously, and it needs to be specific. Be sure your praise supports and encourages your students to develop positive self images and an internal sense of accomplishment and competence in both academic and behavioral tasks.

Praise or Criticize Behaviors, Not the Child

When we say "Bad girl!" or "Good boy!" we know what we mean. However, sometimes the child may be confused by these messages. Remember the exercise from chapter 1 that looked at acceptable and unacceptable behaviors? If the definition of "good" and "bad" can potentially change from setting to setting, how is a young child supposed to make sense of what is expected? By praising or criticizing specific *behaviors*, you can make your expectations become clearer. Zirpoli (2005, p. 422) reminds us, "if a child does something inappropriate and you must say something, talk about the *behavior*, not the child. Although their behaviors may sometimes be bad, *children* are never bad. To maintain the child's dignity and self-worth, describe what the child did that you dislike but do not criticize the child as a person."

Instead of saying "Bad girl!" for example, you can say, "Do not hit, Samantha. If you are angry, you can come tell me." Instead of saying, "Good boy!" you can say, "You are using so many of the measuring tools today. It seems that this will help you finish the building more easily." These statements send clear messages about exactly what the behavior is, and how it is working to keep the child focused on the task at hand in a way that is productive and appropriate for the classroom.

Name and Validate Feelings, Even if the Behavior Is Unacceptable

Children need to learn that their feelings are okay and that everyone has feelings and emotions. Often, when children are upset or very excited, they are told to calm down or settle down, and that stifles their emotional expression. Emotions are natural and should be given voice; however, it is often up to adults to name and validate children's feelings and give them socially appropriate ways of expressing them. For example, if a child is angry with another, she may hit and yell. But instead of saying "Stop hitting," it is better to say, "I understand that you are mad, Mary. Hitting is not okay. So, how can I help?"

Avoid Negative Labels

Children are constantly learning and will live either up or down to our expectations. When they hear they are "bad," "unfriendly," "lazy," or simply "a problem child," they can begin to internalize those traits and fulfill that description. As Kaiser and Raminsky (2007, p. 10) note, "Negative labels can all too easily become self-fulfilling prophecies. They prevent you from seeing the child's positive qualities and may even cause you to lower your expectations of him." It's easy to use those labels when speaking of the child to others (and sometimes even to the child). But children listen to adults more than we might think. Avoid that type of discussion totally. Negative labeling does not provide constructive guidance for anyone. It is destructive and only leads to a downward spiral for child and teacher alike. Remember, "labels are extremely powerful, which is why it is wiser not to use them—or if you do apply them to the behavior rather than the child. Employing language carefully makes a big difference in the way you see a child and think about who he is and what he can and cannot do" (Kaiser & Raminsky, 2007, p. 10).

Pick Your Battles

You do not have to scrutinize everything that a child does; that would be a waste of time and energy. When a child has many challenging behaviors, pick the one or two most critical behaviors to focus on. Instead of cataloguing every wiggle or sound that a child makes as negative behavior, focus on those behaviors that cause the greatest disruption in social relationships or completion of tasks. The less consequential behaviors may begin to fade away as the adults begin to decipher the messages and provide supports for the more critical behavior issues.

Communicate at the Child's Level of Understanding and Ability

Children develop their understanding of language and events at different rates. Do not assume that all children in your classroom can understand everything on the same level. Modify or adapt language and instructions at any time to help children completely understand. This is an integral part of differentiated instruction.

Use Clear, Simple, and Concise Language

Directions that are clear, simple, and concise leave less room for misunderstanding. Once the child is comfortable and the adults know the child's abilities, then the language can be amended to a different level. Conversational language, the language of instruction, and the language used when giving directions will differ, not only depending on the level of the child's understanding, but also on the purpose.

Give Adequate Information

Everyone likes to have enough information to feel totally in control—as if they know exactly what is going to happen, when it will happen, where it will happen, and who will be involved. Use visual supports and verbal reminders to reassure children about their daily schedule and activities.

Be Sure the Child Is Able to Comply

We sometimes forget that children are not little adults. Their minds, bodies, and social skills are still developing. When making a request, be sure to know the child's abilities in all areas in order to assure his ability to comply. This will avoid any embarrassment of the child and need for behaviors to avoid unmanageable tasks.

Be Aware of Your Nonverbal Communication

Just as the behavior and body language of children communicate to us as adults, our behavior and body language communicate to them. Children watch adults. They look at faces, postures, hand gestures, expressions; they listen to sighs, moans, tone of voice, and so on. Often, while our words and voices are saying one thing, our bodies or faces send a completely different and loud message. As Lovett states, "We need to be more rigorous in analyzing our own behavior and recognize our intentions have often differed from our actions" (1996, p. 71). One group of teachers shared with us that there was a young boy who was a "terror" and that every morning they had a prayer circle before school started—praying that he would not show up! Can you imagine what their faces and body language revealed when that child *did* show up at school? What we do is just as important as what we say—sometimes more important.

Tell Children What *to* Do and Avoid Telling Them What Not to Do

Unfortunately, when adults are trying to maintain order in the classroom, the words that come out of their mouths are not always positive. Children hear a great deal of negative instruction every day: "Stop doing that!" "That is not allowed!" Instead, remind children of what *is* allowed—on the playground, in the classroom, with friends, at lunch, and so on. Don't make them have to figure it out for themselves. "Put your spoon on the table" provides a picture of what you want. "Don't throw your spoon on the floor" doesn't tell the child what should happen to that darned spoon.

Often teachers are merely trying to remind the children the rules. One young first-year teacher gathered her third-grade class around her before they headed to the cafeteria and told the students, "Now remember, don't throw your food." The children were silent for a moment, but then the wheels started to turn and grins appeared. What a great idea, they thought—food fight in the cafeteria! This teacher had unknowingly planted a seed in their minds instead of helping them maintain order.

Other common instructions that may embed the wrong information include, "Don't run in the hall," "Don't throw stones," "Don't call each other names," "Don't hit," "Don't yell in the cafeteria," "Don't talk unless you raise your hand," and so on. They are all telling the children what *not* to do. It's more helpful to state rules in a positive manner or tell students what they can and should do. "Walk in the hall," "Only throw balls," "Use your real names," "Keep your hands to yourself," "Use a quiet conversational voice in the cafeteria," and "Raise your hand, wait to be called on, and then talk" are all better and more positive ways to share the same rules.

Sometimes teachers simply shout directions out to the children such as "Stop," "Wait," "Don't do that," or "Cut it out." The children may do what they are told, but only for a few seconds. Then they begin to do exactly what the teachers wanted them to stop doing. Why? They know what not to do, but have nothing to replace the unwanted behavior. This is especially important when supporting students with disabilities, who may take directions literally but then not know what to do instead. Suppose a student with disabilities is poking a peer in the side, and the teacher tells him to stop it. The student stops for an instant or two and then starts right up again. Even though that was not the result the teacher sought, in the student's mind, he had complied with the teacher by stopping for that moment.

Redirect

It is up to us to provide an alternative behavior to use. Instead of merely telling students to stop or wait, give them an alternative and more acceptable behavior. If Danita, who is in fifth grade, constantly watches an activity outside the window during reading time, redirect her to the reading assignment instead of commenting on the behavior. She could be told, "Danita, we are reading right now, and we are on page 17. It is time for you to read from the top of the page." This does not give attention to the unwanted behavior and redirects her attention to what is going on in the class at that moment.

Most children want to do what is best and follow the rules. However, there are times that they are so excited or distracted that they have trouble remembering what it is they are supposed to be doing. If we remind them of the rules in a positive fashion and redirect their attention consistently to the task at hand, children can learn and follow the rules and classroom expectations.

Use Contingencies (First This, Then That) and/or Behavior Contracts

Contingencies are used every day by almost everyone in one way or another. A contingency is basically a "contract" between two entities created before any behaviors occur that states, "First X happens, and then Y will occur." Another way to say it might be, "First you do this, and then you get this." For most adults the most obvious example of a contingency may be your job: first you work, and then you get your paycheck. A contingency can also be looked at as reinforcement for work well done.

A contingency is also a natural way of creating an agreement or a contract between students and teacher that sets goals and defines rewards. For young children contingencies may be simple statements such as, "First we have circle time, and then we play" or "First you wash your hands, and then you can have your snack." For younger children those simple and immediate results are instrumental in illustrating the consequences of their behaviors.

Contingencies can be used in tandem with other positive approaches to help children learn social routines. When Juan wants to ride the tricycle and tries to pull the trike away from Tabitha instead of waiting, he could be told, "First Tabitha will ride for three minutes, and then it will be your turn. I will help keep time." This uses the concept of setting limits as well as the contingency plan. It also helps Juan start to develop the self-control to wait for his turn. Simple, fast, and clear are good rules of thumb for young children and for children with disabilities.

For children with disabilities, the verbal contingency may also have to be augmented with visual accommodations. Using pictures to indicate both the "first" and "then" can assist in making the task clear; for example, using a picture of a work space or table for the "first" and a picture of the reinforcer, such as a video game, for "then." In this way the child can hear and see a simple sequence of events that indicate what will happen. Visual supports are very helpful for students with disabilities and make directions, requests, and sequences clear for just about anyone.

As children get older, expectations for acceptable behavior should be broadened to require a great degree of expectation in more situations with increasingly greater and more complicated demands. As children learn to read, very simple contracts might be incorporated into their day that are explicit about what has to be done and what will be achieved. For example, suppose Mario is in second grade and has trouble turning in his work on time. The teacher and Mario may talk privately and set up a simple contract or contingency that says, "First Mario must turn his work in on time, and then he can have ten minutes on the computer." This could be written out for both the teacher and Mario to sign. For even older students, the tasks could be multiple or longer in order to be successfully completed. Greyson, who is in sixth grade and has a wild imagination and becomes distracted with his own writing during class, may need some additional incentive to pay attention and participate in the class discussion instead of becoming lost in his own stories. His contingency contract may involve more specifics such as, "First Greyson will 1) look at and listen to the teacher, 2) answer three questions during the course of the discussion, and 3) independently complete the assignment, and then he can have fifteen minutes of uninterrupted free time on the computer to write his own story." This contingency uses what is most important to the student and would be a powerful motivator.

A contingency has to be meaningful to the student for whom it's created. Not everyone feels reinforced for their good work with a pat on the back, but some students may be very pleased to receive that sort of attention. This point was brought home painfully at a graduation at which every straight-A student was honored with the same band fanfare and huge applause from the student body. While some students danced across the stage, clearly enjoying the attention, several students opted not to attend the ceremony because they were uncomfortable with the public acclaim. The fact that they had excelled in their classes was enough of a reward. What is reinforcing for one person may be punishment for another. Contingencies must meet the physical and emotional needs of the student involved.

Have Stated, Posted Rules

Rules are created to help maintain orderliness and to help us understand the expectations of each environment. Rules of the road keep us safe while driving; Robert's Rules of Order help keep meetings running smoothly; board game rules help players have an enjoyable and collaborative experience; social rules such as waiting in line to pay for merchandise or to get a ticket ensure that everyone's needs can be met in turn. When we are young, we need to be taught about rules and learn to follow them whether the rules are for being in the community, living at home with a family, or attending school; rules must be explained and taught. Fields, Perry, and Fields (2006, pp. 47–49) note

> Children's limited reasoning ability, coupled with their limited experience, often brings them to conclusions inconsistent with adult logic. This situation often gets children into trouble. Teachers and parents get angry at youngsters for what adults perceive as disobeying rules, telling lies, being selfish or inconsiderate, and behaving in totally irrational ways. To make matters worse, the children don't realize they have done anything wrong. For the parent or teacher . . . this can be totally infuriating.

Thus, rules that are both age-appropriate and explicitly taught are critical for children to begin to learn how to coexist in their varied communities: home, school, or neighborhood. Though all schools have rules that govern the behavior of the student body as well as the adults who are there to teach and support the students, in many instances, school rules are not posted—yet adults still expect students to follow them. In addition to not being posted, the rules are often not stated clearly, nor are the children reminded of the rules until they break one. Students need to know and understand the rules and limits, otherwise they have no way of learning and practicing the expected behaviors.

In anticipation of potential disruptive situations, teachers may want to have a classroom activity about rules to engage their class in discussions about why we have rules and how they help everyone. Children are very willing to talk about what is helpful as well as what creates discomfort and disruption during school. They can be very clear when it comes to acceptable and unacceptable behaviors! A discussion of the rules and how to enforce them is an excellent way to help the students understand the necessity of rules and regulations. The school rules can even be augmented in classrooms by having the students review them and create others they feel may be pertinent to their classroom. As Sailor notes, "When children have some voice in defining a rule, they will be more likely to comply. By giving children a choice, you are giving them some control over the situation" (2004, p. 172).

No Ifs, Ands, or Butts

In a sixth-grade class, several of the students always butted in line and muscled their way to the front. Naturally, other students did not like this and thought something should be done, but many times the teachers were busy and didn't realize what was happening.

In spite of not being a first-hand witness, one teacher was very aware of the issue and decided that perhaps a class discussion about the need for order and cooperation might help. She used a portion of the next day to have a discussion of rules and asked the class to list three things that were bothersome to them on paper and pass it forward. She then tallied all of the issues on the front board, and butting in line came up numerous times. Since the issue did not point a finger at anyone, it was safe to discuss with the group, and no one would be singled out as "the buttinski." The students brought up the fact that everyone has to wait, waiting makes people mad, and perhaps something should be done. The students decided that even though they were in sixth grade, they still needed to know who was to be first in line to go to the cafeteria or elsewhere in the school. Their plan was to have a rotating line leader based simply on the alphabet, and that way everyone, including the teacher (who may not always see someone butt into the line) would know who was supposed to be up front.

With this plan, everyone knew the rule, everyone got a chance to be first, and the consequence for not following the rule was simply that the offender had to go to the end of the line and wait until everyone else was out the door. Since the entire class discussed the issue and cooperatively came to agreement on the solution and consequence, the rule was readily enforceable and the issue decreased dramatically.

When coming up with rules, long lists are neither necessary nor advisable. During an observation in one classroom, an astonishing fifty rules were posted—and over a hundred infraction punishments posted alongside the rules. That is far too many. No one can remember multitudes of rules, but everyone can learn an important few. The rules that are created can be generic and broad. One rule that covers many issues is simply, "No hurting." This takes into account various ways that children can physically and emotionally hurt one another. Other examples are "Walk in the hall," "Hands to yourself," "Stay in your seat," "Come to class prepared," and so on. When generating the rules, be sure the rules are:

- Critically important to the specific group of students (a reasonable number)

- Clearly stated

- Understandable

- Reasonably achievable by the age of child in the class (in other words, rules for fifth graders and kindergarteners may differ, but many will remain constant throughout a student's school career)

This final point bears some discussion. As children grow in their moral development, their understanding of rules changes. For younger children, a rule is a rule is a rule, but as children grow in their understanding of the social constructs that surround the rules, they begin to understand why the rules exist, and the long-term consequences involved in breaking them. While "Walk in the halls" and "Keep your hands to yourself" are important throughout school, the mere physical instruction of those rules will guide the younger children, while the safety and respect for others that make them necessary will guide older students.

Once they are generated, rules should be posted for all to see. This enables any adult who is in the school as a substitute to enforce rules when needed and makes rules always available to the students.

Posted: Kuen's Story

Kuen had a habit of running from one part of the classroom to the next, bumping into desks on her way, which disrupted her classmates. She also ran in the hallways from room to room. One of the school rules was "walk in the halls," and it was posted in the classroom and in the hallways of the school. Whenever Kuen ran, any adult could stop her and point to the rules and verbally remind her that when she was in school, "The rule is to walk in the halls." This reminder was stated in a positive manner and was given to her both verbally and visually. Even if she could not read, she at least knew there was a sign that said something about a walking rule. The use of posted rules can accommodate learning.

Ignore It

Sometimes, the best technique to eliminate a behavior is to simply ignore it. That is *not* an easy task! Ignoring a behavior should not be done in isolation of other supports because it is important to listen to the behavior in order to understand the message behind it. Listening to behavior is demanding, especially when the behaviors are threatening, dangerous, or repeatedly used, as in the case of a student who hits. It can take a terrific amount of control to ignore some behaviors. But sometimes ignoring works!

The students in one of Kim's classes were loud and obnoxious when it came time to answer questions. They would follow the rules of raising their hands to be called on but would make loud grunting noises and wave their hands wildly in order for her to *really* notice them—as if she could not see or hear them in a small classroom. Their behavior annoyed Kim and their classmates. She did her best to ignore their behavior, not even giving them eye contact, and called on others who were quietly raising their hands. On the occasion that the noisy wavers behaved quietly, she would call on them to reinforce that quiet answering behavior. It was tough and took self-control to keep from repeatedly telling them to quietly raise their hand, but they eventually understood. Once Kim had stated that those who quietly raised their hands were going to be called upon, she ignored the unwanted behavior and reinforced the incompatible behavior by calling on quiet students.

The decision to ignore a behavior should be a decision that everyone in the classroom can live with. Consistency, as always, is critical. Some behaviors cannot be ignored due to health or safety. On one instructional team, one member had significant arthritis in her hip; touch was painful. One of the students had a habit of tapping adults on the leg repeatedly until she got the person's attention. Most of the teaching staff simply ignored the student's tapping and went on with the lesson or what needed to be done until she used the acceptable way of requesting attention she had been taught. However, the teacher with arthritis could not ignore the behavior because it was incredibly painful to be tapped once, let alone repeatedly. This simple behavior, which most of the staff agreed could be extinguished by ignoring it, suddenly had to be handled differently. An alternative plan was created that everyone could abide by and enforce. This plan entailed more concerted redirection to a more acceptable means of gaining attention. While redirection had always been part of the long-term plan, the team had to emphasize it earlier to make the plan work for all members. Teamwork is a must!

Teach Children to Listen: Avoid Repetition

Teachers have many techniques to gain their students' attention. One school in which Sue works has a hand-clapping routine that kindergarteners learn on their first day of school, and it is maintained throughout their time there. An entire assembly of children can be quieted in seconds when the principal begins to clap the pattern. Another school has chimes. Rhymes work, too. For example, one teacher with whom we have worked says, "One two three, eyes on me." "One two, eyes on you," respond the students. By the end of September, all her students stop whatever they are doing when they hear the rhyme and look to her for what is coming next. Whatever works for you, teach it explicitly as the cue that means, "Now it is time to listen for directions."

Still, there may be days when you think, "How many times do I have to tell them?" If you say those words out loud to the children, it is already too late. If you ever hear those words come out of your mouth, you are telling them too often. Follow the "three times rule" to help children learn how to listen to adult directions: give them three chances to learn and follow the rule, and then take action.

Is Anyone Listening?

One rainy day, Mr. Rodriguez's class had to have an indoor recess. All the students were fully engaged in their playful activities, gleefully laughing and talking. Eventually, however, recess was almost over, and it was nearly time for studies to start again. Mr. Rodriguez said, "Okay, everyone, it's time to start getting ready for class to begin again. Stop what you are doing and put things away, okay?" Because they were so engaged in their recess time, the students didn't hear him and continued merrily in their play, seemingly ignoring him. He repeated the phrase again and again, but apparently no one heard him at all because no one made a move to get ready to go back to work. Frustrated, Mr. Rodriguez yelled at the class, "Clean up now, and get back to work!" The students all looked at him as if he were wicked and groaned and mumbled to themselves about his behavior. This is not the way to handle this situation!

Here's how the three times rule works. First, be sure you have students' attention before you expect listening. Chimes, lights, clapping rhythms . . . use whatever works for you and your class, and use it consistently. The first time you give the directions clearly and concisely—and without an "okay?" at the end, which implies a choice. Simply say, "It's time to stop what you are doing and get ready for class now." When students are engaged in activities, it's normal for them not to hear you completely the first time, and especially if you have previously had a pattern of repeating yourself numerous times, they will be unlikely to respond. So wait briefly, and then repeat your instructions. If students still are not beginning to respond, within the next minute or so, state your instructions a third time, with specifics: "It's time to stop what you are doing and get ready to work now. Bobby, you put this game back on the shelf; Dorothy, take the papers back to the closet; Rosetta, pass out the books."

By giving the students something specific to do—helping them stop the recess activities and get back to work—you are requiring that they listen and respond to your instructions. If you consistently use this strategy and continually insist they respond when you are speaking, you will help the students learn that teacher's comments require a response of some sort. Teach them to know you mean business and to listen to you.

To review, set up a routine that means it is time to look at me and listen. Then, the first time you speak is basically to get their attention—to let them know you are speaking to them and expecting something. The second time is to remind them of the request and give them another chance to hear you. The third time is to provide some additional direction and physically give them something to put away or do. This can be used in various settings and activities effectively. Once children begin to understand that eventually they will have to act, they will begin to learn to listen the first time and not wait until they are helped to do their task. And don't forget that you can reinforce the students who listen the first time.

Model Appropriate Responses

What an understatement! Our behaviors are the models by which children learn what is appropriate and acceptable, and what is not. Through children's words and actions, we know quite a bit about what children see and hear at home—if parents only knew what we learn about their children's home lives! Many educators have heard profanity that would make parents shudder to know came out of their child's mouth, learned who was sleeping with whom, witnessed pretend drugs being used as props in play—the list could go on.

But the coin has another side. What do our own behaviors, actions, reactions, and words teach our students? Teachers serve as role models for all children in school, not just the ones in a particular classroom. Children watch us and learn from what we do and say. As it says in the song "Children Will Listen" by Stephen Sondheim (1987):

> Careful the things you say,
>
> Children will listen,
>
> Careful the things you do,
>
> Children will see.
>
> And learn.

We always must be fully aware of the power we have all the time. Most of us can remember teachers we enjoyed and those we did not. It is also interesting to recall what we learned from each of them academically as well as about behavior. We may actually use some of the teaching strategies that worked for our own teachers, if we thought they were fair and appropriate. In some cases, children come from families who, while they should be the primary force in their learning and lives, unfortunately are not. Teachers have the potential to be the most consistent adults in a child's life. For that reason, it is critical that teachers are aware of their lifetime impact.

As role models, the areas of influence teachers have run the gamut from observable behaviors, to attitudes about life and learning, to beliefs about self-worth and capabilities. The breadth of the potential impact is great. Be a safe and predictable influence, a person who can negotiate reasonably, model appropriate behaviors when angry, and show students that self-control is cool.

Greater challenges arise when we are confronted with an extreme behavior such as aggression to you or to another child. When that happens, our emotions become inflamed, and it is all too easy to lose our ability to think rationally and clearly. Goleman (1995) says that "in the dance of feeling and thought the emotional faculty guides our moment to moment decisions working hand in hand with the rational mind, enabling—or disabling—thought itself. Likewise, the thinking brain plays an executive role in our emotions—except in those moments when emotions surge out of control and the emotional brain runs rampant" (p. 28). With aggressive students, the key is to remain calm, listen to what is being said via the behavior, and then refer to rules and facts. Be prepared by creating rules and consequences that are simple and clear and understood by everyone. Keep your wits about you, and know what you need to do to help maintain positive behaviors from your students.

Apply Consistent Strategies to Address Behaviors

Once the rules are generated and posted it is vital that the rules are the same for everyone; young or old, regardless of ability. If the rules are altered for one child and not for another, it causes confusion and ultimately friction among the children in the classroom, as well as in the school and at home with family. Kids who get special treatment are seldom looked on favorably. Giving children special treatment can cause them to end up alone and left out.

Smart but Mean: Libby's Story

Libby was an intelligent young student, and all the teachers enjoyed having her in class. However, Libby also had a mean streak and was smart enough to be sneaky about her antics. She would do things like turn the teacher's paper clip bin upside down, hide classmates' books, and even trip some of her peers as they walked up to the board to do classwork. Her peers all knew that she was the culprit, but the teachers would not believe them. In their mind, Libby was a good girl because she was smart. As time passed and Libby got away with her antics and the teachers seemed to turn a blind eye, her classmates played with her less and less and did not include her at lunchtime. Eventually, she became an outcast.

Some children may need more help to understand the rules, but they should always be expected to follow them. It is up to the adults to make sure that there are alternative ways for children to express themselves, especially in the case of children with disabilities who may break some rules with challenging behaviors. Remember, their behavior may actually be the only way they currently have to communicate. Be sure all behaviors are investigated and understood.

> **Not Cute for Long: Bola's Story**
>
> Bola is a very cute young boy with a disability who hits people, adults and children alike. When he hits some of the adults in his classroom, they respond to his hitting with a smile and a gentle question: "What do you want, Bola?" And then they comment to each other, "He is the cutest kid!"
>
> He is not learning the rules and instead is learning that he can hit and no one will redirect him or reprimand him. As Bola grows and becomes bigger in size and continually hits others, it will become harder for him to learn the rule of no hitting—and no one will think he is cute anymore.

Children with disabilities are like all children; they need to learn the rules that allow them to function within a group setting both socially and academically. Some children with disabilities need more time to process verbal information and to get their bodies to move in the way they want them to go. Be sure you've given enough time for everyone to do what you are asking of them.

Consistency in our expectations is critically important, and so is flexibility. We must continue to search for the reasons that behaviors persist, while we make it clear that each student in the class is expected to adhere to the posted rules. Prepare for all ends of the behavioral continuum. Ensure that your children know the rules and understand the expectations. Preparation is fundamental not just for the academic lessons that are found in your lesson plan book, but also to help sustain a positive learning environment for everyone.

When I Am Most and Least in Control of My Behavior

We have been discussing approaches that can help support the nature of the behaviors we find acceptable in classrooms. There may be certain situations or circumstances in which you find you are most in control of your behavior as well. Take a moment and think of everything that needs to be in place for you to be in control of your own behavior. What circumstances or situations might help you be on top of things? List them. Then take a moment and list the things that make you feel out of control. (See page 130 for a reproducible form for group work, or visit **go.solution-tree.com/behavior** to download it.)

Once you have completed your list, examine the lists of typical responses on pages 131–132 that we have compiled from our workshops. Do the responses look like yours? Think about your responses for a moment—are they that different from what children may say they need? We all need support to keep ourselves in check, no matter our age. Remember your needs the next time you are supporting a child's behavior, and be sure the child's supports are in place just as you would want your own to be.

Now go back to your list of Communication Best and Worst scenarios. There will probably be a great degree of overlap. Interesting, isn't it, that the same requirements you have to be at your communication best are also those you need to be most in control of your behavior. When we ask a student who is struggling to "use your words," we are automatically setting up a no-win situation.

Takeaways

- Learn to focus on the positive aspects of your classroom and students.

- Comment on specific behaviors.

- Remember that feelings are genuine; validate and name them to help your students learn how to talk about them. Check with the student to be sure you have interpreted correctly!

- If you want students to feel ownership in classroom rules, include them in the process of identifying priorities.

- Review classroom rules regularly.

- Rules apply to everyone, no exceptions.

- Teach listening by avoiding the repetition of instructions or questions.

- Tell children what they *can* do; redirect them to more acceptable behavior.

- Establish contingencies ahead of time to help children know expectations and consequences.

- Remember that the situations in which we have trouble communicating are the same that can cause us to have less control over our behaviors. This is true for our students as well!

- Always behave like the role model you are.

Most and Least in Control

I am at MOST in control of my behavior when . . .

I am at LEAST in control of my behavior when . . .

Most in Control Situations

Following are typical responses from workshop participants who are asked to identify circumstances when they are most in control of their behavior. Read and discuss with others. What trends do you see?

I feel most in control of my behavior

When I am . . .

Well rested

Secure

Confident

Organized

Informed

Supported

Familiar with surroundings and people

In a safe environment

Alone

Asleep

In my own environment

Affirmed

In a good mood

Around others

On schedule

Prepared

Well

Calm

Comfortable

Competent

In control of situation

Willing

Doing my routine

Doing something I want

Happy

Guarded

When I have . . .

A respectful listener

A lesson plan to guide me

Cooperation

Time

A balance between emotions and rational thinking

Control over routine

Chocolate

A plan

When . . .

I know expectations

I can clearly see the truth

Things are organized MY way

Things go the way I want

I know what to expect

I know the subject

The environment requires it

My needs are met

I like what's going on

I believe in what is being said

Least in Control Situations

Following are typical responses from workshop participants who are asked to identify circumstances when they are least in control of their behavior. Read and discuss with others. What trends do you see?

I feel least in control of my behavior

When I am . . .

Angry

Tired

Sick

Bored

Just awakened

Bitter

Threatened

Lost

Emotional

Stuck in an elevator

Involved in the situation

In pain

Frustrated

Too passionate about subject

Disrespected

Excited

Sad

Unsuccessful

In a tense situation

Confused

Emotionally involved

Physically hurt

Frightened

Waiting

Hungry

Overwhelmed

Not understood

Stressed

Excluded

With teenagers

When . . .

I know someone is lying

I have PMS

My feelings are hurt

I have had too much caffeine

I don't understand the expectations

We have no shared values

The other person loses control

My schedule is disrupted

The environment is chaotic

There are interruptions

I don't have a choice

I don't like choices

No one is listening

I have unfulfilled expectations

Personal Reflection

What types of behavior supports do you currently use?

What are the explicit, written rules for your learning space? Are they clear and concrete? Are they posted?

What do the children learn from simply watching you while you are working?

What is the connection between when it is easiest for you to be in control of your own behaviors and your ability to communicate? How do you see this connection played out in your classroom? Explain your response.

9

Proactive Instructional Strategies

Teachers use many instructional strategies in their classrooms that support positive behaviors. These intuitive methods encourage positive behaviors by ensuring that the instructional environment is as welcoming and supportive as the physical and social environment. They are often very simple ideas, and therefore we sometimes overlook them as a means first to help children learn positive behaviors and second to continually support those desired behaviors—while also continually supporting children's ability to learn.

As teachers create their learning spaces and take all aspects of teaching into account (establishing the physical space, gathering and utilizing materials, and supporting positive interactions), the next step is to plan how to provide instruction that works for the children. Teachers who think in a proactive manner will begin to see better ways to teach and encourage children to learn and grow in all aspects of their development. Their lessons will not only emphasize academic content, but also help children learn to work together, share, and begin to understand the classroom as a community.

In this type of learning environment, social behaviors are as much a part of the curriculum as reading, math, science, and music. Social and academic skills are integrated across the curriculum. With increased skills in behavioral self-control come academic success (McDermott, Mordell, & Stoltzfus, 2001; McClelland, Acock, & Morrison, 2006). We believe that increased academic success will also increase social behavior success.

The following instructional strategies can help maintain positive behaviors. Watch your students for behavioral messages to help clarify in which areas they need more support, and consider in which areas you may need more training or mentoring.

Meet Individual Learning Needs

Several instructional models suggest ways that educators can best meet the diverse needs of all learners. We discuss them here because we know that each of us approaches life, and therefore learning, in different ways. As we consider how to support each child's behavior, we must also look at how to support his or her educational needs. We recognize that both individual children and entire classes struggle to maintain appropriate behavior when one-size-fits-all curriculum, instruction, and assessment practices are used.

One of the foremost theories is *differentiated instruction* (Sizer, 2001; Tomlinson, 1999, 2001). This approach proposes that there are multiple ways for students to take in information and make sense of what they know. As educators, we all know that some children learn best by hearing, others by seeing, some by experience, and many by a combination. Differentiated instruction suggests that our classroom activities should be designed so that any student can access information in the way that is most comfortable and in which he or she learns best. It also proposes cycles of large group, small group, and individual instruction to further address individual learning approaches. Rigidity in instructional methods or practices won't meet the varied learning needs of the children in the class. By designing instruction with multiple ways for students to approach the content (what they learn), the process (how they learn it), and the products (how they show what they have learned), the teacher fills the classroom day with opportunities for children to make meaningful choices.

Another approach that is growing in prominence as its applicability is becoming more clear is that of *universally designed instruction* (Blagojevic, Twomey, & Labas, 2002; Rose, Meyer, Strangman, & Rappolt, 2002; Conn-Powers, Cross, Traub, & Hutter-Pishgahi, 2006). Like differentiated instruction, universal design challenges educators to design and plan learning environments that provide activities and settings in which all children can participate and learn, rather than always adapting existing strategies to meet individual needs; before offering an intervention, universal design suggests, be sure your basic instruction is as effective as possible. Universally designing activities and instruction ensures that all children can access and engage in all learning opportunities, learn from a common curriculum according to their individual strengths and abilities, and demonstrate their learning in multiple ways.

These instructional approaches are *positive* approaches to meeting the needs of all children in a classroom. They both honor individual differences in learners as essential factors to be taken into account as teachers plan. Imagine the impact if each child had the opportunity to engage in learning experiences in ways that tap into his or her learning styles, strengths, and interests! Good environmental and instructional planning go far in reducing children's frustration, need for additional assistance, and subsequent off-task behavior, as well as in supporting learning motivation and efficiency.

When generating learning objectives, think of them in a very broad sense and realize that most can be achieved in an assortment of ways and in a range of settings. By keeping in mind that students need multiple ways to approach ideas, access information, interact with materials, and learn from experiences, it then becomes second nature to build variety into planning and presenting lessons. Thus, the student who needs to listen to learn can find ways to do so, as can the child who is a visual learner, and the one who really needs to move to learn. In physical education, teaching a child to catch can be achieved using a variety of balls, beanbags, or balloons. Literacy skills can be enhanced using books, computers, newspapers and magazines, posters, or even comic books. Math can be taught using manipulative objects, puzzles, shapes, cooking, and science experiments.

Sue recently stepped out of her office to find the hallway filled with children measuring the length of the hall with different devices. How many rulers long was it? How many pencils? Yard sticks? Goldfish crackers? How many of Taryn's scarves? Which of these would be the best measurement to use to tell other people about our school? What fun! The other teachers on that hallway were all prepared, closed their doors, and planned activities that did not require the utmost in concentration. Reminders for volume level were needed, but in this school, educators recognize that excited learning is occasionally not quiet. As long as the teacher is not spending more time reigning in behaviors than she is facilitating the more positive learning outcomes, most behaviors are acceptable.

The students discovered shortcuts (how many goldfish crackers are in one ruler), created graphs, and presented their findings to the other classes, furthering the types of learning offered in that one activity. By the way, the goldfish cracker team worked long into recess just to find out the answer. Talk about motivation! And just think of the dozens of academic and social goals met in this one activity.

Develop a Consistent Routine

We all follow routines in our daily lives, from the time we get up in the morning until the time we go back to bed at night. Without our routines, we can become disorganized, confused, or less productive. Our reliance on routines and the sense of structure they create is usually subconscious. However, when our routines are disrupted, we recognize the role of consistency in our lives; we may even experience challenges unless we can gain some clarification and control of the situation. As fully competent adults, we experience minor disruptions all the time that cause us to forget where we are in our routine—and as a result we misplace keys, put things away in the wrong place, or forget to brush our teeth. The importance of routine is multiplied for children who have not yet developed the level of self-control and organization needed to maintain a day full of demands.

From early infancy, our routines instruct us on the social, language, cognitive, and motor components that make up our lives (Vygotsky, 1978; Fischer, 1980; Bandura, 1986; Dunst, Bruder, Trivette, Hamby, & Raab, 2001). Classroom routines are introduced the first day children start school and continue throughout their school experience. The routines of the school day can help children note similarities and differences between activities, materials, instructions, and outcomes. They can begin to make inferences about certain activities. For example, they may learn the routine, structure, and skills that are involved in center time in preschool, what they need to do in physical education class, or how to work with a math partner. The skills learned through routines that include social skills such as listening, taking turns, social proximity, and group participation carry over to all school settings—and most out of school settings as well.

Routines also help children learn consequences for both positive and negative behaviors. Predictability can help children anticipate events that occur on a regular basis, such as lunch, recess, class, library time, or waiting for the bus. This helps them begin to learn what to expect. They can begin to understand the cause-and-effect relationships in each situation. Previous experiences help the children learn and understand expectations in each situation they find themselves in at school. Consistency and predictability in routines help children learn the conventions and rules of not only the typical behavioral expectations, but also of the underlying social interactions. Consistency and predictability in environments help them learn expectations for appropriate behavior and foster independence.

Many adults rely on organizers, calendars, or planners to keep us on track and remind us of important tasks; we'll talk about these types of supports later. Here we'll discuss the types of daily routines that the adults in a student's life can use to create stability—routines that can become subconscious supports to enable your students to maintain appropriate behaviors and thus take full advantage of the learning opportunities provided. Although rules may be both an explicit and implicit part of every classroom and school routine and environment, they are not the primary focus of this discussion. Instead, we'll look at the routines that guide us through the day and provide a structure that supports acceptable behaviors.

Create Daily Routines

Daily routines are those that tell us what to do when. For example, what is the routine that surrounds coming into the classroom? For the younger students, the sequence probably looks like this:

1. Enter the classroom.

2. Walk (rather than run).

3. Talk quietly.

4. Greet teachers and friends.

5. Find the correct picture/name that indicates cubby/locker.

6. Put away belongings in cubby.

7. Take off outer clothes (for winter or inclement weather).

8. Hang up clothes and backpack.

9. Give lunch/snack/notes to the teacher.

10. Look at the message board.

11. Go to the area of the room in which the next activity will take place.

For older students, the routine will have components of preparation for the lesson, such as being sure they have the required book, paper, writing implement, homework, and so on.

Define Interactive Routines

But these descriptions are just the surface. Within these entry routines are embedded multitudes of expectations about behavior, such as:

• How loud you talk, with whom, and for how long

• How quickly you need to accomplish your task of getting ready for the next step

• How close you stand or sit to classmates, whether there is any touching, and if so, what kind

For the most part, the expectations for entering into a classroom are unwritten social rules. How have the children learned them? They learned through clear expectations, modeling, and repetition of each routine.

Remember the story about the children measuring the length of the hall with yardsticks, goldfish crackers, and scarves? That would have been disastrous in September. By January, the children knew what was expected of them as far as accomplishing the objectives, reporting back to the class, keeping their voices at an appropriate level, collaborating with their classmates, remaining in their own hallway—they knew the rules and the interactive routines.

Interactive routines form the foundation for communicative growth in the same way that the previously discussed classroom routines form the foundation for appropriate behaviors. The ability to behave appropriately is so often intertwined with the ability to communicate effectively that the links between the two sets of skills are inseparable.

Warn in Advance for Transitions and Changes

Transitions and waiting periods are often trouble times for unwanted behaviors; that also makes them prime times for building positive behavior. Transitions generally do not happen randomly, but rather at regular intervals; however, waiting is not always planned and creates many challenges. Plan for those waiting times to support behavior.

Provide routine words and gestures before an action is expected. Warnings before changes in routines reduce the anxiety that can inhibit a comfortable learning experience. If adults are sure to provide consistent verbal cues along with matching gestures to indicate a change in activities is about to take place or something new is about to happen, the unwanted and unacceptable behaviors are less likely to occur.

Some teachers use "lights off" as a cue for all students to attend to their instructions. Some schools have a bell used across all classrooms in all grades that indicates that classes will change in three minutes. The school in which Sue currently works uses chimes as a warning. The kindergarten teachers all say, "One two three, eyes on me," to which the children respond, "One two, eyes on you." One of the classes needed help putting down their work to listen to transition instructions, so the teacher implemented a clapping routine during which she clapped a pattern that the students matched (talk about meeting several goals at one time!). And as always, it never hurts to have information on schedules to which teachers can refer, posted in the room.

For routine transitions, teach the children how you want them to happen. What are the expectations for coming and going from the classroom, from one area to another, from one lesson to another? What is the process for getting ready for lunch or preparing for the end of the day? Routine transition times are good times to implement visual prompts, since the expectations are probably always the same. You always need basic elements: for example, for younger children, they might need their folders with notes to their parents to be put into their backpack, their coats, and their projects. Older students need their homework assignments, their books, their backpacks, and their coats. There is a logical progression to the gathering and organizing of the materials and supplies for any transition. Teach this, and support it visually if necessary, as carefully as any other part of the day. It is one of the most consistently routine times of the day and can be a good time to begin to instill the self-monitoring needed in less structured settings.

If students have to wait in the hall at school, initiate and direct activities to keep them busy. For example, one teacher of younger children keeps a small bag full of notecards with the names of various songs or finger plays. She recognizes a child who is following the rules of waiting (that is, being quiet and still) and lets him pick the first card. The children are then all engaged in the song activity. Older students can be engaged in impromptu spelling bees, math challenges, or geography and history questions. The key is to occupy students so they don't have to occupy themselves. Children cannot simply sit still and wait for long periods of time. If they have to, they generally become fussy, and adults become annoyed or angry. Be prepared ahead of time, plan for transitions, and challenges will diminish.

Be Flexible

Within the structure of routines must be some flexibility. Both teachers and students need the ability to be flexible. This does *not* mean that the lessons are not carefully planned, that the movement and conversations are not carefully orchestrated, or that the teacher is not in full control of the classroom. *Flexibility is not synonymous with chaos.* Instead, it means systematic implementation of change. This is a skill that is good for children to learn in a safe and predictable classroom environment. Being flexible allows us to be in each new and unique situation and adapt accordingly. Since the real world is highly unpredictable, learning how to be flexible and deal with change is truly a life survival skill! Being flexible can allow children to achieve more in their learning and interactions with their peers. If they can learn to adapt and accommodate, they will be more productive learners with fewer behavior challenges.

Most schools are already flexible in some circumstances. For example, when the routine of the bus picking up a student at 7:15 is thrown off by bad weather, we don't then expect the student to meet the usual requirements of arriving at school by 7:45, visiting his locker by 7:55, and sitting in class with necessary supplies at 8:00. Flexibility allows the student to complete all of the remaining steps as fluidly as possible and to enter class without disrupting instruction. Fire drills are another great example of a flexible routine. It is imperative that everyone knows what to do in a fire, but fire drills don't always happen often enough for students to become accustomed to them. Flexibility is needed to break the normal flow, participate in the drill, and enter back into the classroom routine.

State Directions and Limits Clearly and Simply

Directions need to be clear, consistent, concise, and specific. Often teachers give directions that rely on knowledge of social norms and interactive routines, which may not yet be in a child's repertoire. Many will need to be explicitly taught, particularly for younger children, children from another country, or children with disabilities. What exactly does it mean to "be polite," "listen carefully," "touch gently," or "be careful"?

All of us like to know what to expect. If we go to a new place, we ask questions to those who have been there previously. What does it look like where we are going, what should we wear, how long will the activities last, and so on? Letting children know exactly what they will be doing, where they will be going, and for how long can help them cope. Suppose a second-grade teacher who knows exactly how many math problems will be done says to her class, "We will be doing math next." For Missi, who does not do well at math and feels confused and ashamed because she cannot do the work, "doing math" sounds overwhelming. However, if she hears, "It's time for math. Today we will be doing the problems on page five. We will do the first five problems together, and then you will get into your pairs and complete the rest of the odd numbered ones on page five. You will have fifteen minutes to get the work done," she may feel less anxious and overwhelmed because the clear limit has been set. Posting those directions in written format will add to her comfort level, because she does not have to remember what her teacher has said—the instructions are all right there in front of her.

Similarly, the children in a kindergarten classroom are often told to "clean up." If the room has many areas in which children have been involved in industrious and active play, there may be a lot to clean up, and they may not have a clue where to begin. However, the teacher who says, "It's time to clean up. Katya, you put the trucks away. Jacob, you put the books away, and I will meet Millie and Suzy in the housekeeping area," has given explicit instructions, and it is probable that the children in her room now know how to get started on the project.

Mrs. Shonders, a third-grade teacher, will frequently say to her class, "It's time to do our reading. We will read for a little while and answer a few questions before we have recess." She then becomes flustered when some of her students whine and complain. What went wrong? As teachers, we often say, "Let's do it [reading, math, circle time] for a while," "for a little bit," or "for a few minutes." We may tell kids to "wait just a minute, hold on," or we say we will do a *few, a couple,* or *a bunch* of problems. Those instructions are not clear or explicit. Giving instructions should be very intentional.

Make sure your instructions have a concrete and definite limit. The limits can be set with time limits or numbers of repetitions that will be taken. Think about a time when you were listening to a speaker drone on and on; did you get antsy and wonder how long the talk would last? Would it have helped you to know the time frame or limit of the event?

If the original limit seems to create an issue, it is sometimes fine to re-establish the limit and assess what might need to be changed (remember that we can use flexibility to our advantage). If limits are changed, you must always listen to your students' behavior and assess the reason why the activity did not work as originally presented and make the necessary changes for the next time it is attempted. If you don't make changes, the same problems will resurface.

Use Visual Supports

Creating and using visual aids, timers, and/or lists can help children understand limits and boundaries. Incorporating pictures, photographs, or objects into the visual supports can help children know what to expect. Many of us rely on some form of visual support during our day, whether it is a calendar, a list, a recipe, or a picture of something we want to remember. These types of supports help make routines and activities more meaningful and understandable. Sometimes, explaining activities or expectations with more than words is crucial due to the age of the student or due to language issues. Visuals can improve independence and decrease reliance on adults in all situations.

Schedules

Whether we are using paper planners or hand-held digital assistants, most adults use a visual representation of our daily and long-term commitments to keep us on track. In the planning process, we note regular obligations, unusual appointments, jobs that need to be accomplished, and people we need to see.

This same type of organizational strategy is useful for students of all ages. For the child who is reading, written schedules are appropriate. For the younger child, or the child with disabilities, we develop picture schedules. A picture schedule provides additional visual cues (photographs or pictures from a commercially available program) for a student who is not yet reading the printed words. However the information is presented, it serves multiple purposes:

- It tells what is happening.

- It gives the sequence of events.

- It informs if changes (events out of the ordinary) are happening.

- It supports transitions from one activity to the next.

The ultimate purpose of a visual schedule is to create a structure that allows increased independence. Whether they are used to organize a long-term project, a day's activities, or a specific task, visual schedules provide support in a concrete format.

Activity Supports

Visual supports may be used for organizing a specific activity. For example, Ms. Jana has a drawer full of manila folders with instructions for activities. Each folder contains explicit instructions, including photos or drawings, as to how to complete the activity and fulfill goals for her lesson plan for the unit, as well as the requirements of the state standards for this topic. The pictures and visual representations allow both her skilled readers and those whose strengths lie elsewhere to receive information in an additional mode.

Math folders contain instructions for building complex patterns, for classification and reclassification activities with many different materials, and for making cupcakes (yes, cooking can be part of the math, science, and language arts curriculum). Science folders have ideas for experiments, research, and readings on each topic the class will cover this year. Folders have activities that can be completed individually, in pairs or small groups, or in large groups. Depending on the needs of her class on any given day, Ms. Jana can either use the activity folders as part of her teacher-led instruction or offer them as choices during more child-led instructional time.

Graphic Organizers

Graphic organizers come in many shapes and forms, and while they deserve mention here due to their usefulness in making information clear and helping students process and organize content, there are many other sources to which you can turn to find detailed explanations on their construction and use (see the reference section for a list of websites). Our purpose in mentioning them here is as one more example of how the use of visual supports can help focus a child's attention, increase interaction with the content matter, and decrease the likelihood of off-task behaviors. Following are a few examples of graphic organizers.

The first example, taken from a typical kindergarten classroom, is the *word wall*. In this area, each letter of the alphabet has common words with which the children interact regularly, written underneath. As their exposure to words grows, so does the word wall. When the children are engaged in writing activities, their teacher can be heard referring them to the word wall to find the spelling of the word they seek.

The second example, taken from a fourth-grade literacy program, is a *story map*. There are many ways to construct a story map, and the following feature box shows one example.

Story Map

Title: _____

Setting: _____

Where: _____

When: _____

Main Characters: _____

Minor Characters: _____

Plot: _____

Event: _____

Result: _____

Event: _____

Result: _____

Outcome or conclusion: _____

The final example was adapted by a preschool teacher from a middle school science text on the scientific method. Children were encouraged to either draw a picture on each line or write with whatever level of skill they possessed. We like this one because it shows that a good idea is a good idea, regardless of the age or ability. It just might take some tweaking.

What's in the Box?

Hide a common object in a box. Guide the students in discovering what's in the box with the use of the following picture cues.

Feel it 🖐 . It feels like _____.

Smell it 👃 . It smells like _____.

Listen to it 👂 . It sounds like _____.

Look at it 👁 . (There is a tiny hole in the box to allow just a glimpse of the item.) It looks like _____.

Don't taste it!!! 👅

Allow Choices

Choice making is a very fundamental, beginning communication skill, as well as the vehicle that empowers people to give voice to their individuality.

The Value of Choices

On five pieces of paper (index cards, sticky notes, or something similar), write down five choices you make frequently in your daily life, one choice on each piece of paper. These can range from simple (what's for breakfast?) to difficult (how do I tell my significant other that I disagree?). Turn over the papers so that you cannot see what you have written, close your eyes, and take away one piece of paper. Look at the paper you removed. How would you feel if you were told that that choice was no longer yours to make? That someone else would be telling you what to eat or how to respond to your significant other?

Choices are powerful forces in our lives. We make choices that get us what we want and make us feel good. As you continue to read about choices, think about how many ways you can help your students learn to make positive, healthy, and productive choices, that also meet their individual needs. In school, there are ample opportunities for choices to occur throughout a day. Choices can help the students feel more involved in their education and cause them to feel more empowered and interested. Following are some ideas.

Choice of Materials Within an Activity

Many of the activities that are done in school need materials in order to be taught and learned. In each class or activity, the materials can vary greatly. In order to get the task completed and to keep the interest of the students, allow them some real choices.

Bang the Drum: Benny's Story

Benny did not like music class. He would run away when the music teacher came into the room. After a couple of observations and really listening to him and his behavior, it became apparent that he was frustrated because he would ask to play the small drums in music and never got to use them in music class. The small drums were always given to the students who had significant disabilities. Benny was giving up and simply leaving instead of being frustrated each time. Once the music teacher realized it was neither her nor music class that made Benny upset, but rather the fact that he couldn't get his message across, she gave him more frequent choices as to which drum to play, and he became more engaged and enjoyed music class. No more running away. No more frustrated Benny. No more frustrated music teacher. No more frustrated classroom teacher after music class!

We have observed activities turn from struggles to positive experiences with relatively small and apparently meaningless choices being offered. One student was willing to do his creative writing assignments when given options as to the writing implement. He did not like pencils, but markers were fine. Since the project was creative writing, it did not matter what he used. In fact, once the teacher realized that her students liked having that choice and were creative in different ways, she opened up the choice possibilities and had wonderful creative writing success on the computer, with colored pencils, with ink pens . . . creativity flourished when she gave the students some freedom. Were the choices she gave truly small and meaningless? Maybe not—after all, they were critical to the success of her lesson.

Choice Among Different Activities

Within the many lessons that occur each day in school, there are frequently occasions when it is possible, and probably even preferable, to give students the opportunity to decide how they want to approach a specific topic. Mrs. Patterson's class is learning about medieval times, for example. As a large group, students learned about the societal structure and received an overview of life in the middle ages. Mrs. Patterson organized several centers in which students could choose to work individually, in pairs, or with a small team. The assignment was to research the roles of the different levels of power in the society. Students could write essays, draw flow charts, or create small vignettes to be presented to the class. The next day, students chose names typical of the time period and were given roles. They were then asked to create a town. This meant finding out how people dressed, what they ate, how they protected themselves, and so on. Students could choose how to discover the information they needed by using the books or videos in the library, the computers in the classroom, or even interviewing members of last year's class.

While Mrs. Patterson clearly structured the learning outcomes and provided resources and support to the class, the students had a broad range of choice as to how they approached the outcome. They had multiple means of access to information, multiple ways to engage in the process, and multiple ways to demonstrate what they had learned. Content, process, and products all varied depending on the student's needs (see discussions of universal design and differentiated instruction on pages 135–136). Observing this classroom was a truly enlightening and enjoyable experience. There was a constant buzz. The students were all busily working at a variety of tasks. Unwanted behavior was at an absolute minimum. The students' on-task, committed behavior was highly communicative of their excitement about a topic that could have been dry, boring ancient history—literally!

Choice to Refuse an Activity

There may be instances when a child has failed at an activity so many times that he or she will begin to avoid it, and may begin to exhibit some unwanted behaviors. For example, in second grade, Kim hated arithmetic, and especially hated standing in front of the class to recite tables. One time when the teacher had her go up front to read the tables, she actually threw up! Kim was mortified, not only from throwing up but also from not being good at her tables. In this case, if the teacher had given her the option of at least refusing to stand in front of the class, it may not have ended so abruptly. In her seat Kim would have felt comfortable, not so put on the spot and exposed. That simple choice as to how and where to demonstrate her knowledge may have saved Kim some embarrassment—and the janitor a clean up in room 101!

Choice of Learning Allies

Because effective instruction is a flow between large-group, individual, and a combination of different types of small-group activities (Tomlinson, 2001), children will usually be grouped together for at least part of their day. How that happens can impact behaviors. If you let the children choose their own groups and take a close look at what those choices entail, you will learn some important things. The choices they have made are probably children who have similar learning needs, who are supportive of them as individuals, and who get along with them socially.

Kim recalls being in fourth grade and having to work on some of her work with the boy who sat across the aisle from her. She did not like him because he would always announce if she got wrong answers on her paper. Kim was not eager at all to do any of that schoolwork. Her teacher noted this and finally made some adjustments. She allowed the students to choose a new person every week with whom to partner, and that made Kim (and others) more willing to participate fully.

Choice of Location

One of Sue's fondest memories of learning was doing science outside on the hill of her elementary school playground. The students were studying nature (birds, bugs, trees, grasses, flowers, and weeds), and instead of staying inside and looking at specimens that had been brought into the class, the teacher asked if the students wanted to go outside to find as many specimens as they could in ten minutes and then return to the room to share their findings. Of course, almost everyone said yes. Those few who did not want to go out were allowed to stay in the room and read their textbooks. It was wonderful to be allowed outside to explore even for ten minutes—it was something different.

Taking a look at this story from our current educational perspective, this teacher allowed children to choose between multiple ways to approach the content. The location was just the setting. Today, she might have given the children who chose to remain inside the task of designing a basic graphic organizer that would then be used by the children who collected specimens to classify and categorize their findings, and could ultimately be researched, labeled, and used to explain the conclusions of their study of their school's microenvironment.

Not all lessons need to be done while sitting at a classroom desk, nor should they. Some students work better sitting on the floor, in the library, in the hall, or at a table. Forming pods of desks or tables for group work allows children space to work in whatever configuration and physical space suits their needs. It also allows a formal enough set-up for the teacher to conduct large group lessons in a more structured manner if that is needed by the class.

The potential for learning in the community is also great. Consider the amount of excitement generated by a trip outside the classroom. They don't need to be major excursions to the state capitol or a museum on the other side of the city (not to say that those aren't valuable). One innovative teacher set up trips for his third graders to every willing parent's place of employment: farms, the newspaper, the classroom down the hall, the grocery store, and the tractor dealership all became classrooms. Students were not given a choice whether to go, but they were definitely given a choice as to which elements of each setting were comfortable, where they were interested in pursuing closer looks, and how intimately they wanted to become involved with the work that was happening there. Not everyone wanted to touch a seven-hundred-pound hog! Nor did everyone want to walk into the freezer at the grocery or hear the din in the machine shop where tractors were being repaired. Did everyone go to the same place? Yes. Did everyone have identical experiences at each site? No. Did everyone learn from the opportunity? Absolutely.

Lean on Me: Carlo's Story

Carlo was having a tough time. He was in a new school, having moved from a small town where everyone had grown up with him, to a larger community and new fourth-grade class. Carlo was a bright child with typical intelligence; he had many strengths and interests. He also had some significant sensory integration needs that weren't easily apparent to uninformed observers, however. He annoyed his classmates by leaning on them in group time or in line, and he frustrated his teacher by getting out of his seat to lie on the floor during math or while reading. His teacher, Ms. Frazer, was experienced, but just couldn't put her finger on Carlo's needs, and his classmates were getting more and more impatient with his seeming unwillingness to honor their personal space. Sue had supported Carlo from age two and was eager to facilitate an understanding.

It was a real struggle for Sue to convince Ms. Frazer that yes, Carlo really did *need* to lie flat on the floor with his back pressing into the hard surface in order to maximize his learning—otherwise, all he could focus on was how insecure he felt and how at any moment he might fall from his chair. In fact, it took standardized test scores to prove to Ms. Frazer what his behavior had been saying.

Once his teacher had an understanding of what was going on and how she could support his academic and learning needs, she met with Carlo and Sue to decide what to tell his new classmates, and how to support Carlo's sensory needs in group settings so that his social needs could also be met. Carlo wanted his classmates to know all the details of his sensory integration issues because he felt they would be more tolerant and willing to help him out if they knew he wasn't just being a pain. He was right. His class helped problem solve so that during large-group activities, Carlo was always sitting by a wall or bookshelf that he could lean on (instead of one of them). They decided that they needed to rearrange the classroom so they could line up against the lockers, to give Carlo something to push against while standing in line as well. As time went on and the students got to know Carlo, when they noticed patterns in his behavior, they brought them to his and Ms. Frazer's attention proactively, rather than letting potential problems escalate.

The range of experiences was reflected in the variety of products the students generated back in the classroom. The entire class learned from each member of their classroom community as well as from the wider community in general. The ensuing reports were printed, illustrated, then put into a format that could be shelved in the library. Every student in this class had a "published" book on the library shelf. The older students took out the book to see where this year's class had been, and the younger students took out the previous years' books to see where they might be able to go. The number of ways in which this teacher had built in learning opportunities and given his students access to the curricular goals (research, social studies, literacy, writing, and so on) so they could engage in the learning made this single set of activities ideally suited for every student in his class. How amazing!

Choice of When an Activity Occurs

Within every day there are tasks which must be accomplished. Some of them have logical sequences, such as washing hands after using the bathroom or before eating. In many classrooms, it is possible to create flexibility in timing to give children practice in completing tasks within a time frame, yet allow them the freedom of deciding in which order.

In preschool, for example, children generally have a snack and then brush their teeth. Teachers usually insist that the students brush immediately following the snack. However, in one class we observed, instead of telling all children that it was time *now* to brush teeth, the teacher gave students a choice: "Do you want to brush your teeth now or in five minutes?" All of them continued with their post-snack activities and said, "Five minutes." This was acceptable to everyone. And in less than five minutes, all of them had stopped their activities and were headed to the bathroom to brush their teeth. Sometimes that little option of "in five minutes" can bring about the desired behavior more easily than struggling to get it done "now." Power struggles are seldom constructive, and small opportunities for self-regulation of tasks cannot be overlooked as instructional strategies in learning appropriate behaviors.

Sue observed in a classroom where the students created the daily schedule each morning. Whether to have math was not an option; however, whether math came first in the morning or last in the afternoon was the students' choice to make. It was interesting to watch how the class decision making evolved over time. Clearly, some children wanted math first and some wanted it last. So the class created teams that rotated in choosing, the teacher took her turn when she needed to, and the collaboration that started with this scheduling activity flowed into many other times throughout the day. Some groups need a greater degree of structure, and for them this strategy won't work. But the potential for each and every group to make daily choices does exist.

Choice to End an Activity

This strategy may be most useful in those situations when an activity may appear to be going on too long or the students are fidgety or bored. An alert and savvy teacher will read the signs that a change is necessary and ask, "How should we finish this math work? Do you need to stand up and take a stretch break, and then we can finish it up this morning? Or should we review the social studies lesson and come back to it this afternoon? We need to complete both lessons today. Tell me what you need." This can avert escalation of challenges that may already be brewing in the class and give the students a chance to feel heard.

Giving a choice allows some problem solving and decision making on the part of the children. Choice is empowering and allows everyone to feel good, especially those young children or students with disabilities who are given few choices at all. Build this strategy into your program when possible, and see what results you get.

Avoid Giving Unintended Choices

Generally teachers are people who like children. They go into teaching because they like being around them and want to help them grow and learn and become happy, healthy, and contributing adults. When speaking to children, these adults may try very hard to be what they consider "nice and fair." That can sometimes backfire, however. Giving choices is important, but teachers should also take great care to avoid giving unintended choices.

No Unintended Choices, Okay? Jimmy's Story

When Kim was teaching physical education, she would have to go to the classroom to get the students. She had varied responses when she got there. When it was time for Jimmy to come to the gym, Kim went to the door and said, "Hey, Jimmy, are you ready to come to PE?"

He looked up from his desk and said, "No."

Kim grimaced and realized she needed to try again to get him into the gym. She took a breath and said, "Jimmy, don't you want to come to the gym today?"

Once again he simply said, "No." Kim let out a big sigh, and the teacher supporting Jimmy just grinned; some help she was! Third time is the charm, Kim thought.

She said, "I think you should finish your coloring and come to PE, don't you?"

Again, "No."

By this time Kim was getting upset with the entire situation, and she was all set to let Jimmy have it when the teacher said, "Perhaps you simply need to tell him exactly what he should do, without a question attached."

Okay, Kim thought and promptly said, "Jimmy, it's time to come to PE now . . . okay?"

The teacher shook her head as Jimmy once again said, "No!"—and he was perfectly legitimate in his response. Kim was frustrated, and it was entirely her fault.

In this scenario, Kim had allowed unintended choices to be made when she asked Jimmy if he was ready, wanted to come, or thought it was time to go to PE. Each instruction was really a question that allowed him to answer in the affirmative or negative. Of course, since he was doing something he enjoyed, he would say no. When well-intentioned adults use phrases such as, "Wouldn't it be fun?", "Would you like to . . . ?", "Are you ready to . . . ?", "Isn't this fun to . . . ?", "How about we all . . . ", "Could you please . . . ?", "Don't you think we . . . ?" and so on, they are really giving the child the opportunity to simply say no. While having a choice can be an excellent learning tool that teaches children to make meaningful decisions, in many instances, there isn't a real choice, and by phrasing your request in the form of a question, you give the false impression that you are open to either option. When your questions are really meant to be statements, be sure that is what comes out of your mouth. Tell the child what he is expected to be doing. For example, instead of asking a child, "Are you ready to go to the gym?" say, "It's time for gym now. Put your books away and line up to go." This tells him in a nonpunitive manner exactly what he is expected to do. Teachers need to be very intentional about what directions they give and what questions they ask.

If Kim had simply told Jimmy it was time for PE now and to come to the gym, that would have been totally appropriate. She almost did it by the end, but she added that little word—"Okay?"—on the end of her statement. That word turned the instruction into a request, and Jimmy took that bait. Kim literally had to practice saying, "Jimmy, it's time for PE, so come to the gym now" in order to just give him the instruction and not offer him that unintended choice! Once she gave an instruction instead of asking a question, he got up and came to the gym without hesitation.

Our intentional choice of words in all of our interactions can support the behaviors we want to see from our students. If we are not thoughtful, we can create scenarios like this one, where we get frustrated because we are not getting what we want from our students—and that's our fault, not the students'.

Be Prepared

Preparation seems obvious to most people. Teachers write lesson plans, prepare materials, and get their classroom ready for their students. What happens if for some reason the teachers are not prepared for the children? The children, being resourceful, will find something else to do that is interesting and fun, but maybe not an activity the teachers think is so great. The fact that the children become engaged in another activity isn't their fault, but rather the fault of the adults who are not prepared.

Choose Activities and Materials That Foster Positive Peer Interaction

The goal to facilitate positive interaction between the students in your classroom might not be written down in your lesson plan book or in your curriculum. However, in most classrooms, positive peer interaction is an important goal for the teacher. Accordingly, be sure that the materials you select support those goals. If you expect that the children will play or work together to accomplish a task, but the environment or materials limits them, you will probably have behavioral outbursts. For example, the creation of a mural requires enough art materials for everyone's involvement. It does not require a paintbrush for every child—that can be negotiated, another essential social skill. However, if there are not enough paper, fabric, markers, scissors, tape, glitter, and so on, you have created a situation in which unwanted behaviors are the likely way for the children to let you know you haven't planned well.

Turning to another example, collaborative research projects require work groups. Grouping students with diverse strengths and needs creates opportunities for all the children to contribute in different ways. However, collaboration is often a learning process in and of itself, one that happens outside of the specific subject matter. Sue recently complimented Ms. Johanssen, a fourth-grade teacher, on the cohesiveness of her class, the level of commitment they had to learning and to each other, and the great feeling she had whenever she walked into her classroom. After a huge laugh, Ms. Johanssen reminded Sue what a rough experience she'd had at the beginning of the year and how hard she'd worked to create the type of activities that taught the behaviors Sue was observing. Her intentionality about choosing activities to foster positive peer interactions had helped a group of children who had "bad" reputations coalesce into a class of learners whose behaviors allowed each child to be comfortable in the classroom and to succeed academically.

Prepare the Environment

Preparation involves the set up of the environment as well as having the necessary materials available. We cannot stress enough how critical that first step is to supporting positive behaviors. Teachers whose classrooms do not meet the needs of the group in general and of each specific student are starting at a disadvantage. See chapter 7 for more information on creating a physical environment that promotes positive behaviors and learning.

Once the environment is arranged for optimal learning and positive behavior, be sure that it is set up for use and that all materials are ready and within easy reach. If a teacher has to stop a lesson due to the materials not being available or the right number not handy, the students will invariably get busy doing something else.

Prepare a Variety of Materials

One way to help ensure that all materials are with you is to create containers (bins, boxes, and so on) for each activity and fill them with the books and other materials you might need. For example, if you are doing a math lesson, the "math" bin could contain the book, overheads, markers or chalk for the board, eraser, ruler, triangle, protractor, blocks, shapes, coins, or whatever else the lesson might entail, plus any additional items that may come in handy. The same process could be used for science, reading, or even free time. When you have a variety of materials ready, if your first approach to teaching the content isn't clicking with some of the students, the tools needed to expand or elaborate are immediately available.

For choice time or indoor recess, the bins could contain a wider range of items—items that have been carefully chosen for the purpose. Indoor recess is a challenge behaviorally. In what kinds of activities do you want the children to engage that will be a good break for them mentally and physically, yet provide enough structure that behaviors don't spiral out of control? Remember, you need to be ready to tell them *what* to do, not just what not to do.

Prepare a Variety of Teaching Strategies

Another way to be prepared is to be completely familiar with the activities you intend to do during the day. Most teachers would say they are very familiar with all of the activities they are going to implement in their classroom. However, many times when we are planning, we don't think about the "what ifs."

Being prepared and thinking through each activity completely ahead of time can prevent challenges. The antithesis of preplanning to address the needs of all learners in your class is embodied in the term *car curriculum*—that is, creating the day's activities in the car on the way to work. "What should I do for math today?" generally does not work well and can cause confusion and challenges for your students. It is hard to have a clear foundation for our expectations if we have no plans. If we as teachers are not ready and familiar with the activities and expectations, we cannot expect our students to do well.

Planning ahead of time, setting limits, giving warnings, and being very clear and intentional about objectives and instructions each contribute to the behaviors that children will exhibit in school. Teachers are capable of setting the stage for success. With a little preparation, classes can run smoother and everyone will enjoy the time spent in school.

Duck, Duck, Goose

When teaching a physical education lesson to a group of preschool children, Kim thought she had everything figured out for the lesson. That day they were going to play Duck, Duck, Goose. There were children with varying abilities in the class, but Kim explained the game to them and figured, how hard can this be? As the class started, the first player started tapping each classmate on the head, saying, "Duck, duck, duck, duck, duck . . . " and continued around the circle three or four times before Kim realized he needed to be reminded to say "Goose!"

Then the child he selected said, "I don't wanna be the goose!" and sat crying.

The next player walked around the circle banging on each head; he needed to be quickly assisted to a more appropriate touch. The next goose got up and simply ran all over the room and then out the door, and the final goose just kept running and running around the circle and would not sit down. The game was simple; Kim knew the rules and how to play, had explained it, but had not thought of all the what-ifs. Those exceptions to the rules caused anxiety for the other students, created the need for some immediate adaptations, and changed the expectations for the game on the spot. She had not anticipated any of the challenges and became flustered, which transferred to the rest of the class. The group became a bit unruly as Kim chased students or helped them accommodate. It was definitely not a great lesson for anyone, despite the fact that Kim as the teacher was familiar with the game and knew how to play it just fine.

Takeaways

- Everyone learns differently, so teachers should prepare lessons for a variety of learners.

- Routine and structure are important in everyone's life; some routines are intentionally created, and others become automatic through repetition.

- Routines help children learn both academic skills and social rules.

- Clear limits and boundaries encourage interaction and willingness to engage.

- Making choices within a daily routine is a powerful strategy teachers can use to encourage learning, participation, and engagement with others.

- When teachers are not intentional in their instructions, they can offer unintended choices and create unnecessary challenges.

- Be sure to have variety in activities and in teaching strategies. Giving advance warning for any and all changes can reduce students' anxiety and help maintain positive behaviors.

Personal Reflection

Have you added to your definition of the term *proactive strategies*?

What are the proactive instructional strategies that you use?

What kinds of routines do you have in your life? What routines do you create for your children?

What types of visual supports do you use in your life, and what visuals do you provide for your children?

Explain the power of choice, and name some of the choices allowed in your learning space. Would other choices alleviate any behavioral issues?

How many ways and what do you use to prepare your children for transitions?

10

Reactive Strategies

So what do we do when our proactive strategies don't work; how then do we go about helping students change unwanted behaviors? The reactive techniques discussed in this chapter are necessary in some situations. But what is also true is that the proactive techniques, team approach, and positive perspective on the child's strengths discussed in other chapters also work. Proactive strategies can create more positive environments and help everyone achieve success. They are not always easy; they take dedication and people who are willing to support one another as well as the student. They require people who are willing to constantly reevaluate their plans, the student's behaviors, and what the adults are doing that might be part of the problem as well as part of the solution. Teamwork, honest communication, and egoless involvement can create a wonderful atmosphere. As we delve into the topic of reactive strategies, the question that should always be in the forefront of our mind when dealing with behavior is: *what is this child saying?*

This chapter is not a discussion about how to control the behavior of others. We cannot substitute control tactics for meaningful and engaging interactions. Instead, this is a discussion about how our *own* behavior influences others, how we can help instill a sense of *self-control* in children, and how we can teach them to communicate in a socially acceptable manner to a broad audience (particularly at school). Educators are not in the "power business" of gaining control over others. We are in the business of creating learning environments in which everyone can participate and grow. The basic philosophy of respect for each child, each child's individual strengths and needs, and each child's culture (familial, ethnic, socioeconomic) remains the foundation for everything in this chapter as it is throughout the book. We hope that the suggestions in this chapter will be implemented with respect for each child and the belief that win-win solutions to unwanted behaviors are possible. Remember, our first question is always, what is the message of the behavior? And our second question must then be, how can we support the child in "getting the message across"—getting her needs met in an acceptable way?

Simple Responses

We have all been in situations in which children don't use the most socially acceptable behaviors. We also know that, try as we might, we cannot always anticipate every behavior in every setting. So we have to plan some reactive strategies. What follows are strategies that are quick and easy responses to unacceptable behaviors. As you can see, several of the behavior strategies you already have learned as proactive strategies can work for you in different ways. And as always, remember that there is no magic response for every behavior, because each behavior functions to send a unique message depending on the sender and the situation.

Proximity

Proximity can be used to support behavior. Standing near a child who is talking out of turn or who is passing notes or wiggling around at naptime may send a message of "settle down." An adult nearby causes the child to be aware of his behavior and change it to avoid "getting in trouble." Remember, as a proactive strategy, you can use this by having the more challenging child sit or stand near you for classroom activities—before trouble starts. However, this technique is an effective reactive strategy as well.

Nonverbal Cues

Putting a finger to our lips to *shhh* children, shrugging our shoulders when we do not know an answer, holding up a finger or hand to mean "wait," or giving the "evil eye" to stop a behavior are all examples of nonverbal cues. They are a natural form of communication that seems to be universally understood!

Restructuring the Lesson, Environment, or Activity

Some days, nothing goes right and things seem to fall apart. Those are the times to simply take a deep breath and start over again, with either something completely different or a modification of the activity. There is no reason to plod along if the lesson or activity is not working or if the environment is disturbing to a child. Adaptations and modifications are fine. If children are upset and disrupting the situation, no one will learn anything—other than it is not fun to be here right now. Be flexible and gentle with yourself and your kids, and simply regroup. Allow yourself to take advantage of a learning opportunity, and restructure what needs to be restructured. Often a simple change is all that is necessary to mend a situation that can quickly get out of hand.

Reinforcement Theory

Some people spend their lives and careers studying behaviorist theory, which is also called reinforcement theory. Reinforcement theory is based on two principles: (1) any consequence that is rewarding will perpetuate a behavior, and (2) any consequence that is punishing will decrease a behavior. Accordingly, this theory suggests that if you want to make a behavior appear more often or more intensely, when you see that behavior, reward it. If you want to make a behavior appear less frequently or intensely, punish it.

Simple! What's the big deal? The big deal is this: no behavior serves the same purpose every time for everybody. Additionally, what is rewarding to one person may be punishment to another. The tough thing about applying reinforcement theory is that reinforcements are defined by how they work for any student within any given context at any given time. There is no always-successful reinforcement, as we all are reinforced in different ways. This is the second main reason that this book is not a collection of prescriptions where you can look up "biting" and find a solution for it. (As a reminder, the first reason is that every behavior has a unique message.)

To complicate matters, many factors affect the successful implementation of reinforcements—factors not under our control. Because strict behaviorists only look at the behavior that is observable and measurable, things like the emotional state of the child are not taken into account. This is one example of factors that are not under our control. How the actions of the class in general impact each individual student's thoughts and feelings are not under our control. This is another example.

The techniques underlying reinforcement theory are very widely used, but the theory remains not only a bit messy in terms of how it works for humans (as opposed to pigeons or rats) but controversial. Let's examine some basic components of this idea and discuss what pieces of it we can take for our daily use.

Positive and Negative Reinforcements

As adults, we are responsible for maintaining, encouraging, and supporting the acceptable behaviors we observe in children, and for helping shift their unacceptable communication behaviors into more acceptable forms. When a student does something repeatedly, he "gets something out of it"—a benefit or *reinforcement*. *Positive* reinforcement strengthens the likelihood that the behavior will happen again by providing a pleasant consequence following a behavior. For many of us, one of the positive reinforcements that keep us going to work each day is a paycheck. Marathon runners talk about a "high" they get when they run. Having dinner with friends is positively reinforcing for many adults, just as hanging out with friends is positively reinforcing for many children. In each of the previous examples, the consequence of the behavior was positive for the person in that specific example. When something is added that increases the likelihood that a behavior will happen again, this is positive reinforcement.

Negative reinforcement also increases the likelihood that a behavior will happen again, but this time because something unpleasant is removed. When a kindergartener throws the blocks when it is time to pick up, the teacher removes the child from the area—which means all the other children pick up the blocks while he does something more fun! If a fifth grader gets an A on her math test, she may not have to do math homework for the next week. The removal of the undesired activity (picking up blocks or doing homework) is negative reinforcement. Both positive and negative reinforcement increase the likelihood that a behavior will happen again. Don't confuse "positive" with "reward" and "negative" with "punishment." Teachers may unintentionally use positive reinforcement by giving attention to behaviors they'd actually like to reduce.

Table 10.1 (page 158) gives examples of positive and negative reinforcement. Remember, these are simply examples. Depending on the student, the situation, and the message of the behavior, these may or may not be appropriate responses to the behaviors presented. They are generalized scenarios to illustrate a point. *Always* ask yourself, what is the message this behavior is sending? Then provide alternate, more acceptable ways to get the message across.

One really tricky thing about all forms of reinforcement is that people react differently to the same stimulus. Some children love videogames and find them positively reinforcing; they'll do anything to avoid going outside to play. Others hate videogames and would rather go outside or curl up with a book. Most children want attention from the adults in their lives, and the manner in which they seek this attention varies greatly. Depending on the way we react and interact with the children in our care, we can cause either desirable or challenging behaviors to persist. The consequences children experience as a result of their behavior influence whether the behavior is eliminated or perpetuated. We can teach children to look at what they are communicating through their behaviors (what they want or need) and help them learn how to accomplish this communication task in ways that produce the desired results.

Table 10.1: Reinforcement and Punishment

	Reinforcement (increases the likelihood behavior will happen again)	**Punishment** (decreases the likelihood behavior will happen again)
Positive (something is added)	Teacher calls on a student who is waiting quietly (attention is given). Teacher reprimands a student who is noisily waving her hand (attention is given). Teacher allows additional trips to the library when students demonstrate that they have read the books they have taken out (library time is added). Teacher encourages students who extend themselves, explore new ideas, and take educational risks (attention and praise are added).	Teacher gives additional math problems to students who understand but do not finish the work (work is added). Teacher asks a child who knocks over books to pick up the stack and reorganize the rest of the bookshelf (task is added). Teacher gives a child who is disruptive in the cafeteria the task of helping the custodian collect the trash at the end of lunch (work is added, and the attention of other students, which may or may not be wanted).
Negative (something is taken away)	Teacher assigns no spelling homework when students get 100 percent on the quiz (homework is taken away). Teacher helps the kindergarten group that starts cleaning up most promptly (some clean-up work is removed).	Teacher ignores student who is noisily waving her hand (attention is taken away). Teacher asks student to complete unfinished homework during recess (some recess time is lost).

Different Ages, Different Behaviors, Same Message: Melissa and Manny's Stories

Kindergartener Melissa wanted to be the calendar person every day. She would jump up and start the task, even though it wasn't her turn, and finally when she was redirected back to her seat consistently (jumping up didn't work), she raised her hand and grunted enthusiastically. Mr. Bailey, reinforcing children for other behaviors that were incompatible with Melissa's, would pointedly say, "Jonas, you are sitting so quietly and waiting, will you please be our calendar person today?" However, Melissa was not yet deterred. Her message was not only "Pay attention to me," but also "I am not understanding the expectations of this meeting time" and "I don't have experience sharing the attention of adults." Clearly, the other children had learned the appropriate meeting-time behaviors, but Melissa needed some additional help. She needed some direct instruction on what was expected behaviorally.

With Sue's help, Mr. Bailey wrote a script for Melissa. "During meeting time, all the children take turns with jobs. Some days it will be my turn to be the calendar person. Some days my friends will be calendar person. I can sit quietly and wait for my turn. Mr. Bailey will call my name when it is my turn." After a few readings of the script, and consistent follow-through by Mr. Bailey, Melissa was able to raise her hand and wait appropriately for her turn. Her "Pay attention to me, pick me" behaviors virtually disappeared after she understood the routine and the expectations, and got called on consistently when she adhered to the expectations of meeting time.

Fourth-grader Manny sat sullenly in the back of math class in his new school. He seldom opened his book, almost never had his homework, and refused to participate when called on. It looked as if he wanted to melt into the floor and disappear. After a few weeks, Mrs. Gould discovered that he had an extremely hard time with math and needed to have the ideas explained in multiple ways. However, being new, he was not going to raise his hand to ask for help. So his message was not only, "Pay attention to me," but also, "I'm not getting it, I don't understand, I don't know how to get help without embarrassing myself."

Mrs. Gould and Manny created a code together, by which he could indicate to her that he wasn't understanding without letting the rest of the class know. As a nice side-effect of the changes she made for Manny, the grades of other students in Mrs. Gould's math class improved after she began explaining concepts in more and varied ways.

Melissa and Manny were both asking for attention (although Manny would probably have denied it), albeit in very different ways, and with need of different solutions. Both children needed to be explicitly taught how to gain attention appropriately to meet their individual needs in a specific situation. Hopefully, they both had skills added to their repertoire that they could utilize later. Melissa learned how to share desired activities and wait patiently, while Manny learned that asking for help in Mrs. Gould's class didn't entail public humiliation, and that by letting someone know what he needed he could successfully negotiate a potentially failing situation.

Using Reinforcements Effectively

Even given their weaknesses, in practical application, behaviorist ideas are still useful and important concepts for every educator to understand. Behavioral change happens for a reason. Children will behave in ways that give them positive feelings and accomplish their goals. They will avoid behaviors that result in unpleasant consequences or that do not result in meeting their needs. Thus, the entire rationale that underlies this theory is that behavior is learned, and can therefore be unlearned or replaced by more acceptable behaviors (Parkay & Hass, 2000). By recognizing the message the behavior is sending, acknowledging and acting upon this message, teachers can foster positive classroom behaviors and discourage behaviors that interfere with learning.

Following are some basic guidelines to understanding how reinforcement can be one tool in your repertoire of assisting children in using socially acceptable behaviors. Remember, the first rule is to understand the message the behavior sends and validate it, even if you don't like the behavior.

Use Effective Reinforcers

Believe it or not, not everyone likes chocolate! What qualifies as an effective reinforcement varies depending on the individual, time, place, and message of the behavior. Learn first what the message of the behavior is, then what the child enjoys or seeks, and use the child's preferences as the reinforcement for positive behavior and work.

Prespecified reinforcers are decided in advance. Earlier in this book, we talked about getting paid for doing your job; a paycheck is a prespecified reinforcer that is quite effective. However, sometimes teachers specify reinforcers that don't support or reinforce the message of the communication (such as stickers, for example). *Naturally occurring reinforcers*, those that logically follow from a behavior, are more effective. For example, for most children whose ability level places them in academic programming, stickers may no longer be desirable, may be seen as too childish, and are an artificial addition to a classroom routine. Therefore, "When you've finished your math, you can use the computer to play a game" makes more sense than "When you've finished your math, you can have a sticker." The computer is more likely to be a pleasurable consequence for finishing an assignment and to hold the students' attention for longer than a sticker. As a result, its potential to reinforce learning objectives is greater than that of stickers.

What reinforces one person may be punishment for another. Knowing the function of the behavior is crucial! Consider these two examples: Jody interrupts class and is reprimanded and asked to leave class. Jody, a typically good student, has her feelings hurt and will not interrupt class again. This was punishment for Jody because she enjoys class. Though her interrupting behavior had socially positive consequences (attention from her peers), she later realized those consequences didn't carry as much weight as the negative attention from her teacher. Chelsea also interrupts class and is also reprimanded and asked to leave. Chelsea performs poorly in this class and has been dreading it all day. She's gotten just what she wanted—out of class! This has been a negatively reinforcing event for her rather than a punishment, and it has ensured that she will interrupt often.

Reinforce As Soon As Possible

When you want to strengthen a desired behavior, reinforce it as close to the time the behavior occurred as possible: "Charlie, thank you so much for clearing your work off the table so the next group will have a place to set up their projects." The positive behavior has been noticed, the student has been reminded that he knew and followed a classroom rule, and a social reinforcement (the attention of the teacher) has been given. (Of course, this assumes that adult attention is reinforcing for this student. Don't forget that not everyone is reinforced by social interactions!) The reinforcement is much more powerful given right away, to this specific student, than it would be if the teacher commented at the end of the day that everyone had been really good at putting away their stuff. Remember, although not all behavior is *intentionally* communicative, we can attribute meaning to any behavior we can observe.

When a child has learned a communicative alternative to a previously unacceptable behavior, the reinforcement for that alternative must happen quickly and often in order for the child to associate the acceptable behavior with the desired outcome. For example, in order to get the teacher's attention, Ariel yells, "Hey lady, listen to this!" While this certainly does gain the teacher's attention, it is not the most appropriate method. The teacher reminds Ariel that she only needs to raise her hand to be called upon. As the lesson progresses, the teacher takes great note of Ariel, and when she sees Ariel's hand go up, she immediately calls upon Ariel to respond. The teacher knows she must do this consistently until it becomes habit for Ariel. If the teacher misses too many raised hands, Ariel will revert to calling, "Hey lady!"

Reinforce Only the Behavior You Want to Increase

If a child receives attention for both appropriate and inappropriate behaviors, the process of learning the acceptable behaviors will be delayed. Call attention to the behaviors you want to perpetuate or increase, and ignore or redirect behaviors you want to decrease. Remember to say what students *should* be doing instead of what they should *not* be doing.

Consider Sam, who got teacher attention every time he deliberately dropped his book on the floor. Dropping his book only meant he had to pick it up—but his teacher paid attention to it and thereby drew the attention of his peers to this behavior. What was the message of Sam's behavior? "I want to make noise"? Probably not. "I want to bend over and pick up this book"? Also unlikely. Sam's message was probably, "Pay attention to me!" (For a refresher on this topic, revisit chapter 4.)

His teacher should also question why he needed attention. Was the subject matter boring? Too hard? Too easy? Why was the attention he received from his peers so important that he was willing to get repeatedly reprimanded? We'll come back to Sam and his teacher's response in the next section.

Remember, every child who drops his book is not sending the same message. Every behavior deserves consideration as a unique message.

Use Frequent Reinforcers

This guideline complements the preceding one nicely, particularly when initially trying to shape a positive behavior or change a negative one. If an unacceptable behavior has "worked" in the past to get the desired response, the child will need a great deal of reinforcement each time he uses the desired behavior.

Let's reconsider Sam, the book dropper. If his teacher pays attention to him when he drops his book, she positively reinforces that behavior, even if she yells at him. Take a moment to think about this seemingly counterintuitive idea. Why would yelling at Sam be positively reinforcing? Because his message was "Pay attention to me," and in response he got attention. Once Sam's teacher decides to reinforce only on-task work behaviors, she has to do it often. Why? Because the book-dropping behavior is an active part of Sam's communication repertoire, it always worked before, and she has to prove that Sam can get his need for attention met by behaving in appropriate ways. In order to do this, she has to demonstrate to him that his on-task behavior can get him as much attention as dropping his book on the floor.

With another student, however, the needs might be completely different. If the student's message had been "This book is too heavy, and I can't hold it" or "These math problems are too hard, and I can't do them, help me," yelling would not be a positive reinforcement; it would be a hurtful and harmful consequence for an inability to physically or cognitively complete a task.

Use Contingencies

Using a contingency means allowing the student to receive reinforcement only after he or she has completed a requested task. Most of us use contingencies in our daily lives. For example, adults may delay having a cup of coffee until after they put in a load of laundry, or they may tell themselves they can use the Internet after they write at least five pages of a report. Our lives are filled with contingencies. First walk the dogs, then feed the cats, then sit down with the morning paper. First work, then play.

In order to make contingencies understandable for children, state them in a positive manner such as, "First go wash your hands, and then you can have a snack." This tells children what they will get to do *if* they follow directions. The reward is simply stated and positive.

Contingencies are not bribes. Children see through bribes quickly. Think about the sticker charts that are sometimes used in early elementary classrooms. Do they work for every child? How long do they work? Why do they stop working? Contingencies need to be naturally occurring consequences or logical events within the daily routine. Examples of contingencies are, "First you clean your plate, and then you can have dessert" or "First you clean your room, and then you can have an allowance." Bribes are not naturally occurring consequences. If a student refuses to go to class, and a teacher says, "If you go to this class and do your work, I'll take you out for breakfast second period," the teacher has offered a bribe.

The difference is whether the contingency has been established prior to behavior. If no plan or contingency is already established, as in the breakfast example, the statement made by the teacher was a bribe used to make the behavior go away. It was not a plan, not proactive, and not teaching what had been intended. Bribes can often teach that a behavior "works"; in other words, the student learned that her unwanted behavior can result in breakfast during second period.

Contingencies are intentional, used to help support positive behaviors, and are goal driven: students work for a reward that has been established in advance. Bribes are last-ditch efforts to make a behavior go away and are usually not well thought-out.

Reinforce Others for the Desired Behavior

Sometimes the challenging behavior can be seen while the child is involved in group activities. In those situations, when the opportunity arises to point out and praise the positive and desired behaviors of others, do so in a very obvious manner. Continually provide the attention and praise to the desired behavior, and ignore the undesirable behavior.

Waiting for a Turn: Ethan's Story

While consulting with the third-grade teacher in a class where Sue was doing therapy, several children came up to talk. Candice came up and stood next to the two of them, waiting to be acknowledged. Ethan stomped up and immediately started in: "It was my turn and Jacob took the markers away and . . ."

When a logical pause occurred in the conversation, Mrs. Rebecca turned to Candice and said, "I really like the way you waited for a turn to talk." Sue and Mrs. Rebecca proceeded to talk, totally ignoring Ethan's "It was my turn!" Mrs. Rebecca had reinforced another child for appropriate waiting behavior that was incompatible with interrupting. Of course, she also needed to help Ethan learn the appropriate rules for interrupting an ongoing conversation, but at this moment, she was reinforcing Candice for her positive social communication skills.

Changes do not come overnight, so stick with any behavior change strategy for at least four to six weeks before ruling it out. It may take that long for the child to learn the more appropriate way to convey his or her message; after all, that behavior had always worked before. Be sure the communication form is as efficient as the old one and that it sends the same message.

When reinforcing other children for the behavior you want to see, take care that this technique doesn't backfire. If Mrs. Rebecca was always praising Candice for her good behavior, sometimes doing it in front of the whole class, the rest of the children could easily come to resent Candice. Older children can see through this type of praise and realize that it is a form of manipulation, and it then loses its power. Children know when praise is thoughtful and genuine. Authentic praise does not feel manipulative, and is therefore more likely to be reinforcing.

Redirect Behavior

Remember, any kind of attention to a behavior is a consequence; whether that consequence is perceived as positive or not depends on the student. Therefore, when confronted with an unacceptable behavior, try redirecting that behavior into a more desirable one that cannot be accomplished without abandoning the unacceptable behavior.

Block That Behavior! Marissa and Tonya's Story

Marissa and Tonya are playing with the blocks. Their teacher notices that the towers are becoming a bit tall and that there is a lot of crashing when the girls deliberately knock them down. While this is okay on some days, today there is a puppet show being developed in the learning area next to the blocks. Their teacher sits down to play and gently says, "You are building great towers today. What would you think of building a whole town for the rest of the children to see when they come to the puppet show? You could build roads, stores, bridges, houses . . . anything you want. And just because today is special, you can use the whole rug instead of just the block area."

Not only has their teacher reinforced their nice cooperative play, she has also suggested an extension to their construction activity that is incompatible with tower building. She has redirected their activity to a larger horizontal scope without ever saying, "Stop building towers."

Getting the Hang of It: Lowell's Story

Lowell is having some trouble expressing his frustration with creating his artwork the way he wants it on the computer. His keystrokes are becoming louder and louder, his sighs and groans are audible from across the room, and the other children are starting to attend to his behaviors. Mr. Marcos intervenes by saying, "Lowell, I understand you are frustrated. How can I help? Let's look at what happened and see if we can figure this out together." The two of them spend a few minutes to backtrack and discover that Lowell is in a different part of the editing program than he thought, and once this is rectified, Lowell moves on to complete his project without further assistance or disruption.

Mr. Marcos validated Lowell's frustration, labeled it for him, and redirected him into a problem-solving mode that can teach him how to solve dilemmas without throwing a fit in the future.

Redirecting also means supplying an alternative way to communicate the same message. Be sure that the alternative you provide sends the same message—that it serves the same function as the undesirable behavior. After making sure it sends the same message, make sure that it is at least as efficient as the undesirable behavior. Asking an angry child to jump through a number of hoops to get his message across is not going to work. Asking a frustrated child to engage in a difficult communication exchange is not going to work, either. Both these examples create a situation in which the alternative is harder to accomplish than the unwanted behavior, and is likely to fail.

Let's pull all of these ideas related to positively reinforcing behaviors together by taking another look at our book dropper, Sam. Don't forget that this is a simplistic example for the sake of learning some complicated ideas. Life is seldom this simple.

If the behavior of dropping his book consistently has always gotten the desired results, Sam's teacher will need to:

- Look for the message ("Pay attention to me!")

- Find ways to pay attention at moments when the behavior is appropriate (reinforce only the behaviors she wants; reinforce behaviors that are incompatible with the unacceptable one)

- Teach Sam ways to gain her attention that are not disruptive to his learning, his classmates' learning, or her teaching, but at the same time are as efficient as dropping his book (teach acceptable communication alternatives to the unwanted one)

- Make a concerted effort to catch Sam during on-task times and times that he appropriately requests her attention, and reinforce the behaviors she wants to see often

- Redirect or ignore the behaviors she does not want to see

Remember, this is a snapshot. We have not discussed some pieces of this picture for the sake of simplicity. What if dropping the book was to gain the attention of Sam's peers and not his teacher? A whole different scenario would emerge, with a different set of solutions needed. The essential question remains: what is this behavior communicating?

Ignore the Behavior

Ignoring is the strongest way to eliminate a behavior, yet it is often the hardest strategy to implement. Many times, it takes persistence and strength of character to outlast a child who is incredibly motivated to get her message across.

Here is how ignoring works. Suppose a child who raises her hand to speak also makes lots of groans and noises at the same time; teachers may not enjoy that behavior or the disruption it causes. Instead of calling on that student or telling her to be quiet when she raises her hand, the teacher could call on someone whose hand is up and who is quiet. That behavior could be pointed out in a positive manner, thus sending a message to the louder student: "Rickie, thank you for quietly raising your hand." The teacher will have to consistently call only on the children who are raising their hands quietly, or it will lose its power. Ignoring is a powerful way to extinguish unwanted behavior, but never forget to look for the underlying message and provide an alternate way for the child's needs to be met.

Ignoring does not work for all behaviors. Hitting, for example, must not be ignored. And because behavior is communication, if we choose to ignore the behavior, the *first* thing we need to do is establish the meaning of the behavior and supply the student with a socially acceptable way to get her message across. If we fail to do this, and the message is important to the sender, she will continue to use the unacceptable behavior to get us to understand. It is always better to "listen" to the message, give the student another way to get the message across, and then ignore the unwanted behavior.

Remember, when you start to ignore a behavior that has worked in the past, *the behavior will escalate.* The student will try harder and longer to get the desired response because the behavior has always worked before! Therefore, carefully consider the behaviors you are choosing to ignore, and always provide an alternative way in which the message can be delivered.

Use Intermittent Reinforcement

Intermittent reinforcement—sometimes paying attention to the behavior, and sometimes not—is extremely strong. This can work for and against a teacher. For example, if a child persistently taps an adult and says, "Teacher, Teacher, Teacher," to gain attention, his teacher may want to give the child a more appropriate way to gain her attention and to ignore the behavior. Behaviors don't change overnight, however. What if the child reverts to the old behavior and the teacher abruptly can't handle it anymore and responds to renewed tapping with, "What do you want?" In this case, the child learns to be persistent: "If I tap and talk longer and harder, Teacher will eventually pay attention!" When ignoring a behavior, it is imperative to truly ignore it. Don't give into the temptation to respond. And of course, before ignoring, be sure to provide another way for the child to get his message across and reinforce that behavior instead.

Use Punishment

Punishment diminishes or eliminates behaviors. It is a quick fix; it stops the behavior for that instant, but does nothing to promote any learning or alternative means of expression. The only thing punishment does is tell the child what *not* to do. It gives no information about acceptable alternatives, nor does it provide support for sending the message in more appropriate ways.

Punishment shifts the focus away from the message of the behavior and from the lesson of what a more appropriate way to communicate the message might be to the question of who is in control. The type of relationship that develops from punishment is typically a power relationship in which the adult controls the child's behavior, and the child's responsibility for controlling his or her own behavior is not supported. Children who receive punishment rather than a lesson on communication alternatives learn:

- To depend on adults to control their behaviors

- To let adults think for them

- To behave only when they will get caught doing otherwise

- To use power to solve their problems

When punishment is used, the consequences for behaviors do not take into account the message sent by the behavior, and are seldom logical, or related to the behavior itself. Whether the punishment is verbal (shaming, ridiculing, using cruel words) or physical (slapping, spanking), it impacts a child in many ways that defeat self-esteem and do not produce positive results.

When the Going Gets Tough

Sometimes children need more than a signal, proximity, or redirection, however. If children become aggressive, self-injurious or otherwise out of control, more adult assistance is needed to maintain safety for the student as well as peers or others around the child. At these times, a more invasive or hands-on approach may be needed. Some schools have strict rules about physically touching or assisting children; be sure to learn those guidelines before school starts. Each school district is different as well in how parents feel about physical assistance of their child. If it becomes necessary to use these techniques—the last-ditch efforts—first meet with parents and an administrator to clarify the issues and proposed techniques. Keeping all information on the table and having open and honest lines of communication among everyone is imperative if the child is to succeed.

Quiet Place

Everyone needs a place to regroup, pull it together, or simply "chill," but this need is often overlooked in the course of a child's day. Sometimes the environment is too chaotic, noisy, or confusing; at other times the child may not feel well or secure and need a getaway. A quiet place is not intended to be an escape from activity, but instead a place to reorient oneself to the task at hand within a certain environment.

There are different ways to create quiet places in classrooms or at home. Remember being a young child and creating a fort out of blankets and a clothesline or sitting under a table with a long tablecloth? Those are examples of quiet places created by children that give them their own private space. Try large appliance boxes with a door and maybe a window cut out to provide a comforting confined place, or put up pup tents in a corner of the room.

Easy Does It: Rakim's Story

One small classroom in Iowa had very little space to spare, but the teachers knew a quiet place was very important, especially for one young boy, Rakim. The transition from home to bus to classroom was quite stressful for him. He couldn't enter the classroom successfully without first allowing himself time to regroup and gather his wits. If he didn't have the time, his behaviors were less than desirable. The only spot the teachers could spare was under an eight-foot table, so under this table they placed a reading bolster, some books, a blanket, and a stuffed animal that the children enjoyed.

Afterwards, transitions worked like clockwork for Rakim. He would enter the room and dash to this spot as soon as he entered, coat on and book bag with him. He would simply sit and recline against the support and watch what was happening in the room as the other students entered. No one bothered him, other than one teacher greeting him briefly with "Good morning. Glad to see you." Rakim sat under the table for no more than five minutes and then emerged on his own, hung up his coat, put his book bag in his cubby, and then joined his classmates for the rest of the day.

Another teacher we know had a unique idea for her quiet space. She sewed together a pair of old adult-sized sweat pants and a sweatshirt, stuffed the entire thing with soft material, and then sewed all the openings shut, thereby creating an adult-sized human-like form. The children in her class could go to the stuffed adult, sit on its lap, and pull the arms over themselves to get a hug and relax. They loved it! Quiet spaces can be unique, simple, and inexpensive and should be a part of both home and school spaces.

Time Out

Many school programs and families use time out—often in the wrong way, as a threat for any and all behavior infractions. This is not an effective use of time out. Because putting a child in time out takes him or her away from instructional time, and does nothing to teach alternative behaviors, it is often counterproductive. This technique must be thoroughly planned by the entire support team, including parents or caregivers. Since it's only to be used as a last resort, everyone must agree and be able to identify what behavior qualifies for time out. The chosen behavior should be the most crucial behavior: usually, when a child is aggressive towards others or to themselves. It is a safety issue almost as much as it is a behavior intervention.

The team decides upon how to implement this strategy well in advance. In many instances, other meetings about a specific child's specific behaviors are the perfect place to discuss all the particulars of this strategy. Where will the time-out spot be located? In the classroom, in the hallway, or in a separate room at school? Will it be in the child's bedroom or in another room at home? How will the space be created, and what will be in the space? Will it be empty or contain furniture such as a beanbag chair? What will be the verbal response of the adults before the child would be taken to time out? Everyone should send the same message consistently so its meaning can become clear to the child. Each person, at home and at school, should learn the phrase that is used and when to use it.

Time out should only be used for a brief period of time for the student and/or the support person to calm down before reuniting to work once again. Both people need to be calm in order to move forward with the lesson or activity. If one of them is still upset, those feelings will impact the lesson and the other person. One to three minutes is usually sufficient; if the child is in time out much longer, it may be considered a teacher/parent time out! The longer a child is in time out, the less time a teacher or parent has to deal with the chance that the behaviors would occur again. If this becomes the case, something is very wrong and should be looked at in depth.

When a child is in time out, it is a time away from any and all positive reinforcements, which means no eye contact, because that can be very reinforcing for some children. This also means do not answer any questions, comment on what they have done to get to time out, or otherwise become engaged. Time out is a time out of any sort of interaction and attention.

The use of time out as a last resort should not be a surprise to the child or to any other adults in the vicinity. No one should question or wonder why it happens, because everyone who supports the child would have been included in any planning and discussion of time out. Everyone would be absolutely clear as to the reason, how it was communicated, where the child would be going, and what the adults involved would need to do. No one should have any doubts or questions.

Finally, all who support the child should be clear about one more issue: time out should never be used as a response made in anger. It should be used in a matter-of-fact manner: you broke a rule, and this is what happens. If a situation occurs that creates anger in an adult, get assistance from someone else. That means that in school, everyone should be alert to particular sounds that may indicate an eminent challenge that needs assistance; at home, one parent could call another. It may not always be easy, but if at all possible, get help from someone else to allow yourself time to cool down and avoid any unnecessary repercussions. Dealing with such challenging behaviors must be total team effort; it should never be left to only one person. That is unfair and would also ultimately cause that person to burn out and lose hope. Hope is what is always needed to keep moving forward!

Physical Assistance

Sometimes children need an extra hand to get started on a task. They may be refusing to participate, or they may be confused and not know where or how to begin. When those situations arise, some gentle physical assistance from one adult may be useful. Here are several examples.

A classroom can be quite messy and filled with toys or other play materials. When the announcement to clean up comes, some children find the room totally overwhelming. They may have no idea where to begin and, the words, "Clean-up time," are not very clear or concrete directions. Those children may try to leave the situation because it is so chaotic. In those situations, it might be helpful to say to the child, "It's time to clean up, and I need your help. Take this toy [hand it to the child], and put it on that shelf. Then come back, and I will give you something else to put away."

If the child attempts to move away or avoid the situation, it is acceptable to have him "on hand" and take him over to the shelf to put the toy away and then go back to get another. Do all this in a matter-of-fact, neutral fashion, and always give a verbal warning of "I will help you" before touching the child. The child needs to know he will be physically assisted to complete the task.

Sue often finds herself walking through the hall during class changes, a notoriously difficult time for children to maintain quiet, orderly behavior. Sometimes just the fact that she is walking beside a student is enough to reestablish calm (the proximity strategy), sometimes an explicit reminder of the expectations is enough, but occasionally, Sue says, "I can see that this is a rough day. Why don't I help you get to your next class?" She gently hooks her arm into the student's and guides him or her to their destination. This is done with a smile, a gentle touch, and with students familiar with the way Sue works, so it is not a surprise. It could never be misconstrued as a physical threat; the tone of the physical assistance and the unambiguous message that it is being done with a positive outcome in mind are never in doubt.

Physical Restraint

Some school districts offer training programs on safe physical restraint; these courses are both helpful and necessary before school staff can resort to this technique. Remember, this should be a last-ditch effort to keep a child from hurting self or others. Staff must be trained and know the proper techniques for using any physical restraint so that neither staff nor the child is injured or has the potential for injury. The National Disability Rights Network has examined all state laws, policies, and guidelines of the fifty-six states and territories of the United States and found:

- 41% have no laws, policies or guidelines concerning restraint or seclusion in schools

- Almost 90% still allow prone restraint

- And only 45% require or recommend that schools automatically notify parents or guardians of restraint/seclusion use. (National Disability Rights Network, 2009)

In addition, in some states, each local education agency creates its own rules and guidelines regarding policy on restraint. Therefore it is imperative to discover what your local school district's policy is on the use of restraint; for your safety and for the safety of the children. It is truly a last-ditch effort that should only be undertaken with proper training and knowledge of regulations and alternatives.

Do not take this strategy lightly. All circumstances leading up to it and while it is happening must be noted and well documented. Most school districts have strict rules, policies, and forms that must be filed when any sort of physical restraint or physical incident occurs. The Council for Children with Behavioral Disorders (www.ccbd.net) and the Crisis Prevention Institute (www.crisisprevention.com) have suggested guidelines available.

A Values-Based Approach

Behavior theory needs to be used with our eyes wide open. We play a role in the behaviors we observe, whether they are those we want to encourage or not. So whenever we are using any method that "modifies behavior," it is a values-based approach; we are deciding which behaviors are acceptable based on our own belief system. We are exerting control over another person's right to be heard, and consequently over the value of their message.

It is natural to avoid doing things we do not find pleasant. When was the last time you were excited about a staff meeting? Our job as educators is to find ways to teach that engage our students in activities they find meaningful, interesting, and rewarding. When we find ourselves faced with behaviors we find frustrating, the first line of attack should be to listen to their message and act on it. Are we meeting the needs of that individual child? Are we meeting the needs of all the children in our class? Respect for the child and message comes first.

Accordingly, when we find ourselves thinking about behaviorist techniques, including reinforcement schedules, the first thing that we need to do is be absolutely certain that we are using them for the benefit of the child and not for our own benefit. Looking inside is never easy. Whose behavior is creating the tension in the situation that causes the child to act in ways that are unacceptable? Our message needs to be, "I hear you and understand what you are saying. How can we come together to make this situation work for both of us?"

The bottom line is that teaching is the practice of constantly making decisions about how to support learning, and that includes the support of the positive behaviors that allow children to fully engage in the learning opportunities available to them. In their book *The Moral Dimensions of Teaching: Language, Power, and Culture in Classroom Interaction*, Cary Buzzelli and Bill Johnston (2002, p. 157) say, "Teaching is inherently, unavoidable, and primarily moral action and interaction: that is, moral contact. This is the case whatever kind of teacher you are and whatever context you work in." The decisions you make about supporting behavior are among the most personal ones you will make in your teaching career.

The Jellybean Jar

Sue attended a workshop a number of years ago during which the presenter put a picture into her head that has remained a powerful image of the long-term influence of punishment and discipline.

Think of a child as an empty jar. Every time a positive experience happens—something fun or a learning opportunity, including constructive discipline—a green jellybean goes into the jar. For every negative experience that damages a child's self-image or ability to grow and learn, a red jellybean goes into the jar.

When the child reaches inside to pull out a skill, a behavior, a response to a situation, what color jellybean will he or she find? If the majority of the jellybeans are red—if negative experiences are predominant—the child will be more likely to respond in a way that demonstrates physical or verbal violence against another person.

If, on the other hand, the child's life experiences have been that the messages of unacceptable behaviors have been heard and valued, and the guidance that has happened as a result of this is discipline, the child will have a wealth of green jellybeans from which to choose. He will have experienced guidance in resolving conflict and in finding appropriate ways to gain attention or to voice his unhappiness. The number of ways he has to communicate appropriately his needs, wants, and ideas will have been expanded.

What color of jellybeans do you want to add to the jar?

Takeaways

- Our own behaviors influence children's behaviors. What we do can either perpetuate or diminish the behaviors we see.

- Many proactive strategies can also be used as reactive strategies.

- Reinforcement helps children begin to learn consequences of their actions.

- What is reinforcing varies for each and every one of us.

- Timing is crucial for the success of any type of reinforcement.

- Unless teachers are intentional in their words and actions, they can reinforce both positive and negative behaviors.

- Ignoring is a powerful way to eliminate an unwanted behavior, but it only works if the child has another way to communicate needs.

- Time out is a strategy that should be thoughtfully planned and executed. It removes a child from the opportunity to learn and can therefore be counterproductive.

- Physical restraints have guidelines that dictate their use in schools. Physical restraint should be used only for protection of self and/or others.

- The decisions you will make about supporting children's behavior are among the most complex and personal ones you will make in your career.

Personal Reflection

What does the term *reactive strategies* mean to you?

What are your personal beliefs around the ideas of reinforcement and punishment? How do those beliefs impact what you do in your classroom?

What sorts of reactive strategies have you used in the past? How did they work?

How do the reactive strategies work to solve the challenges you face long term?

How do you provide reinforcement to your children? Do you still like the way you have done it in the past?

What are your school guidelines on time out or physical restraint?

11

A Child-Centered Approach

The central theme of this book is that all behavior communicates. If we seriously consider all behaviors as communicative and listen to their messages, then we create environments and patterns of interaction with and around people that are positive, respectful, and affirming. No place is this more important than in our classrooms as we form relationships with children.

Children come into the classroom with a file full of academic history. Unless you are a preschool or kindergarten teacher, you will have information about how each child did academically in previous years. You may also have the story about each child. What a delight Sara is! What a ball of behaviors Marissa is! What a brilliant child Austin is! All of this data helps you begin your year. Or does it?

As you have been reading this book, you will have noted that the issues that we have identified and discussed might be described by some as "minor" challenges compared to other challenges that teachers in some schools face. Sadly, stories of student involvement with weapons, drugs, gangs, and extreme aggression are becoming all too common. These horrifying behaviors still send messages; however, they are usually very child-specific and can require more resources than schools can provide. It is important to stay connected with your local community and know what sort of help is available. As the saying goes, "It takes a village to raise a child." Call in reinforcements when the messages of behaviors are so extreme that they pose a danger or threat to the individual or to others.

The good news is that because everyone reacts differently to different people and situations, each child has the potential to start fresh in your classroom: to have an entirely different year than ever before. Your behavior can tell your students that you respect each one of them as an individual and that you strive for an environment where each child feels safe and can succeed. You can design your classroom to support both their academic and their socioemotional needs, and you can use the proactive strategies discussed in the previous chapters.

However, some children will still confuse us with unwanted and challenging behaviors. Often, in those cases, a great many meetings are held in order to "solve the problem." Many adults come to the table, each bringing his own story of the child's behavior and how it impacted him and the classroom environment. The initial moments of those meetings can set a tone for the remainder of the session.

You Think That's Bad?

At one school where Kim worked, she attended biweekly staffing meetings about the children. They were all very challenging students: highly aggressive, self-injurious, and sometimes very difficult to manage. The staff all needed to share stories and let people know what had been happening. While it is important to share, the meetings became unproductive. During the initial minutes, various people would show their wounds and discuss in great detail the horrors the particular student created for him or her. Then the next person had to "go one better" and find something equally if not more horrible to share. By the end of the meeting, the tone had once again been reinforced that this was a tough kid who could hurt others and needed to be "managed" by the adults in "charge." "Let's just get rid of the behavior, make it go away," was the mood that was set. This always felt uncomfortable to Kim, as if the team was not really seeing the entire child or looking at life through the child's experience and eyes.

The same thing sometimes happens on consultations. Of course, Kim is called in to observe a child not because things are going great, but because the situation is very challenging. In meetings with staff, almost everyone wants to share their nasty experiences with the particular child, again setting a tone that says, "Why are we even bothering to attempt to teach this child? There is no way to control her, and she is completely disrupting my ability to teach. Kids like her need to be elsewhere and not here, where they can monopolize my time. I guess we will do what we can—but only because we have to. This is a hard kid, and we need you to help us manage her." This tone prevents the staff from thinking in a more positive way; all they can see is the very challenging negative behavior instead of any message that child might be trying to send. Their focus on the negative will lead them to find more negative things, day after day. If anything positive happens, they will be blind to it.

It can be demoralizing to have a student we cannot figure out. We begin to doubt our own capacity to understand the message and provide necessary support. But while behaviors can be exceptionally difficult, it is still critical that someone listens and responds to the student's message. Make a concerted effort to break the negative cycle.

What can we do to ensure that our conversations focus on the positive when the child and situation are challenging? First, remember that the child is a person who has feelings, desires, wants, and may have a hard time clearly communicating those to the adults in every situation. Even adults can have a hard time "using their words" when they are feeling extreme emotions or desires, and children are still developing—not only their ability to self-regulate their behaviors, but also their ability simply to talk about their emotions and internal state.

Many times when teams meet, challenges or deficits are very clear to everyone. However, most teams don't spend enough time looking at the child's positive aspects, and every child has positive aspects that can be utilized in his education and life. Begin meetings with everyone around the table contributing one positive comment about the child. Sometimes this can be quite difficult. In those situations we have heard some people say, "He has a great smile" or "It was a good hair day." While those are not major compliments, they begin to change the tone and allow the adults to see the child as a real person and not a bundle of daily behavior problems.

Get to Know the Child

This activity will help your team get to know the child and use that knowledge to improve your relationship with the child and the child's learning experience. (See page 184 for a reproducible form to use with groups, or visit **go.solution-tree.com/behavior** to download it.)

Part I: Identify Strengths and Frustrations

As a team, create two lists. First, list the student's strengths, interests, and preferences. Second, list the student's fears, frustrations, and dislikes. Each team member should contribute. The lists will grow and change as the student changes (see fig. 11.1, page 176).

These lists can provide guidance in how to engage the student in any type of planned activities. For example, if a younger child is interested in trains, he can read about trains, draw trains, sing songs about trains, or play games involving trains. An older child could do math, geography, social studies, and written projects involving trains. The interest areas can be built into many activities that may be either formal or used as reinforcements, and will help the student stay focused and engaged. Temple Grandin, a woman with autism, often says that we should take the "interest areas and broaden them out" (cited in Davis, 2001b).

On days full of challenging behaviors, teachers can look at the two lists for the students to see what the balance may be between the two lists. Is the student engaged in more fearful, frustrating, or disliked activities, or are her strengths, interests, and preferences worked into the day to bolster the areas that need improvement? If there are more fearful or frustrating engagements, the child's behaviors may reflect those feelings. Try to incorporate as many strengths, interests, and preferences into the day, and use them to teach skills that the student may need in the future.

Part II: Identify Areas Needing Support, Learning Profile, and Appropriate Strategies

The team can create two additional lists in order to get a more complete picture of the student: a list of areas needing more support and learning, and a list of the child's learning styles and appropriate strategies. Once again, if the team spends time creating these lists, the priorities for the student will become clearer to everyone. Lists should reflect ideas from both home and school and should be incorporated into the child's individualized education program (IEP), if she has one (for more information on IEPs, visit www.ed.gov/parents/needs/speced/iepguide/index.html). Figure 11.2 (page 177) continues the example of Michael's lists.

Strengths

Uses acceptable communication skills to ask and answer questions and to express feelings

Can wait and be patient when activities are interesting to him

Has empathy for classmates

Shares materials well

Negotiates a compromise when faced with disagreements

Volunteers answers in class appropriately

Follows routines independently

Sits in his seat at appropriate times

Follows basic health and safety rules and routines

Reads at a level of understanding for grade-level work

Writes and draws for pleasure and as part of classroom assignments

Demonstrates age-appropriate number skills

Takes turns in play and conversation

Can use the computer

Works and plays independently

Follows directions

Talks with peers and enjoys being with his friends

Uses social pleasantries (please, thank you, excuse me)

Asks for help when needed

Is quiet when he is engaged in meaningful activity

Interests

Animals

Music, especially country

Mechanical objects, from power tools to automobiles

Computer games

Being read to

Drawing

Preferences

To be engaged in meaningful activities (as opposed to waiting or worksheet-type repetition)

To receive direct questions or instructions (indirect or implied questions are confusing)

To be "right" or do things correctly (need to be careful to provide challenging instruction without being too difficult)

To know exactly what to do

To know and follow the rules for each situation

To be with his friends (try to create work groups that include both friends and other students who are at a compatible learning level)

Learning activities with movement components (when ideas are tied to movements)

Learning both visually and auditorily (needs the visual component)

Fears, Frustrations, and Dislikes

Tasks that are uninteresting or meaningless

Not having enough time to process information

Receiving too much verbal information too fast

Unclear limits or expectations

Being asked to sit at one task for too long

Coordinating all of his senses to follow the rules: processing information, remembering, raising his hand to talk before he can speak, waiting, and so on

Not finishing an activity in the allotted time, and therefore, not turning in his work on time

Figure 11.1: Getting to know Michael, Part I.

Areas Needing Additional Support for Learning	Learning Profile and Appropriate Strategies
Staying with an activity through completion	Learns better when a visual component is included
Asking for help only after having made a good attempt at solving the problem	Build on his love of books and skill in reading
Waiting during activities uninteresting to him (in line for lunch or the bus, for a turn during physical education, to answer a question in class)	Utilize visual schedules and planners
	Make a plan for turning in work on time
	Accommodate his preferences for rules and order
Entering a group (cooperative learning activities in class, basketball games during recess)	Build on his enjoyment of spending time with peers by using them as supports
Getting work turned in on time	

Figure 11.2: Getting to know Michael, Part II.

The information you compile can become integral aspects of the planning and implementation of activities to enhance the student's learning. Many of these identified strengths can be used and needs met as part of everyday classroom routine and instruction. All students will benefit from your efforts to identify and meet typical student needs for explicit expectations, assistance in demonstrating on-task behavior, or a visual presentation of information. This style of planning typifies the universal design and differentiated instruction principles discussed earlier. These instructional methods promote multiple ways for students to access and engage with information, and multiple ways for them to demonstrate their knowledge.

Part III: Set Important Goals

Next, the team can work together to establish goals that are important for the child, not only in the immediate classroom setting, but over the long term of the child's education and life. For example, being able to persist in a task without asking for help until having first attempted to solve the problem independently is a good goal for your classroom and will also be a valuable skill for employment. Many of the important goals for the children in your class are not academic!

Consider Michael, the child in our example. It appears that he has many strengths and preferences, but is a bit impulsive and doesn't always have the degree of control necessary to be a consistently responsible member of the classroom learning community. This is particularly true when he is challenged by information that pushes him beyond what he finds easy or comfortable to understand. Following are some sample goals:

- Attend to a task until it is completed, whether a formal part of the daily routine (such as a large-group, small-group, or independent learning activity) or an unstructured part of the day (such as playing on the playground).

- Hand in work on time.

- Have short conversations with classmates about a shared interest.

Part IV: Maximize Strengths and Minimize Fears

Next, look at the list of the student's strengths, interests, and preferences to see if you can use anything from the list to help him work toward his goals. Using the student's own strengths, interests, and preferences to support his learning will increase his motivation to learn. Everyone is more motivated to work when the task is personally meaningful and enjoyable (see fig. 11.3).

Have him sit with a peer to team-read or buddy-read assignments.

Teach Michael how to use visual organizers for planning both short-term and long-term assignments and projects.

Use him as a mentor for math lessons.

Figure 11.3: Plan to use Michael's strengths, interests, and preferences in learning.

Along with inserting the student's strengths, interests, and preferences into the curriculum, create ways to decrease the student's fears and frustrations. If you can reduce his anxiety, confusion, and stress, it will be easier for him to learn. As the student's fears are reduced and activities become more interesting, he'll gain skills (see fig. 11.4).

Use visual schedule to introduce the day, and create a work plan.

Be exact with number of repetitions for activities or amount of time to spend on an activity.

Build in extra time for him to move by having him help with setting up the room, running errands, and so on.

Allow flexible time to process information.

Incorporate review of his schedule throughout the day to remind him of the tasks at hand.

Figure 11.4: Plan to reduce Michael's fears and frustrations.

Part V: Identify Instructional Strategies

Finally, as a team, discuss what instructional strategies and physical settings work best. Remember that the environment and all it entails contribute to the success or failure of a child's learning, as well as the materials that are used to encourage learning. Ask more specific questions regarding the best all-around ways to help the child, literally from the ground up: classroom set up, where he is seated, lighting, sounds, distractions, where materials are kept, how he obtains materials, and how the student-teacher interactions are carried out. The team should ask themselves questions that may include:

- Does the student need a work area that is freer from distractions than many of the other children?

- How can you accommodate, in a directed way, the student's need to move in order to reduce off-task wandering?

- Is there a way to take advantage of the student's academic strengths to focus his attention to new and difficult tasks?

- Does the student work best with cues?

- How does written work need to be adapted?

- How does the child obtain and use materials for each activity?

- What types of interaction from the teachers work best for the child?

- Does the child need warnings for changes? How far in advance?

- Are there sensory issues to consider when giving instructions, so the child can see and hear them?

Once again, this list can be modified as time passes to maintain a current listing of strategies that all of the student's teachers might utilize (see fig. 11.5).

Be very clear and specific with instructions for each activity.

Use both visual and auditory modes to instruct and as reminders for classroom behavioral expectations.

Incorporate the interest of mechanical objects into his tasks. For example, he could use math to learn about dimensions, weights, or measurements; in science and history, he could learn how the mechanical objects have been used; spelling tests could contain words about these objects, and he would be reading about them as he uses them or encouraged to check out library books for further reading. This would help to keep him on task.

Create work groups that include both friends and other students who are at a compatible learning level.

Use the computer to augment any activities or classroom homework.

Call on Michael when he raises his hand so that he is included in discussions.

Figure 11.5: Instructional strategies for Michael.

This method of getting to know a student and working as a team can help alleviate some of the stress for everyone involved. Teamwork can be challenging in itself, but if your team remembers that the meeting and lists are about the individual child and not about personal egos, you can make progress. Truly listening to one another and knowing that each team member has valuable information is crucial. Success is great positive reinforcement for students and instructional teams alike. When we reframe our thinking about these meetings as well as about each child we support, the results are outstanding.

Use Individual Visual Supports

Visual supports can take many forms. We discussed classroom schedules and posted rules earlier; these are examples of visual supports for the entire class. They remind students of what will be happening and what the behavioral expectations are for the class. Some classes implement schedules, planners, or visual organizers for all students in the class. While this can start as early as kindergarten, with a simple checklist of the activities that will be accomplished before the end of the day, it is more common as students begin to be given more responsibility for completion of tasks.

Turning It Around: Toshi's Story

Fifth-grader Toshi was barely passing several of her classes because she was not turning in her homework on time. Now she uses her planner to keep track of when her assignments are due. Her mom looks at it with her daily to see if Toshi needs support in making time to do her work, help with the subject matter, materials or supplies, or just some gentle reminders. Her planner has not only helped Toshi to pull up her grades, but has also improved her relationships with her teachers and her mother, who were tired of the nagging and cajoling that had been the previous pattern. Toshi is in control of her planner and her work now.

As learning opportunities become more complex, so do the ways in which students approach them. This is when the universally designed classroom that employs differentiated instruction techniques becomes critical in meeting the individual needs of the students. While some students approach content in a linear way, others discover the same content through more creative avenues. In order for students to take advantage of the type of learning available to them, they need to be able to organize their time and be responsible for their learning. Visual organizers or schedules can be as basic or as complex as needed.

Picture This: Grant's Story

Kindergartener Grant was having meltdowns all day, every day. He didn't seem to be able to move from one activity to the next without throwing a temper tantrum. In response, his teacher created a daily picture schedule and corresponding activity mini-schedules. Grant's daily schedule directs him to circle time. His mini-schedule tells him to go to the assigned area, sit on his carpet square, listen to the story, sing the song, participate in the calendar and weather activity, pick up his square, and then go back again to refer to his daily schedule to find out what is next. The daily schedule then reminds Grant that it is time to have a snack. This entails washing hands (in the bathroom, a schedule pictures the sequence of water, soap, rinse, turn off water, paper towel, throw in the trash), coming to the table, and so on. Since implementing the daily picture schedules to help him understand the specific expectations of each individual activity, Grant's misbehaviors have decreased greatly.

While this level of visual support is difficult both to implement and to maintain, it may be what some children need to gain a sense of control over their environment and subsequently, their behavior. Grant's schedules took time to create and to teach him to use, but the amount of time and energy the teaching staff spent to support him behaviorally decreased once he learned the expectations. Long-term gains for everyone resulted.

Know Your Expectations for Each Child

When thinking of activities for your daily routine, always keep in mind the ultimate goal of that activity—and be very clear about what that goal is.

Directions for activities often contain confusing messages for children. The directions may disguise the real goals or assume that everyone hearing the directions has the same understanding of the expectations. For example, many kindergartens have story time. The children are often told, "Come to story" or "It's time to listen to the story for today." The children move to the area, and the teacher begins to read the story. However, the teacher spends much of the story time telling the students to sit up, hold still, sit on their rumps (instead of laying down), or stop wiggling and listen. The real goal of the activity becomes being in the upright ready position instead of listening to the story.

This unspoken goal is strange when we consider that as adults, we don't necessarily read sitting in a chair with our feet squarely on the floor and the book in an upright position; we read and listen in many different positions. Sue once observed a most wonderful reading of a piece of classic fantasy writing during which the entire class was enraptured by the story, and everyone was listening in a different way. Some children were lying in front of the teacher, others sat at their desks, and still others relaxed in the beanbag chairs provided for independent reading. Each child found the position that best allowed him or her to engage in the story. For several of those children, it would have been impossible to listen while sitting at their desks. Not one child interrupted the entire twenty-minute reading. This teacher clearly met her goals without having her students in the upright and ready position! Having clear goals will determine what we do or don't do in classes, how we interact with the child, and what we expect from the child in each activity.

It is also important to know whether or not the child *can* meet the goal. Is it feasible to expect a six-year-old child to sit for an hour through an assembly, or is arranging for the kindergarteners and first graders to be present for just part of the gathering a better choice if we want behaviors that are acceptable? Can an elementary student always contain his excitement at holiday time during that same all-school assembly? Making expectations smaller and breaking things down can help a child accomplish what we are asking. For example, instead of expecting a younger child with a disability to sit for all of the activities, the expectations for that child could be, "We'll stay for two songs, and then we will go get a drink and come back for the rest of the circle time." If more than one child is having trouble attending to any given lesson or activity, it is time to check the activity itself.

Children have varying abilities and interests and can succeed when teachers are flexible with the amount of time spent in an activity or adjust the difficulty level or material used or amount of support given. Some teachers have expressed that it is not fair to make adjustments for a student, even if the adjustments are helpful. Richard Lavoie (1989), who educates teachers on learning disabilities, has said, "Fair is not that everyone gets that same thing. Fair is that everyone gets what they need."

This is an excellent mindset to have when teaching diverse children and also preparing lessons with a proactive, positive approach to education.

Getting It Write: Dieter's Story

Vesta, a paraeducator, once showed Sue an example of a boy's handwriting that was not as neat or as organized as his third-grade teacher hoped for. She explained that every day she picked out a sentence for Dieter to copy and gave him the paper and pencil to do the task. Vesta was absolutely right that he needed practice; his cursive writing was unreadable!

For some reason, the day of the observation, Vesta made a change. She told Dieter it was time to practice his writing. She had the paper ready for him, but this time gave him a choice of writing instrument—pencil, pen, or marker. She also told him she had not picked out a sentence for him; instead, he could make one up on his own or copy one from his favorite book.

When Dieter finished the assignment—in record time—his result was totally different from previous tries. The writing was entirely legible, neat, and tidy. Everyone was surprised and pleased. What made the difference? The goal was still "handwriting," but the student had some say in the matter. First, he had chosen to write with a marker (bright lime green) instead of a pencil because he knew that regulating the pressure on the pencil (to write without either pressing too hard, breaking the lead, or too softly, making no mark) was frustrating for him. Second, Dieter had chosen to copy a sentence from his favorite book and wanted to write it perfectly because it was important to him! When the goal was handwriting—with an additional, unstated expectation of using a #2 pencil and a prescribed sentence—the result was poor. However, the *critical* goal of handwriting was still achieved with minor adaptations or accommodations that allowed the student to be successful and find meaning in the work. The student's behaviors were changed due to a simple change in adult expectations.

Assess and Evaluate Progress

The vast array of ways in which teachers can evaluate the academic progress of the children in their classroom (including portfolios, rubrics, and performance-based assessment) allows children with differing cultural and educational backgrounds and with differing educational abilities to demonstrate their knowledge and skills in the way that best suits their needs. Anne Donnellan, a professor in the School of Leadership and Education Sciences and director of the Autism Institute at the University of San Diego, says, "Why would you do a standardized test, in a standardized way, with learners who have not a standard experience or course of development and come up with a standard score that's meaningful?" (personal communication, August 24, 2009) Test taking is a skill which must be learned, just like any other, and as such, is susceptible to the ability of each student to focus, attend, and recall information. Ongoing evaluation may be a better option for many students.

Because this is an important concern in determining what and how much each student is learning, it deserves note here, but this book cannot cover the many issues surrounding assessment and evaluation of progress. More information can be found at www.ed.gov/admins/lead/account/saa.html and each state's special education department website.

Understand the Needs and Focus on the Positive

Using a child-centered approach, especially with those children who have difficult behaviors, can take some adjusting and time. With so many students, taking the time to really get to know one child may seem overwhelming. Yet when that child disrupts lessons and causes the teacher to stop teaching the whole class, putting time into getting to know that specific child can lead to fewer class disruptions. This approach can ultimately relieve stress for both the teacher and the child, thereby promoting learning for all, a better self-image and self-esteem for the child, and a more positive feeling to the entire learning process.

Takeaways

- Even major behavior issues send messages, so we must learn to ask for help from other associations when needed and work together to explore more intensely to find the reasons for some behaviors.

- Getting to know the whole child is imperative. Instead of focusing only on the weak areas, identify and discover strengths, preferences, and interests.

- Build those strong points into activities to help ensure success and decrease challenging behaviors.

- Reduce the fears and frustrations for the child whenever possible.

- Understand that accommodations *are* fair when they are needed to help support a child to be successful.

- Assessment is ongoing, and teachers should be aware of each child's circumstances before going into formal assessment situations to ensure that accommodations are in place as needed.

Getting to Know the Child

Fill in the following information, then compare your responses with those from others.

Part I

What are the child's strengths, interests, and preferences?

Strengths	Interests	Preferences

What are the child's fears, frustrations, and dislikes?

Fears	Frustrations	Dislikes

Part II

What are the areas where the child needs additional support?

Areas Needing Additional Support

What is the child's learning profile?

Learning Profile

Part III

What are the important learning goals for the child? Remember, they may not all be academic.

Important Learning Goals

Part IV

How can the child's strengths, interests, and preferences be used to support learning, reinforce acceptable behaviors, and increase motivation?

Ways to Build on Strengths, Interests, and Preferences

How can the child's fears, frustrations, and dislikes be minimized?

Ways to Reduce Fears, Frustrations, and Dislikes

Part V

What instructional strategies and physical environments will work best for this child?

Appropriate Instructional Strategies

Other:

Guiding Questions for Supporting Behavior

Answering these questions can help you determine whether you have met your obligations in supporting a child's behavior.

1. **Is the environment conducive to positive behavior?**

   - What are the traffic patterns?

   - Are work areas clearly defined?

   - Are there adequate materials?

     – Are there enough of the popular item(s)?

     – Are there materials for all developmental levels and interest areas?

2. **Are expectations for behavior clear?**

   - Do staff understand the rules?

   - Are classroom rules posted?

   - Are rules for each area clearly understood by all involved?

3. **Are my expectations realistic regarding the student's:**

   - Attention span

   - Ability level

   - Interests

4. **Why is this behavior occurring, and what makes it "a good idea" from the child's perspective?**

   - Describe the behavior.

   - Why is this particular behavior an issue?

   - Does this behavior happen at predictable times?

   - Is this behavior typically seen during the same activity? (If yes, go back to question 1. If one activity is typically problematic, something has been overlooked in planning.)

   - Are the same students usually involved when this behavior occurs?

1 of 2

5. **What happened?**

   - What more acceptable ways to get the message across were tried first?

   - What responses did those initial attempts to get the message across generate?

6. **What was the message of the behavior?**

7. **Was the message heard and acknowledged? What did I do to let the child know I heard the message that was so important that the child believed acting out was the only way to get me to hear it?**

Personal Reflection

What does a *child-centered approach* mean to you? Do you think it would take more time (in the long run as well as short term)?

Can you name the strengths, interests, and preferences of any one of your students? How do you infuse them into your lessons?

Can you name the fears, frustrations, and dislikes of any one of your students? Can you elaborate on how those might impact behavior?

How can you make your teaching more child centered in general?

Epilogue

By this point, we hope you have taken the journey from looking at behavior as a struggle and something to eliminate to a way for anyone—particularly children—to communicate some need or desire. Instead of seeing behaviors as bothersome, you are starting to see them as messages and ways to gain insight into the children teachers support every day in classrooms in schools across North America. Behavior does communicate. The more anyone—again, particularly a child—feels supported and safe, the better able he'll be to use acceptable communication behaviors.

Take a few minutes to review and compare your responses to the "Communication Best and Worst" and "Behavior Acceptable and Unacceptable" activities. Undoubtedly, you will see a pattern begin to emerge, sometimes subtly, but more often forcefully: the times when you communicate the best are the times you feel the most in control of your behavior. The opposite is also true: the more in control of your behavior you feel, the better you communicate. Notice all the conditions we require as adults to "keep it together" and to be "on top of" situations. Do we always create those conditions for our students? If we need to feel supported, listened to, respected, or rested and well, won't our students feel the same way?

Behavior and communication are truly connected. As we learn to see that connection, we become better able to support the children we teach and care for—and better able to support one another, in and outside of the school setting. When we know how to listen with more than just our ears, we can create positive learning environments for everyone.

Internet Resources

Visit **go.solution-tree.com/behavior** for live links to these sites and more.

Positive Behavior Supports

The Council for Children with Behavioral Disorders website has references concerning physical restraint, as cited in this text, as well as much more worthwhile information.
www.ccbd.net

The Crisis Prevention Institute provides training on safe, respectful, and noninvasive methods for managing disruptive and assaultive behaviors.
www.crisisprevention.com

The Technical Assistance Center on Positive Behavioral Interventions and Supports was established by the Office of Special Education Programs, U.S. Department of Education, to give schools capacity-building information and technical assistance for identifying, adapting, and sustaining effective practices that support positive behaviors.
www.pbis.org

Graphic Organizers

The S.C.O.R.E. Language Arts website has templates for many types of graphic organizers, among other ideas for teaching language arts.
www.sdcoe.k12.ca.us/score/actbank/torganiz.htm

Graphic organizers are also illustrated on the North Central Regional Educational Laboratory site.
www.ncrel.org/sdrs/areas/issues/students/learning/lr1grorg.htm

Houghton Mifflin Harcourt's Education Place also has a multitude of graphic organizers for teachers to print and use.
www.eduplace.com/graphicorganizer

Child Welfare

The National Disability Rights Network website has a wealth of information regarding the laws that govern how discipline is used in the schools.
www.napas.org

Help Guide is an organization that focuses on understanding and preventing child abuse and neglect. This link will take you to the page that describes warning signs of abuse and how to report it.
http://helpguide.org/mental/child_abuse_physical_emotional_sexual_neglect.htm

The Children's Bureau of the U.S. Department of Health and Human Services hosts a very informative website called the Child Welfare Information Gateway.
www.childwelfare.gov/index.cfm

For information specifically on the topic of mandated reporting of suspected abuse and neglect, visit
www.childwelfare.gov/systemwide/laws_policies/statutes/manda.cfm

Differentiated Instruction and Universal Design

The following website offers information, sample lesson plans, and more resources on differentiation. It is monitored by Carol Ann Tomlinson.
http://differentiationcentral.com/

The Center for Applied Special Technology (CAST) website does a nice job of synthesizing the concepts of both differentiated instruction and universal design.
www.cast.org/publications/ncac/ncac_diffinstruc.html
www.cast.org/publications/UDLguidelines/version1.html

The Center for Universal Design is a national information, technical assistance, and research center that evaluates, develops, and promotes accessible and universal design in the development of environments and products. This site is interesting in that the principles and foundational work for universal design in education began at North Carolina State University, at this center.
www.design.ncsu.edu/cud/

The National Early Childhood Technical Assistance Center (NECTAC) has a nice section on universal design.
www.nectac.org/topics/atech/udl.asp

Learning, Lighting and Color: Lighting Design for Schools and Universities in the 21st Century by Randall Fielding provides classroom layout ideas to enhance student learning.
www.designshare.com/articles/1/133/fielding_light-learn-color.pdf

References and Resources

Allen, D. (2000). Recent research on physical aggression in persons with intellectual disability: An overview. *Journal of Intellectual and Developmental Disability, 25*(1), 41–57.

Bandura, A. (1977). *Social learning theory.* Englewood Cliffs, NJ: Prentice Hall.

Bandura, A. (1986). *Social foundations of thought and action.* Englewood Cliffs, NJ: Prentice Hall.

Bandura, A. (1997). *Self-efficacy: The exercise of control.* New York: W.H. Freeman.

Bennett, D. S., Bendersky, M., & Lewis, M. (2002). Facial expressivity at 4 months: A context by expression analysis. *Infancy, 3,* 97–113.

Bertoncini, J., Bijeljac-Babic, R., Jusczyk, P. W., Kennedy, L. J., & Mehler, J. (1988). An investigation of young infants' perceptual representations of speech sounds. *Journal of Experimental Psychology, 117,* 21–33.

Blagojevic, B., Twomey, D., & Labas, L. (2002). *Universal design for learning: From the start.* Orono, ME: University of Maine. Accessed at www.ccids.umaine.edu/facts/facts6/udl.htm on January 13, 2009.

Bodrova, E., & Leong, D. J. (2008). Developing self-regulation in kindergarten: Can we keep all the crickets in the basket? *Young Children, 63*(3), 56–58.

Borkowski, J. G., & Thorpe, P. K. (1994). Self regulation and motivation: A life-span perspective on underachievement. In D. H. Schunk & B. J. Zimmerman (Eds.), *Self-regulation of learning and performance* (pp. 45–73). Hillsdale, NJ: Erlbaum.

Bronson, M. B. (2000). *Self-regulation in early childhood: Nature and nurture.* New York: Guilford Press.

Buffum, A., Mattos, M., & Weber, C. (2008). *Pyramid response to intervention: RTI, professional learning communities, and how to respond when kids don't learn.* Bloomington, IN: Solution Tree.

Butterworth, G. E. (2003). Pointing is the royal road to language acquisition. In S. Kita (Ed.), *Pointing where language, culture, and cognition meet* (pp. 9–34). Mahwah, NJ: Lawrence Erlbaum Associates.

Buzzelli, C. A., & Johnston, B. (2002). *The moral dimensions of teaching: Language, power and culture in classroom interaction.* New York: RoutledgeFalmer.

Canter, L. (2006). *Classroom management for academic success.* Bloomington, IN: Solution Tree.

Capone, N. C., & McGregor, K. K. (2004). Gesture development: A review for clinical and research practices. *Journal of Speech, Language and Hearing Research, 47,* 173–186.

Carpenter, M., Nagell, K., & Tomasello, M. (1998). Social cognition, joint attention, and communicative competence from 9 to 15 months of age. *Monographs of the Society for Research in Child Development, 63*(4), 1–143.

Center for Applied Special Technology (CAST). (2008). *Universal design for learning guidelines version 1.0.* Wakefield, MA: Author.

Conn-Powers, M. (2009). *Designing effective early education programs that meet the learning needs of all children: Application of multi-tiered and universal design teaching strategies.* Accessed at www.iidc.indiana.edu/styles/iidc/defiles/Universal%20Design%20in%20Early%20Ed_Draft.pdf on October 25, 2009.

Conn-Powers, M., Cross, A. F., Traub, E. K., & Hutter-Pishgahi, L. (2006). The universal design of early education: Moving forward for all children. *Beyond the Journal: Young Children on the Web, September.* Accessed at www.naeyc.org/yc/pastissues/2006/september on October 25, 2009.

Cross, A. F., & Dixon, S. D. (2004). *Adapting curriculum and instruction in inclusive early childhood settings* (Rev. ed.). Bloomington, IN: Indiana University, Indiana Institute on Disability and Community.

Council for Exceptional Children/Division of Learning Disabilities. (2007). *Eight practical tips for parents of young children with challenging behavior.* Accessed at www.education.com/reference/article/Ref_Behavior_Tips/?page=2 on October 25, 2009.

Davis, K. (2001a). Movement difference: A closer look at the possibilities. *The Reporter, 6*(3), 15–24.

Davis, K. (2001b). *Untapped talents: Pursuing employment* [video]. Bloomington, IN: Indiana Institute on Disability and Community.

Department of Health and Human Services Centers for Disease Control and Prevention. (2004). *Developmental disabilities.* Accessed at www.cdc.gov/ncbddd/dd/default.htm on October 25, 2009.

Division for Early Childhood of the Council for Exceptional Children. (2007). *Promoting positive outcomes for children with disabilities: Recommendations for curriculum, assessment, and program evaluation.* Missoula, MT: Author.

Dobrich, W., & Scarborough, H. S. (1984). Form and function in early communication: Language and pointing gestures. *Journal of Experimental Child Psychology, 38,* 475–490.

Doherty-Sneddon, G., Bruce, V. Bonner, L., Longbotham, S., & Doyle, C. (2002). Development of gaze aversion as disengagement from visual information. *Developmental Psychology, 38,* 438–445.

Doherty-Sneddon, G., & Kent, G. (1996). Visual signals and the communication abilities of children. *Journal of Child Psychology and Psychiatry, 37,* 949–959.

Donnellan, A. (1984). Analyzing the communicative functions of aberrant behavior. *Journal of the Association for Persons with Severe Handicaps, 9*(3), 201–212.

Donnellan, A., & Leary, M. (1995). *Movement difference and diversity in autism/mental retardation.* Madison, WI: DRI Press.

Donnellan, A., Leary, M. R., & Thelan, E. (1998). *Autism, movement difference and the dynamic system.* Workshop conducted in French Lick, Indiana.

DuFour, R., DuFour, R., & Eaker, R. (2008). *Revisiting professional learning communities at work: New insights for improving schools.* Bloomington, IN: Solution Tree.

Dunn, R., Dunn, K., & Perrin, J. (1993). *Teaching young children through their individual learning styles: Practical approaches for grades K–2.* Boston, MA: Allyn & Bacon.

Dunst, C. J., Bruder, M. B., Trivette, C., Hamby, D., & Raab, M. (2001). Characteristics and consequences of everyday natural learning opportunities. *Topics in Early Childhood Special Education, 21*(2), 68–92.

Fields, M. V., Perry, N. J., & Fields, D. (2006). *Constructive guidance and discipline: Preschool and primary education.* Upper Saddle River, NJ: Merrill/Prentice Hall.

Fischer, K. W. (1980). A theory of cognitive development: The control and construction of hierarchies of skills. *Psychological Review, 87*(6), 477–531.

Fox, L., Dunlap, G., Hemmeter, M. L., Joseph, G., & Strain, P. (2003). The teaching pyramid: A model for supporting social competence and preventing challenging behavior in young children. *Young Children, 58*(4), 48–52.

Fox, L., & Harper Lentini, R. (2006, November). You got it! Teaching Social and Emotional Skills. *Beyond the Journal—Young Children on the Web.* Accessed at http://journal.naeyc.org/btj/200611/pdf/BTJFoxLentini.pdf on October 25, 2009.

Fox, L., Jack, S., & Broyles, L. (2005). *Program-wide positive behavior support: Supporting young children's social-emotional development and addressing challenging behavior.* Tampa, FL: University of South Florida, Louis de la Parte Florida Mental Health Institute.

Gillingham, G. (1997). *Autism, handle with care! Understanding and managing behavior of children and adults with autism.* Arlington, TX: Future Horizons.

Glaser, C., & Brunstein, J. C. (2007). Improving fourth-grade students' composition skills: Effects of strategy instruction and self-regulation procedures. *Journal of Educational Psychology, 99*(2), 297–310.

Goleman, D. (1995). *Emotional intelligence.* New York: Bantam Books.

Goode, T. D. (2002). *Key definitions.* Washington, DC: Georgetown University Center for Child and Human Development, National Center for Cultural Competence.

Greenman, J. (2005). *Caring spaces, learning places: Children's environments that work.* Redmond, WA: Exchange.

Gurian, A. (2005). Learning right from wrong. *Child Study Center Letter, 10*(2), 1–4.

Harms, T., Clifford, R. M., & Cryer, D. (1998). Early childhood environment rating scale (Rev. ed.). New York: Teachers College.

Harms, T., Cryer, D., & Clifford, R. M. (2003). *Infant/toddler environment rating scale* (Rev. ed.). New York: Teachers College.

Harms, T., Cryer, D., & Clifford, R. M. (2007). *Family child care environment rating scale* (Rev. ed.). New York: Teachers College.

Harms, T., Jacobs, E. V., & Romano, D. (1995). *School age care environment rating scale.* New York: Teachers College.

Hodgdon, L. (2000). *Visual strategies for improving communication.* Troy, MI: QuirkRoberts.

Honig, A. S., & Thompson, A. (1994, April-May). Helping toddlers with peer group entry skills. *ZERO to THREE,* 15–19.

Howell, R., Patton, S., & Deiotte, M. (2008). *Understanding response to intervention: A practical guide to systemic implementation.* Bloomington, IN: Solution Tree.

Howse, R. B., Calkins, S. D., Anastopoulos, A. D., Keane, S. P., & Shelton, T. L. (2003). Regulatory contributors to children's kindergarten achievement. *Early Education and Development, 14,* 101–119.

Jones, W., & Lorenzo-Hubert, I. (2006). Culture and parental expectations for child development: Concerns for language development and early learning. In S. E. Rosenkoetter & J. Knapp-Philo (Eds.), *Learning to read the world: Language and literacy in the first three years* (pp. 187–212). San Francisco: WestEd.

Kaiser, B., & Raminsky, J. S. (2007). *Challenging behavior in young children: Understanding, preventing, and responding effectively.* Boston: Pearson/Allyn & Bacon.

Kendon, A. (2004). Review of Susan Goldin-Meadow's Hearing gesture: How our hands help us think. *Gesture, 4,* 91–107.

Lavoie, R. D. (1989). *Understanding learning disabilities: How difficult can this be? The F.A.T. city workshop.* Alexandria, VA: PBS Video.

Leary, M., & Hill, D. (1996). Moving on: Autism and movement disturbance. *Mental Retardation, 34,* 39–53.

Levine, D. A. (2003). *Building classroom communities: Strategies for developing a culture of caring.* Bloomington, IN: Solution Tree.

Lifter, K., & Bloom, L. (1998). Intentionality and the role of play in the transition to language. In S. F. Warren & J. Reichle (Series Eds.), & A. M. Wetherby, S. F. Warren, & J. Reichle (Vol. Eds.), *Communication and language intervention series: Vol. 7. Transitions in prelinguistic communication* (pp. 161–195). Baltimore: Paul H. Brookes Publishing Co.

Lovett, H. (1996). *Learning to listen: Positive approaches and people with difficult behavior.* Baltimore: Paul H. Brookes Publishing Co.

Mahnke, F. (1996). *Color, environment and human response.* New York: John Wiley and Sons, Inc.

Marion, M. (2007). *Guidance of young children* (7th ed.). Upper Saddle River, NJ: Pearson/Merrill Prentice Hall.

Martin, G., & Pear, J. (2003). *Behavior modification: What it is and how to do it* (8th ed.). Upper Saddle River, NJ: Merrill Prentice Hall.

McClelland, M. M., Acock, A. C., & Morrison, F. J. (2006). The impact of kindergarten learning-related social skills on academic achievement at the end of elementary school. *Early Childhood Research Quarterly, 21,* 471–490.

McDermott, P. A., Mordell, M., & Stoltzfus, J. C. (2001). The organization of student performance in American schools: Discipline, motivation, verbal learning, nonverbal learning. *Journal of Educational Psychology, 93*(1), 65–76.

McIntyre, T. (1996a). Does the way we teach create behavior disorders in culturally different students? *Education and Treatment of Children, 19,* 354–370.

McIntyre, T. (1996b). Guidelines for providing appropriate services to culturally diverse students with emotional and/or behavioral disorders. *Behavioral Disorders, 21*(2), 137–144.

Meerwein, G., Mahnke, F. H., & Rodeck, B. (2007). *Color-communication in architectural space* (4th ed.). Basel-Boston-Berlin: Birkhauser Verlag.

Murray-Slutsky, C., & Paris, B. A. (2005). *Is it sensory or is it behavior? Behavior problem identification, assessment, and intervention.* San Antonio, TX: PsychCorp, Harcourt Brace Assessment.

National Center for Cultural Competence. (2004). *Bridging the cultural divide in health care settings: The essential role of cultural broker programs.* Washington, DC: Author.

National Disability Rights Network. (2009). *School is not supposed to hurt: Investigative report on abusive restraint and seclusion in schools.* Accessed at www.ndrn.org/sr/SR-Report.pdf on October 25, 2009.

Nazzi, T., Floccia, C., & Bertoncini, J. (1998). Discrimination of pitch contours by neonates. *Infant Behavior and Development, 21,* 779–784.

Normandeau, S., & Guay, F. (1998). Preschool behavior and first-grade school achievement: The mediational role of cognitive self-control. *Journal of Educational Psychology, 90*(1), 111–121.

Ozcaliskan, S., & Goldin-Meadow, S. (2005). Gesture is at the cutting edge of early language development. *Cognition, 96*(3), B101–B113.

Parkay, F. W., & Hass, G. (2000). *Curriculum Planning* (7th ed.). Needham Heights, MA: Allyn & Bacon.

Parvizi, J., Anderson, S. W., Martin, C. O., Damasio, H., & Damasio, A. R. (2001). Pathological laughter and crying: A link to the cerebellum. *Brain, 124,* 1708–1719.

Pretti-Frontczak, K. L., Barr, D. M., Macy, M., & Carter, A. (2003). Research and resources related to activity-based intervention, embedded learning opportunities, and routine-based instruction: An annotated bibliography. *Topics in Early Childhood Special Education, 23*(1), 29–39.

Rose, D. H., & Meyer, A. (Eds.). (2006). *A practical reader in universal design for learning.* Boston: Harvard Education Press.

Rose, D. H., Meyer, A., Strangman, N., & Rappolt, G. (2002). *Teaching every student in the digital age: Universal design for learning.* Alexandria, VA: Association for Supervision and Curriculum Development.

Sailor, D. H. (2004). *Supporting children in their home, school, and community.* Boston, MA: Allyn & Bacon.

Sandall, S., & Ostrosky, M. (Eds.). (1999). *Practical ideas for addressing challenging behaviors.* Denver, CO: Division for Early Childhood, NAEYC.

Schuler, A. L., Wetherby, A. M., & Prizant, B. M. (1997). Enhancing language and communication development: Prelinguistic approaches. In D. J. Cohen & F. R. Volkmar (Eds.), *Handbook of autism and pervasive developmental disorders* (pp. 539–571). New York: Wiley.

Seefeldt, C., & Wasik, B. A. (2006). *Early education: Three, four, and five year olds go to school.* Upper Saddle River, NJ: Pearson/Merrill Prentice Hall.

Siegel, D. J. (1999). *The developing mind: How relationships and the brain interact to shape who we are.* New York: Guilford Press.

Sizer, T. R. (2001). No two are quite alike: Personalized learning. *Educational Leadership, 57*(1), 6–11.

Sondheim, S. (1987). Finale: Children will listen. On *Into the woods* [CD]. New York: Nonesuch.

Stormont, M. (2007). *Fostering resilience in young children at risk for failure: Strategies for grades K–3.* Upper Saddle River, NJ: Pearson/Merrill Prentice Hall.

Thompson, S., & Thurlow, M. (2002). *Universally designed assessments: Better tests for everyone! (Policy Directions 14).* Minneapolis: University of Minnesota, National Center on Educational Outcomes. Accessed at http://education.umn. edu/NCEO/OnlinePubs/Policy14.htm on October 25, 2009.

Thurlow, M. L., Elliott, J. E., & Ysseldyke, J. E. (2003). *Testing students with disabilities: Practical strategies for complying with district and state requirements* (2nd ed.). Thousand Oaks, CA: Corwin Press.

Tomlinson, C. A. (1999). *The differentiated classroom: Responding to the needs of all learners.* Alexandria, VA: Association for Supervision and Curriculum Development.

Tomlinson, C. A. (2001). *How to differentiate instruction in mixed-ability classrooms* (2nd ed.). Alexandria, VA: Association for Supervision and Curriculum Development.

Tomlinson, C. A. (2003). *Fulfilling the promise of the differentiated classroom: Strategies and tools for responsive teaching.* Alexandria, VA: Association for Supervision and Curriculum Development.

Tomlinson, C. A., & Eidson, C. C. (2003). *Differentiation in practice: A resource guide for differentiating curriculum.* Alexandria, VA: Association for Supervision and Curriculum Development.

Turnbull, A., Edmonson, H., Griggs, P., Wickham, D., Sailor, W., Freeman, R., et al. (2002). A blueprint for school wide positive behavior support: Implementation of three components. *Exceptional Children, 68*(3), 377–402.

Vygotsky, L. (1978). *Mind in society: The development of higher psychological processes.* Cambridge, MA: Harvard University Press.

Warren, S. F., & Yoder, P. J. (1998). Facilitating the transition from preintentional to intentional communication. In A. M. Wetherby, S. F. Warren, & J. Reichle (Eds.), *Communication and language intervention series: Volume 7. Transitions in prelinguistic communication* (pp. 365–384). Baltimore: Paul H. Brookes Publishing Co.

Weiss, N. (1999). It may be non-aversive, but is non-coercive? The ethics of behavior change in the modern age. *TASH Newsletter, 25*(11), 20–22, 27.

Weiss, N. R., & Knoster, T. (2008). It may be nonaversive, but is it a positive approach? Relevant questions to ask throughout the process of behavioral assessment and intervention. *Journal of Positive Behavior Interventions, 10,* 72–78.

Wetherby, A., & Prizant, B. (1989). The expression of communicative intent: Assessment guidelines. *Seminars in Speech and Language, 10,* 77–90.

Wetherby, A. M., & Prizant, B. M. (1992). Profiling young children's communicative competence. In S. F. Warren & J. Reichle (Eds.), *Communication and language intervention series: Volume 1. Causes and effects in communication and language intervention* (pp. 217–254). Baltimore: Paul H. Brookes Publishing Co.

Wien, C.A., Coates, A., Keating, B. L., & Bigelow, B. C. (2005). Designing the environment to build connection to place. *Beyond the Journal: Young Children on the Web.* Accessed at www.journal.naeyc.org/btj/200505/05Wien.pdf on October 25, 2009.

Williams, L., & Golenski, J. (1978). Infant speech sound discrimination: The effects of contingent vs. noncontingent stimulus presentation. *Child Development, 49,* 213–217.

Zirpoli, T. J. (2005). *Behavior management: Applications for teacher.* Upper Saddle River, NJ: Pearson/Merrill Prentice Hall.

Index

thoughts, 88
multitasking difficulty, 86
muscle tone, changes in, 19

N

National Disability Rights Network, 169, 193
nature, in the classroom, 108
negative labels, avoiding, 118–119
nonsymbolic communication, 18
nonverbal cues, 156
nonverbal communication, 18–24, 119–120

O

"101 Ways to Praise a Child," 34
orientation, 20

P

Parkinson's disease, 83
pathways, 103
perceptions, difficulty with, 88
Perry, N. J., 122
philosophical foundations, 3–4
physical assistance, 168–169
physical restraint, 169
physical settings. *See* environments, supportive learning
picture communication systems, 23, 25–26
pinching, 34–35
pointing, 20–21
positive approaches, 96
postures, difficulty with, 87
praise, how to give, 117–118
preparation, need for, 150–152
Prizant, B. M., 27
proprioception, 87
proximity, 20, 156
punishment, reinforcement versus, 158, 166

Q

quiet place, 166–167

R

Raminsky, J., 118
reaching, 20–21
reactive (redirective) strategies
personal reflection, 172
physical assistance, 168–169
physical restraint, 169
quiet place, 166–167
reinforcement theory, 156–166
simple responses, 155–156

time out, 167–168
values-based approach, 169–170
redirecting behavior, 120–121, 163–165
reinforcement
of behavior you want to increase, 161
contingencies, 162
effective use of, 159–166
frequent use of, 161–162
group activities and, 162–163
ignoring behavior, 165
intermittent, 165
naturally occurring, 160
negative, 157–158
positive, 157–158
prespecified, 160
punishment versus, 158
redirecting behavior, 163–165
use as soon as possible, 160–161
theory, 156–166
responses, modeling appropriate, 126–127
Robert's Rules of Order, 122
rooting reflexes, 20
routines
daily, create, 138
example of what can go wrong, 152
familiar, 68
flexible, 140
importance of safe consistent, 73–74
interactive, 138–139
need for consistent, 137–140
transitions, warn in advance for, 139–140
rules
three times, 125–126
use of stated and posted, 122–124
running, 32

S

Sailor, D. H., 123
scatter plots, use of, 60–62
schedules, 141–142
self-injurious behaviors, 22–23, 27
self-regulation, 95–96
self-stimulatory behaviors, 22, 36
sensory and natural elements, 106–108
sensory behavior, 36–39
sensory needs, 76–77
overload, 108
shoestring story, 37–38
Simple Communication Assessment, 40, 45–48
skill fluency, 82
sleeping in class, 78

smells, 107
social density, 103–104
social environment, 108–110
Sondheim, S., 126
sounds, 106–107
spatial variety, 102
speech, difficulty with, 88
starting difficulty, 85
stereotypic behaviors, 22
stopping difficulty, 85
storage areas, 99, 106
story map, 143
switching difficulty, 86–87

T

talking to children, tips for, 53–55, 57–58
teaching strategies, need to evaluate and monitor, 77–78
Technical Assistance Center on Positive Behavioral Interventions and Supports, 193
temperature, room, 106
thoughts, difficulty with maintaining, 88
three times rule, 125–126
time out, 167–168
touching, 21
Tourette's syndrome, 83
transitions
difficulty in making, 86–87
warn in advance for, 139–140

U

universally designed instruction, 136, 194

V

verbal warnings, 52
visual displays, 107
visual impairment, 81
visual supports, 55, 121
activity supports, 142
graphic organizers, 142–143
schedules, 141–142
use of, 141–143, 179–180
visual warnings, 52

W

Wetherby, A., 27
word wall, 142
work spaces, defined, 102–103

Z

Zirpoli, T. J., 118

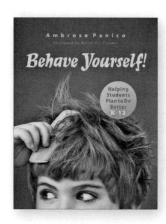

Behave Yourself! Helping Students Plan to Do Better
Ambrose Panico
Learn specific strategies for developing behavior intervention plans (BIPs) that lead to long-term, positive change for general and special education students. The author outlines a practical five-step Plan to Do Better approach and provides reproducibles that ease the information-gathering process.
BKF267

Pyramid Response to Intervention: RTI, PLCs, and How To Respond When Kids Don't Learn
Austin Buffum, Mike Mattos, and Chris Weber
Foreword by Richard DuFour
Accessible language and compelling stories illustrate how RTI is most effective when built on the Professional Learning Communities at Work™ model. Written by award-winning educators, this book details three tiers of interventions—from basic to intensive—and includes implementation ideas.
BKF251

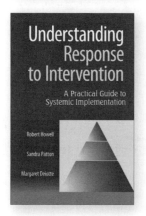

Understanding Response to Intervention: A Practical Guide to Systemic Implementation
Robert Howell, Sandra Patton, and Margaret Deiotte
Whether you want a basic understanding of RTI or desire thorough knowledge for district-level implementation, you need this book. Understand the nuts and bolts of RTI. Follow clear examples of effective practices that include systems and checklists to assess your RTI progress.
BKF253

Making Math Accessible to Students With Special Needs: Practical Tips and Suggestions
r4 Educated Solutions
These manuals offer grade-appropriate research-based strategies for increasing confidence and capability among students with special needs. Reflective questions and tasks make this a perfect book for self-guided or group study. Appendices offer sample answers and additional supports.
Grades K–2: **BKF288**   Grades 3–5: **BKF289**   Grades 6–8: **BKF290**   Grades 9–12: **BKF291**

Solution Tree | Press a division of
Solution Tree

Visit solution-tree.com or call 800.733.6786 to order.